In memory of
Derek and Jeannie Tangye

THE
MINACK
CHRONICLES
REVISITED

THE STORY OF DEREK & JEANNIE TANGYE

⸺∞⸺

Including a special 50th Anniversary Edition of
the first of Derek Tangye's Minack Chronicles

'A Gull On The Roof'

'A Gull on the Roof' first published 1961 by Michael Joseph Ltd
'The Minack Chronicles Revisited' first published in 2011 by
Old Well Studio, Lamorna, Penzance, Cornwall TR19 6BQ
and sponsored by The Friends of Minack Society

The Friends of Minack Society

ISBN 978-0-9559688-1-5

A catalogue record for this book is
available from the British Library

All images reproduced with permission
Typeset in Minion Pro

Design, typesetting and artwork
by Old Well Studio
www.oldwellstudio.co.uk
Printed and bound in Cornwall
by Headland Printers, Penzance

CONTENTS

DEREK TANGYE

A GULL ON THE ROOF

WITH ORIGINAL SKETCHES
BY JEAN TANGYE

(Paginated separately between pages 46-47 of The Minack Chronicles Revisited)

INDIVIDUAL SPONSORS AND CONTRIBUTORS

We are grateful to the following individuals who made personal donations to the Fund set up by FOMS to finance this publication. Without their generous assistance, and also of those who donated anonymously, it would not have been possible.

Mike & Mary Ackroyd	Judy Lewis	Lorna Roberts
Anne Atkins	Joan & John Loader	Gail Robertson
Gill Bilcliffe	Patricia Lockwood	Yvonne Robinson
Caroline Bliss	Anne Macaulay	Don & Margaret Russell
Joan Burns	Lilian & Andy McCartney	Mary Simpson
Jan Carlson	Beryl Mc Diarmid	Tessa Skola
Elizabeth Carnaby	Dorothy McIsaac	Adrian, Rachel
Jan Dellar	Vic & Pat Machin	& Rupert Smith
Christine Dickson	Jeannie Matthews	Audley Smith
Yasmin Donlon	Marta Merrifield	Pauline & Vic Stevenson
Pauline Downing	Avril Lesley Moody	Anne & Malcolm Sutton
Rachel Eyre	Karen Morgan	Brian Tandy
Davina Fennemore	Nuala Morris	June Teece
Jon Fenwick	Kath Mulligan	Ann Tomlinson
Joan Frost	Jennie & Gerald Murrish	Jennie Towan
Pauline & Eric Gibbons	Mim & John Nash	Gloria & Eddie Townsin
John & Jaqueline Hards	Julia Norridge	Michael Troon
Iris Hare	Juliet Nowak	Tricia Twose
Barbara Hargreaves	Joanne Ottley	Margreta Von Pein
Sylvia & Roland Hargreaves	John Owen	Jane Walker
Jeff & Linda Hartley	John & Gill Owen	Terence & Sheila Wall
Annette Holmes	Theresa Pattie	Jean Wallbank
Jane & Bryan Jackson	Josie Paver	Stuart D. Ward
Cynthia & Demelza Jupp	Grant Pendergrast	Sybille Weber
Alan Kendall	Marion Penfound	Basil & Helen West
Gary Kennon	Gill Pudenz	Jean Whatton
Nick & Lorna Knight	Valerie Pysden	Moira & Roy Wickens
Lynette Laramy	Barbara Reese	Patricia Wilnecker
Sue & Dave Law	Ann Rivers	David & Mary Young

Introduction

HOW MANY of us, faced with the relentless realities of maintaining a modern lifestyle, have indulged ourselves in the dream of escaping the rat race to find a slower, 'back to basics' life somewhere in the country? Judging from the popularity of reality TV programmes on the subject, quite a few. The concept of living simpler, but more fulfilling lives, once seen perhaps as being just the pipe dreams of a few hippy dippy new agers, is increasingly being considered as a realistic alternative to the consumerist merry-go-round. As more and more of us recognize the scale of the ecological damage that decades of industrialization have inflicted on our planet, we've increasingly accepted that we need to find ways of reducing our personal impact on the environment. The recent near collapse of the global financial system and the recession that followed brought anxiety and sometimes real suffering to millions of people, but it also prompted many to pause and reconsider where they were going with their lives. The media has responded to this change of mood with a plethora of articles, books, web sites and television programmes about greener lifestyles, creating eco-friendly houses and growing your own food, mixed with nostalgic repeats of the 1970s TV series 'The Good Life'.

In reality, although demand for allotments may have rocketed, and many people are making real efforts in their everyday lives to reduce their personal 'carbon footprint', a really radical change in lifestyle will remain a dream for all but the most determined. This book is about two people with just such a determined and pioneering attitude. *Pioneering* because their adventure into an alternative lifestyle was long before the modern green movement existed and certainly long before the fictional Tom and Barbara Good dropped out and turned their back garden in Surbiton into a smallholding. Convinced that their previous conventional pursuit of material things was shallow and unfulfilling, they voluntarily turned their backs on the prosperous and glamorous lives they'd been leading in London and stepped out, hand in hand, into the unknown. Their names were Derek and Jeannie Tangye, and their new home was a dilapidated, isolated, centuries old granite cottage, with no running water or electricity, on the beautiful but windswept cliffs of the far west of Cornwall. Its name was 'Dorminack', but it was known locally as just *Minack*. The year was 1950.

John Nash

SO, WHO were Derek and Jeannie Tangye and what was it in their past that brought them together? What led them to be so certain that the answer to the deep, personal questions they asked themselves lay in the drastic cutting of virtually all their former ties, for a future that was, at best, unknowable? From the research I did for this book and talking to local people that knew them during their time at Minack, I came to respect them both, primarily for their courage in persevering with their dream. When you realize what they went through, there must surely have been times when it looked as if their dream was turning into a nightmare - but then perseverance was perhaps one of the defining characteristics of their generation. Much more extensive research into their earlier lives had already been done - in 2000, four years after Derek died in 1996 and fourteen years after Jeannie had succumbed to cancer in 1986, the writer David Power published what was effectively a dual biography of them both, called simply, *'Tangye'*. Although an admirer of Derek's writing, Power clearly felt that it was Jeannie who was Derek's lodestar rather than the other way round, and she was the real strength behind their partnership. Derek certainly, like all of us, had his weaknesses, but whether David Power's analysis truly reflects the dynamics of their long and loving relationship must be to some extent personal speculation. Nevertheless, I am much indebted to David's extensive research, which I gratefully acknowledge, as well as the autobiographical writings of both Derek and Jeannie Tangye themselves, for the story that follows.

Derek Tangye was born on 29th February, in the Leap Year of 1912, at Earls Court in London. Despite his birthplace, he always considered himself, with justification, to be a Cornishman. His father, Richard Trevithick Gilberstone Tangye, was a barrister whose work at the Law Courts meant that he needed a permanent London home, and the whole family stayed there together for much of each year. Theirs was a happy, prosperous, upper middle class family who could trace their

Glendorgal in the early 20th century

Cornish roots back many generations, and indeed the main family home was *Glendorgal*, a rather grand residence, now an hotel, near Newquay on the north Cornish coast. Derek's background then, was one of considerable wealth, within a loving home, which was staffed by the usual domestic servants appropriate to the family's status. In

Harrow School 1927 - Derek Tangye is in the back row, second from the right. The author and playwright, Terence Rattigan, is also in the back row, seventh from the right.

his education he followed his two older brothers, Colin and Nigel, firstly as a boarder at Copthorne Preparatory School in Sussex and later, at 14 years of age, as a boarder at that quintessentially English public school, Harrow. Apart from an unfortunate tendency in adult life to offend tradespeople and employees by addressing them solely by their surname, this rarified background seems to have left few long term ill effects; although in the eyes of potential employers his expensive education seemed to have left no perceivable effects at all, for Derek left school having failed all his examinations.

Unable, therefore, to go on to university, he drifted for a while, playing the upper class social calendar and making the most out of his Harrow old school tie to obtain invitations to parties, dances and balls as a *debs' delight*. Although his father managed to get him a 'proper', albeit very junior job working in the offices of Unilever, Derek somehow contrived to combine this with his considerable social commitments, using his daytime uniform of bowler hat and black city suit to give off a reassuring air of being 'something in the City'. He relied for sustenance though on his evening social invitations, where he would eat his fill at the buffet and then surreptitiously, between dances, stuff the hidden pockets in the long tails of his evening dress with free sandwiches. On one occasion, after a particularly energetic spin with a debutante around the dance floor, he was mortified to discover he'd left a tell-tale trail of purloined cucumber sandwiches in his wake.

The pointlessness of this existence caused the youthful Derek a great deal of soul searching about his future, and he took solace in reading, in particular the works of Marcel Proust, whose 'À la recherche du temps perdu' made a life-long impression upon him. He dreamt of travelling around the world, visiting exotic and far flung places, but the reality of his straitened financial circumstances ensured this remained just that - a dream. His quest for a new direction in life was then brought, quite literally, to a head by a lunchtime visit he made to a phrenologist at Ludgate Circus. This soothsayer, having felt the bumps of Derek's head and thereby divined his future, advised journalism as an appropriate career and confidently exclaimed that, whatever else he did, *"you must not barter"*. As his only chance of advancement at Unilever was likely to be in the sales department, he immediately returned to his office and resigned on the spot.

Derek, the 'Debs' Delight'

Using his social connections now in a more positive way, he managed to engineer an interview with Max Aitken, owner of the Daily Express, and made sufficient impression upon him to obtain a two week trial as a junior reporter with the Manchester Daily Express. Starting at the bottom, which for a junior reporter meant night shifts ambulance-chasing and hanging around police stations, this job nevertheless proved to be the breakthrough he needed and he went on to spend eighteen successful months in Manchester, learning both the craft of journalism and, just as importantly, a great deal about the hardship and suffering in the lives of ordinary people.

He returned to London where initially he worked for the Sunday Referee; hardly the most prominent paper of the time, but it gave him the opportunity to work as a columnist wearing a number of different hats; reviewing theatre, radio, cabaret and music. In each of these roles he was showered with invitations to social and showbiz events, widening his contacts enormously, and it was not long before he was invited to rejoin the Max Aitken stable as a staff reporter on their flagship paper, the Daily Express. He was becoming increasingly well known as a skilled and successful journalist, and this led to him being given the opportunity of a very high profile job indeed with the Daily Mirror.

For years the legendary journalist Godfrey Winn had been writing a regular and very popular 'advice' column, offering sympathy and support, including, in certain circumstances, financial support from a special fund to readers with all sorts of personal problems. Winn had just given up this role and Derek, probably much to his own surprise, was appointed to take over. Suddenly he found his own image everywhere, staring down at him from buses and hoardings in a national poster campaign designed to project him as the Daily Mirror's bright, new, but at the same time wise and compassionate sage, whose advice could be relied upon to resolve life's problems and ease the furrowed brows of the more vulnerable amongst the Mirror's readership. In later life, as a much older man, Derek did indeed assume the role of a wise advisor in many of his readers' minds, but at this earlier stage of his life he lacked not only the gravitas, but also the theatrical charisma of his famous predecessor to carry it off. The column's popularity declined and eventually the Mirror decided to resolve the problem by dropping it altogether and Derek, having temporarily scaled the national heights, found himself potentially back in the pack as a jobbing journalist. He skilfully took the opportunity though, with the Mirror's support, to avoid humiliation by dressing up the termination of his contract as a voluntary resignation in order to release him to pursue his lifetime's ambition - a journey around the world.

Financed by his settlement cheque from the Mirror and the sale of the Buick car he'd acquired as part of the trappings of his former life, Derek set off on his great adventure, initially crossing the Atlantic by ship to New York. His excitement was tempered by the fact that this was now June 1938 and ominous war clouds were gathering across Europe. Derek was very patriotic and politically he was completely opposed to the appeasers of Hitler. He anguished

A page from Derek's scrapbook - not quite the Express' leading story that day, but he somehow convinced the editor that bus stops were front page news.

about the situation in his letters home, cursing *"the mad Mullah of Germany"*, and he knew in his heart that, if war broke out he would have to return to England. In the event, it was more than a year before Great Britain finally declared war on Germany and Derek was able to complete his circumnavigation, which, having crossed America via Greyhound bus to California, included an extended stay on the south sea islands of Tahiti and Toopua. The simple and uninhibited life he experienced there, where he lived in a basic wooden beach hut and developed a very close relationship with one of the native girls, must have had a considerable influence on his future attitudes to life. He returned home via Samoa, New Zealand, Australia, the Phillipines, Hong Kong, China, Japan, Korea, Manchuria, Russia, Poland, and Germany - where he stopped for a breather and snatched *"a sight of Hitler shouting"* - then on to France and finally across the Channel to England. He arrived back in Cornwall in the summer of 1939 and, renting a cottage near Truro he immediately sat down to write the full story of his travels. This was his first book, called *'Time was Mine'* which, when completed and published the following year, led to him meeting Jeannie for the first time.

The new recruit

In the meantime though, his two older brothers having joined up, Derek felt that now he had to conform and do his duty. Just a few days before the declaration of war, he enlisted with the Duke of Cornwall's Light Infantry and was initially assigned to patrol duties in the docks at Falmouth. When word of his recent travels in Asia and Europe reached the War Office though, he was summoned to London, promoted to Captain and given a special monitoring role, eventually being appointed to MI5.

Just a few months before this, an attractive *20 year old* girl by the name of Jean Nicol had been appointed to the post of secretary in the publicity office of the Savoy Hotel, just off the Strand in London.

Jean Everald Nicol was born on 23rd March 1919 at Chiswick, near Kew Gardens, London. When she was two years of age her parents moved to Ayrshire in Scotland, where Jean's younger sister, Barbara, was born, but the family soon moved south again, to St Albans, where their father built a house to his own design, named Bryher Lodge, after the small island in the Scillies. Both sisters were sent to Westgate, a boarding school near Margate in Kent for their education, where Jean excelled in all the arts subjects, particularly English, which encouraged her to consider journalism as a future career. After Westgate, she returned home to St Albans to complete her education at St Albans High School, followed by a period at the local college, where she learned the secretarial skills of shorthand and typing. These skills were later to be invaluable to Derek, for it was to Jean that Derek turned to type up the manuscripts of his books, often running to several proofs on each.

On leaving college and keen to break into journalism, she wrote and typed up a number of articles which she submitted to various newspapers and magazines, accepting the inevitable rejection slips as part of the probationary experience. By a strange coincidence, she was eventually to gain employment at the Daily Mirror, where she was given the role of 'agony aunt', answering letters from readers seeking advice on emotional problems. Sadly her inexperience, at 19 years of age, led to her being sacked from this job, by the same editor, at the same newspaper, in the same building, that would eventually sack Derek from a similar post - indeed he was already in this post, but for some reason their paths had not crossed there once. Perhaps fate was biding its time.

She was not unemployed for long and in April 1939 she started work at the place that would define her very existence for the next ten years - the Savoy Hotel. Her first role was a very junior one, as secretary to the assistant to the publicity manager, but with the war now only just over four months away, nobody could be very certain of what the future had in store. She was on holiday at a farmhouse near Newton Abbot on 3rd September when Prime Minister Neville Chamberlain came on the radio with his famous announcement that Britain was at war with Germany. Phoning her office for advice, it at first seemed likely that, with her boss about to be called up, there would be no job for her to return to. Desperately disappointed she returned to her home in St Albans, and a few weeks later she got a call to let her know that her old boss had indeed been called up. Instead of confirming that this meant she had no job to return to, she was pleasantly surprised to be offered *his* job as assistant to the publicity manager. She returned to the Savoy, overjoyed at her good fortune, where she now had the opportunity to make her mark working directly as assistant to Jean Lorimer, the experienced journalist who was now the Savoy's Publicity Manager.

In those dangerous days of the war, where fear for the future was a constant companion, the concept of *'fate'* was very real to many people. It now seemed that fate, which had intervened once to steer her towards the Savoy, and then again into an important job there that she loved, was about to intervene for a third time. Jean was summoned to a meeting with one of the directors of the Savoy and she went with considerable trepidation, wondering why a director wanted to see her and whether her youth and lack of experience meant that she was about to be replaced. As she sat at his desk, fearing the worst, he explained to her that her boss, Jean Lorimer, had decided that she wanted to return to full time journalism. There was therefore a vacancy and Jean had so impressed the management that, despite her youth, they wanted to offer her the role of Publicity Manager for the Savoy Group. So it was then, that Jean Nicol, at just

21 years of age, stepped into the job that would raise her to the very top of her profession.

Although the Savoy's location in the heart of London meant it was extremely vulnerable to the Luftwaffe's bombing raids, far from business being reduced it became the headquarters for journalists from around the world, especially the Americans, who would congregate at the 'American Bar'. Senior visiting politicians would often base themselves at the Savoy, as would the American entertainers and film stars that came to London to help keep up morale. Jean was much in demand, both for her energy and efficiency, but also because many thought her to be more beautiful than most of the glamorous film stars she looked after during their stays at the Savoy. It was her role in charge of publicity that first brought her into contact with an officer from the Intelligence Corps - Captain Derek Tangye.

Derek had completed and published his book *'Time was Mine'* and was now unashamedly looking for ways in which he could promote it. On a freezing day in January 1941 he contrived to get a mutual friend, Ronald Hyde, the news editor of the Evening Standard, to come with him to the Savoy and introduce him to Jean. After exchanging the usual brief pleasantries, Derek immediately announced that he'd written a book, and asked if she would display it on the Savoy bookstall. Jean agreed, and Ronald helped him seal the deal by buying them both lunch at the Grill. In his biography, *'Tangye'*, David Power relates how Derek had in fact another, and perhaps more significant motive for this visit - he'd already dined at the Savoy on a previous occasion and had been struck by Jean's poise and natural good looks. Perhaps publicity for his book was really just a convenient excuse to engineer an introduction. If so it was also the cause, in the eyes of Jean's parents, of him being firmly discounted as an appropriate suitor for their daughter's hand. When Frank and Dora Nicol read *Time was Mine*, especially his account in it of his adventures in the South Seas and his liaisons with nubile young native women, they were horrified. Derek Tangye, ex Harrow, respected journalist, well-spoken Captain in the Intelligence Corps, was in reality a louche and degenerate beachcomber. He became, most definitely, *persona non grata*.

Jean herself, although she continued to enjoy occasional dates with other male friends, was attracted to Derek and was secretly seeing more and more of him. In the meantime Derek had rented, along with two American journalists, Cholmondeley House, a property by the river at Richmond and here he often played host on Sunday afternoons to Jean and large numbers of mutual friends. In the congenial atmosphere they created there, animated debates would take place about politics and the Government's conduct of the war. In their official duties, both of them were brought into personal contact with large numbers of important politicians and political commentators, who'd often then join them on Sunday afternoons at Cholmondeley House, along with exiles from all over war torn Europe. Whilst living there Derek edited another book - 'Went the Day Well?' - a collection of essays that he'd commissioned from their friends and acquantances about those who had made the ultimate sacrifice in the war. He skilfully edited these together into one volume and adapted the title from an anonymous entry he'd once seen in a visitors' book, relating to the first world war:

Went the day well? We died and never knew.
But well or ill, Freedom, we died for you.

During these often desperate days of the war, as Britain stood alone against Hitler's apparently invincible war machine, Derek and Jean drew closer together. Gradually, as Hitler overstretched himself by turning on the Soviet Union and the Japanese attack on Pearl Harbour brought America into the war, the tide looked as if might at last be turning. Still the visitors came - as Derek later wrote in *'The Way to Minack'*, one of the Minack Chronicles: *"Jeannie never knew who might be there when she arrived at Cholmondeley House; and quietly took over the role of hostess."* Notice that Derek had now dropped the more formal 'Jean' and begun to call her affectionately, 'Jeannie'. He went on: *"Then at last she became the resident hostess. 'Will you marry me?' It was seven o'clock in the Coalhole, the pub in the Strand, and I had been waiting for her for an hour; and she had expected a row as she came up to the marble topped table where I was sitting. 'Yes' she said quickly, glad to be let off."* They were married at Richmond Parish Church on February 20th 1943.

Jeannie's parents were not entirely reconciled to having Derek as a son-in-law, but they were sensitive enough not to spoil their daughter's wedding day. Frank Nicol led her into the chapel of Richmond Church and the reception, held at Cholmondeley House, went off without a hitch, apart from the Thames bursting its banks and threatening to flood the house. It had done so before, but on this occasion it stopped just short and the happy couple were able to tip toe along a stone wall to the car which was waiting, wheels under water, to take them to Victoria Station. Their honeymoon was spent in Brighton, a time of hope for the future that Derek later recalled with great affection.

Cholmondeley House now became the marital home and it was here that Jeannie first acquired 'Monty', a stripey, marmalade kitten with white paws that Derek originally disapproved of, but who was to be the first of a number of pets that played an important part in their future lives. There was some temporary disruption when they were given notice to quit the house and after a difficult spell of house hunting they finally moved to another house by the river, Thames Bank Cottage, at Mortlake. This had the advantage of being situated right by the finishing line of the famous Oxford and Cambridge boat race, creating an annual opportunity for a giant party which they never let pass without doing it justice.

As the war moved slowly towards its bloody conclusion, they both continued with lives that Derek described as being *"at the heart"* of national affairs. He is referring here to the fact that, because of the potential usefulness of Jeannie's everyday contacts with leading international personalities and American newspaper correspondents, he had enrolled her into MI5. As a result she would have been privy, with Derek, to sensitive security issues and was exempted from the normal call-up. Ostensibly still happy and fulfilled in their work, they probably didn't yet realize that the seeds of future doubts about the *"spinning top"* of their lives, were already being sown. Derek had also been working constantly, since soon after publishing 'Went the Day Well?', on another book - this time an exhaustive survey of the British Empire, entitled 'One King'.

As part of my research, I'd tracked down a copy of 'Went the Day Well' without too much difficulty and happily read right through it, finding the various contributions about individual sacrifice during the war quite moving. Copies of 'One King' however, proved much more elusive. I searched the internet and the hardback shelves of local second hand bookshops - a survey of the Empire sounded as if it would make a hefty tome. The worthy sounding title, 'One King', troubled me a little though and I sensed that I might find some of Derek's political views uncomfortable - his friend David Cornwell (the writer John le Carre) had once written that although Derek was completely classless, *"...his radical right wing opinions would have had Genghis Khan choking in his soup"*. Many books with patriotic themes published during this period can seem absurdly jingoistic from our 21st century perspective and normally I'd sooner set fire to myself rather than wade through one. When I then read that Field Marshall Montgomery had written a letter of thanks to Derek for *'One King'* and that it had then become his favoured bedtime reading, my preconceptions were confirmed and I quietly dropped my search for a copy. Then, several weeks later, I received a parcel from a lady that had visited us a year earlier, who'd promised to send some memorabilia she had collected from a long friendship with Derek and Jeannie. Amongst the parcel was a copy of *'One King'*.

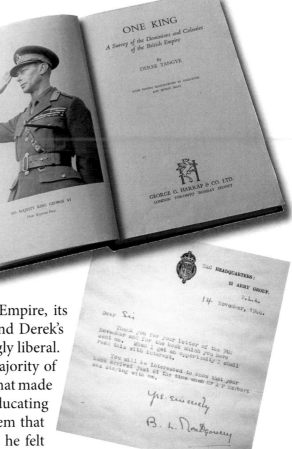

My concerns proved to be unfounded - whilst not exactly what most modern readers would call a page-turner, it is a well researched analysis of both the origins of the British Empire, its status at the time of writing - late 1944 - and Derek's opinions on its future. These were surprisingly liberal. In it he decries the ignorance of the vast majority of people about the inhabitants and territories that made up the Empire and argues that only by educating the public will it be possible to convince them that it was right to invest the large capital sums he felt were essential to help the more backward of Britain's overseas possessions move towards eventual self government. He manages to put up a valiant defence of the benefits that Britain had brought, whilst taking a generally enlightened view about what the future should be for the native peoples of the Empire.

If only because he is looking at the issues from the viewpoint of 1944, and we have the benefit of hindsight, parts of the book did make fascinating reading. He describes with some balance, for example, the situation in the then Mandated Territory of Palestine and the mutually incompatible promises made by the British government to first, the Arabs and then the Jews. For him, the impossible position Britain then found itself in filled him with foreboding and he finalises his chapter on Palestine with the prescient heading: *'Trouble is Coming'*. Likewise, his chapters on South Africa and India, written before the momentous events that were to take place in the following decades, show that he was a serious and thoughtful observer of the global political scene. His chapter on Australia praises their transferable voting system as *"an example for electoral reform to the Mother Country"*, a progressive opinion that nearly seventy years later, the mother country is only just getting around to putting to a referendum.

At the same time, Derek was writing from the social paradigm of 1944, and the spirit of comedian Harry Enfield's creation, Mr. Cholmondley-Warner, can occasionally be discerned, especially when he somehow contrived to allocate twenty five pages to describing the entire history of Australia, its discovery and colonisation, its vast outback, the convicts and immigrants, the development of its land, its rise to a powerful modern democracy and its role as a partner in wartime, with only a fleeting, single line mention of the original, but dispossessed, owners of the place - the Aborigines.

THE immediate post war years saw Jeannie Tangye firmly establish herself as probably the best Publicity Manager the Savoy had ever had. Although she enjoyed her job enormously, it did seem to her to have had more genuine purpose during the war years, and now during peacetime she was aware that her abilities and connections were sometimes taken advantage of by people with trivial commercial intentions. Then, late in 1947 there came a major test of her public relations abilities. An Italian waiter at the Savoy, named only as 'P', was sacked by the management amid suspicion that he was an agitator, planted there by the Revolutionary Communist Party, to stir up trouble. As a direct result of his sacking though, trouble certainly was stirred up, as it led to a large number of staff going on unofficial strike in his support, thus causing severe disruption to the hotel's ability to function properly. This would have needed some delicate public relations at the best of times, but the problem for Jeannie was made far worse because it occurred in the immediate run up to the wedding of the then Princess Elizabeth, the future Queen, to the Duke of Edinburgh. There were fears that the strike would disrupt the royal nuptuals and, with dozens of notables and assorted crowned heads of state due to stay at the Savoy, the idea that there might be reds under the Savoy's beds sent the establishment into a flat spin.

Communist agitators made wonderful copy for the Press and consequently the cause of something approaching paranoia within the post-war Labour government - three days before the wedding the Cabinet met to discuss its grave concerns about the strike. Recent releases of the Cabinet secretaries' notebooks in the National Archives show how concerned the government was: *"Danger if C. Party get control over Ldn. hotels. Managers open to blackmail. Centre for espionage etc."* If 'P' really was a 'plant', whoever planted him must have been laughing their little red socks off at the success of their dastardly plans. When the Savoy was heavily criticised in a leading newspaper article, poor Jeannie came under extreme pressure to pull their chestnuts out of the fire and resolve what was becoming a public relations disaster. Professional as ever, she stepped up to the mark and rallied support amongst the staff that hadn't gone on strike, who apparently felt that the attack on the Savoy was grossly unfair. She managed to get a letter of protest, signed by these staff, published on the front page of the Sunday Express, along with a leading editorial supporting them and opposing such unofficial strikes at a time when the country was desperately trying to recover from the effects of the war. Jeannie later called this episode *"one of the most miserable experiences of my life"* and went on to comment that the rewards of a glamorous job can be worthwhile *"if you are tough and have no other interests; but if your ambition is to enjoy life, you must have the luck to recognise the moment when it is time to go"*. She added: *"I had that luck."*

Derek, like Jeannie, suffered from a similar sense of post war ennui as most of his important war work came to an end. He felt *"restless and unsure"* despite the fact that he was still very much in demand as a journalist. Always a staunch patriot, he hinted with a rather conspiratorial overtone in his subsequent book *'The Way to Minack'*, there was still an ongoing arrangement with MI5 that he *"might have to operate on certain missions should the necessity arise"*. When I read this, I couldn't help wondering whether 'certain missions' might have included a clandestine operation to winkle out subversive Italian waiters, but if so, be assured that Derek maintained a discreet silence on the subject.

In later life he would talk quite freely about his experiences with MI5 and often included stories about it in his books. His MI5 work had brought him into close working contact with Kim Philby, Guy Burgess, Donald McClean and Anthony Blunt, members of the notorious ring of 'Cambridge spies' that had infiltrated to the very heart of British intelligence. Many years later, when his one-time MI5 chief, Guy Liddell, was accused, some twenty years after his death, of being a KGB agent, he was highly sceptical and pointed out how many writers were now making a very good living, thank you very much, out of encouraging 'secret agent' speculation. *"So easy to smear the reputations of those who are dead"* he wrote, unaware that he and Jeannie would one day be subject themselves to the very same posthumous speculation. In 2000, a national Sunday newspaper ran a story announcing that recently discovered KGB files suggested that Derek and Jeannie Tangye were both double agents and had carried on even after moving to Minack - presumably digging potatoes in all weathers or picking daffodils with an icy wind whistling around their derriéres simply as a cover for their more nefarious activities. The story was never substantiated, but it made good Sunday afternoon copy and inevitably went on to appear as front page news in the *Cornishman* and *Western Morning News*. It was met with incredulity by their friends who were outraged that such a smear could be published when they were no longer here to defend themselves - or sue for damages. To be fair, they were given plenty of column inches by the local press to refute the claims, but it's a sad fact of life that mud sticks, and actual evidence isn't required in order to get some people to believe even the most wildly improbable conspiracy theories.

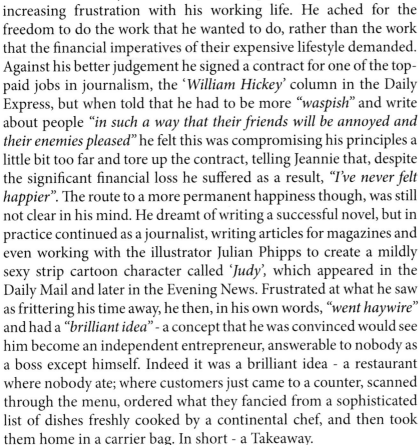

Back in the immediate post war period though, whether he was still involved in any clandestine security work or not, Derek expressed increasing frustration with his working life. He ached for the freedom to do the work that he wanted to do, rather than the work that the financial imperatives of their expensive lifestyle demanded. Against his better judgement he signed a contract for one of the top-paid jobs in journalism, the 'William Hickey' column in the Daily Express, but when told that he had to be more *"waspish"* and write about people *"in such a way that their friends will be annoyed and their enemies pleased"* he felt this was compromising his principles a little bit too far and tore up the contract, telling Jeannie that, despite the significant financial loss he suffered as a result, *"I've never felt happier"*. The route to a more permanent happiness though, was still not clear in his mind. He dreamt of writing a successful novel, but in practice continued as a journalist, writing articles for magazines and even working with the illustrator Julian Phipps to create a mildly sexy strip cartoon character called *'Judy'*, which appeared in the Daily Mail and later in the Evening News. Frustrated at what he saw as frittering his time away, he then, in his own words, *"went haywire"* and had a *"brilliant idea"* - a concept that he was convinced would see him become an independent entrepreneur, answerable to nobody as a boss except himself. Indeed it was a brilliant idea - a restaurant where nobody ate; where customers just came to a counter, scanned through the menu, ordered what they fancied from a sophisticated list of dishes freshly cooked by a continental chef, and then took them home in a carrier bag. In short - a Takeaway.

Sadly it was at least ten years or more ahead of its time. The great British public, used to plain wartime food and whose only foreign travel, unlike Derek, was likely to have been in a troop carrier on Army rations, were singularly unimpressed. And, just as importantly, most of them simply couldn't afford it. Despite his best efforts, working long hours behind the counter himself and even co-opting Jeannie in to work on Saturday afternoons, the business folded. This brought on a period of intense introspection between Derek and Jeannie, who often talked about their future late into the night. Their experiences had, if anything, strengthened their marriage, and they were increasingly of the same mind - they just needed a way of life that they could really believe in, something with integrity, honesty and above all, independence.

Left to right: A P Herbert, Dave Golding, Derek, Jeannie and Frank Bowles MP (later Lord Bowles), at the opening of 'The Larder'

They both loved Cornwall and, as Derek regarded himself as a native Cornishman, it was natural that they should take their holidays there. Like many townspeople on holiday in the countryside, relaxed and away from the pressures of their busy everyday lives, they enjoyed indulging themselves in the dream of getting away from it all to a life of honest and independent endeavour somewhere in a rural setting. For most people it's just a pleasant fantasy; a part of the enjoyment of temporary escape, and as practical considerations reassert themselves at the end of the holiday the dream is reluctantly put away in the suitcase with the other souvenirs. On previous holidays, this was pretty much how it had been for Derek and Jeannie. They had vague ideas of an old and isolated cottage, close to the sea, and a life tilling the soil, but as long as nowhere that fitted the dream actually presented itself, action could be delayed indefinitely.

DEREK and Jeannie found their future in the spring of 1949, when they were staying at Lamorna Cove, on the far south western coast of Cornwall, just a few miles from Land's End. They'd been playing their 'looking for a cottage' game, and on this occasion were now sitting outside the village pub, the *Lamorna Wink*, enjoying a quiet drink. They confided in one of the locals, who'd then told them that there was a vacant, but tumble-down cottage on the cliff land to the west. They immediately decided to try and find it. Having then walked some half a mile along the overgrown cliff path from the Cove, admiring the blue sweep of Mount's Bay and taking in the hazy outlines of the Lizard peninsula, they'd arrived at the rocky outcrop known as Carn Barges. This huge carn marks a ridge on the coastal path and is an ideal point at which to take a breather, to shelter for a moment if there's a strong breeze, or to simply immerse yourself in a place that has changed very little in thousands of years. On this coast the air, coming straight off the ocean, can be almost intoxicating in its purity, and Carn Barges gave them a breathtaking vantage point, looking downwards across jagged rocks to the sea below and westwards along the cliffs and moorland to the next headland of Tater Du. As you picture this scene, listen now to Derek as he brings his considerable descriptive powers, honed by years as a professional journalist, fully to bear when describing, in 'A Gull on the Roof', this seminal moment in their lives:

Carn Barges with Tater Du in the distance

"Jeannie suddenly pointed inland. "Look!" she said, "there it is!" There was never any doubt in either of our minds. The small grey cottage a mile away, squat in the lonely landscape, surrounded by trees and edged into the side of a hill, became as if by magic the present and the future. It was as if a magician beside this ancient Carn had cast a spell upon us, so that we could touch the future as we could, at that moment, touch the Carn. There in the distance we could see our figures moving about our daily tasks, a thousand, thousand figures criss-crossing the untamed land, dissolving into each other, leaving a mist of excitement of our times to come."

What they could see in the distance was 'Dorminack', known locally just as 'Minack', a 400 year old cottage, isolated from the outside world by its position at the far end of a bumpy, mile-long farm track. Damp, worm eaten, rat infested and abandoned, its lack

of any sort of modern facilities must have added immeasurably to its sense of isolation, but in a perverse way only added to its initial attraction to Derek and Jeannie, along with the sheer wild beauty of its setting. They resolved to find the owner.

They were, of course, eventually successful in winning Dorminack and *A Gull on the Roof* is primarily the story of their early lives there. Initially, few people had given them much of a prayer, especially some of the locals. You can hardly blame them - local people were well used to visitors, having been seduced by a relaxing holiday far from all the cares of their everyday lives, passing their final evening in the pub by indulging in a dream of a new life in a traditional Cornish cottage. Minack was indeed in an idyllic setting that could easily beguile the senses in the long, balmy days of a Cornish summer. It would, however, require a major effort to make the building even remotely habitable, let alone to clear its overgrown meadows and then make a living from them. Neither of them had any agricultural experience at all and Jeannie must have seemed a mere slip of a girl, quite unsuited to hard, outdoor physical labour. In summer the Cornish sea and coastal views may indeed be quite wonderful, but wait until the Cornish winter, when this same coast is assaulted by Cornish gales, and grey, horizontal Cornish rain is rattling the doors and lashing against the windows - that would be the real test of what this upcountry couple were made of.

Derek and Jeannie proved they were made of pretty tenacious stuff, and went on to win the respect of many local farmers. It was a respect won by perseverance and hard physical work, bringing the cliff meadows back into commercial production, and becoming more self-sufficient by growing their own vegetables and keeping

chickens. Derek frankly admitted how frequently he was afflicted by worries and fears for the future, but at times like these he also credited Jeannie with strengthening his resolve by her quiet but unwavering conviction that they had chosen the right path. Jeannie, who in many ways had given up the most to pursue their dream, was often the rock upon which their new life was now being built. Step by step, day by day, beset by difficulties and sometimes outright

"..there was the continuing challenge to prove that we were not flirting with the tedium of manual labour...that we possessed staying power which could earn respect."

disasters; encouraged by occasional successes, and always buoyed by the exhilaration of existing literally on the edge, they started to give Dorminack a new life. In the process they were building for themselves new and, despite the problems, infinitely more fulfilling lives.

For anyone thinking of giving up the rat race for the 'good life', *A Gull on the Roof* is both a warning and an inspiration.

DEREK and Jeannie must, in their hearts, have realized from the beginning that trying to live entirely off the proceeds of this remote smallholding, however heroic the effort they put into it, was probably unrealistic. They became as self-sufficient as possible and Derek's garden diaries are full of notes about crops and planting times and other information that show how important this was to their philosophy of life. They brewed their own wine, and Derek at first claimed, putting on a brave face, that it had been good enough to serve over dinner and fool a connoisseur friend. Later he ruefully owned up and admitted it was scarcely drinkable. Lovers of classical music, they entertained themselves during the dark winter evenings playing records from their collection. "*The blessing of enthusiasm is its ability to deceive pleasantly*" he wrote of those early days of hope. They worked hard though, and treated their smallholding as a deadly serious business, employing experienced staff, branching out into different crops and sinking whatever capital they could scrape together into equipment and greenhouses. Had they not been able to find another source of income though, it is likely that their venture to find the good life at Minack may well have failed. Writing was the obvious answer, but it was not Derek who first turned to the pen as a way of supplementing their income - it was Jeannie. Her first book was '*Meet me at the Savoy*', a novel based upon her experiences in her former life as the Public Relations Officer for the hotel and published under her maiden name. Initially turned down by larger publishers, it was eventually published by Museum Press in 1952 and then serialised in *John Bull* magazine. Although only a modest financial success, it helped to keep the wolf from the door, supported the business, and paid for a few much needed improvements to the cottage - just small things - like running water.

When I say 'running water' I mean that, courtesy of a new well and a pump, water could at least usually be persuaded to *run in* to a tap. The luxury of it running out again had to wait until they could afford drains. But it was enough to encourage Derek to start writing again.

As an experienced journalist he knew there was always an

appetite amongst the public for stories about the hopes and struggles of real people in real life. No doubt he also realized that many people yearned, in their imaginations at least, to be transported away from the austere dullness of life in post-war Britain. In 1955 he decided to start work on an autobiographical book telling the story of their first few years at Minack. Somewhat slow in gestation, *A Gull on the Roof* was eventually published in 1961 - it was to be the first of a series that would make Derek one of Britain's most popular writers.

Derek's second book, published the following year, was *A Cat in the Window*, unashamedly dedicated to their cat, Monty, who played such an important role in their lives, both before and after moving to Minack. Monty *"the colour of autumn bracken"* was named by Jeannie after General Montgomery, as he'd come into her life at the same time that the famous wartime Commander of the 8th Army had arrived in London to report back to Winston Churchill on the North Africa campaign. Jeannie had met Montgomery in her role as Press Officer for the Savoy Group, and on this occasion had been given the task of ensuring that his presence *wasn't* reported in the press. It was Monty (the cat, not the General) that converted Derek, stage by stage, from an irrational but inbuilt antipathy to all members of the feline race, to being a cat lover.

Along with Jeannie, he now regarded all the creatures that shared Minack with them to be their special friends, giving both the wild and the domesticated ones pet names. They were in fact almost as likely to give pet names to places and inanimate objects as they were to their actual pets, thus imbuing their surroundings with a heightened reality. The books abound with nicknames like 'the Ambrose Rock', 'Monty's Leap', 'Oliver Land' and 'the Confusion Room'; names that would acquire special meaning to his regular readers and that often then became the titles for his books. Some might find this attitude a little too sentimental, but Derek never considered honest sentimentality a vice, and in any event he much preferred it to the false metropolitan sophistication both he and Jeannie had come to hate in London. At Minack they could be as 'sentimental' as they liked - this was *their* world, the one they'd created, and there was nobody else in it with the right to sneer or criticize.

In the third book of the series, *A Drake at the Door*, Derek introduced his readers to the widening circle of people and animals that enriched their lives at Minack, bringing their story vividly to life and ensuring that each future book was awaited by a growing army of readers eager for another glimpse of the magic of Minack. As the years passed and the number of titles grew, the books became known collectively as *The Minack Chronicles*. *A Drake at the Door* was followed by *A Donkey in the Meadow*; next came *Lama,* and then *The Way to Minack* and *A Cornish Summer*, each one building upon a readership that had now expanded well beyond the shores of Britain.

Such success as an author gave Derek much greater financial security, but brought with it new responsibilities. Book launches require the presence of the author to maximise publicity, and this meant travelling up to London. Temporarily at least, Derek and Jeannie had to return to the world they'd worked so hard to escape from. Their circumstances were now quite different though, and they made use of the contrast of these occasional sabbaticals to refresh themselves. Jeannie especially enjoyed the opportunity to get out her best clothes and spend a few days away from wearing working corduroys. They would stay at the Savoy, eat their evening meal at their old table and indulge in a little nolstagia as they looked out from the hotel's large windows at the familiar view across the Thames. Anxious about their animals though, they were always glad to get back and Derek often described how, after a few days away in London, they would whoop and cheer as they turned their car into the lane that led to Minack.

Although it was Derek's books that became best sellers, Jeannie continued to write and followed *Meet me at the Savoy* with three other books - *Hotel Regina; Home is the Hotel,* and *Bertioni's Hotel.* A naturally creative person, she'd always supplied the line drawings for Derek's books and went on to develop her skills as a painter in the quiet little hut that was set aside as her personal studio.

In 1970 *Woman's Weekly* magazine started to serialize abridged versions of the Chronicles and thus started a relationship that would last for many years. Between 1970 and 1990 they published eleven of the books in this format, liberally illustrated with photographs and helped to expand an ever widening readership. Derek and Jeannie's lives at Minack were now being followed by readers all over the world - at their peak, whether you were in the coldest depths of Canada or somewhere in the searing heat of Australia, the chances are there was someone not too far away from you that was reading one of The Minack Chronicles, and being transported in their mind's eye to a far distant world that revolved around a tiny cottage and a few acres of a remote Cornish cliff. The full series of books would eventually comprise eighteen separate titles, plus four additional compilation and omnibus editions, and span thirty five years. The final book, *The Confusion Room*, was published in 1996, the year of Derek's death. He was to carry on writing almost to the very end of his life at Minack; amongst his papers found at the cottage were the initial workings of yet another book, which he'd provisionally entitled 'Shadows'

I F YOU'VE ever been on a walking holiday in Cornwall, you can probably already appreciate why Derek and Jeannie regarded it as a very special place. Even if just driving down here for a few days to enjoy our beaches, scenery, restaurants and tourist attractions, many people are somehow aware that, by crossing the Tamar, they seem to be entering a different country. In many ways, of course, that's exactly what they are doing - for this great river, which practically bisects the land from the north coast to the south, all but makes Cornwall an island, a boundary that for centuries has kept it as a place apart. There are many today who claim that the Tamar still defines Cornwall, more than a thousand years since the English King Athelstan first did so, as being a place *next to,* not *part of* England - just like Wales and Scotland.

The more you then travel further west, past the Eden Project and the white 'alps' that mark the china clay pits around St Austell; on to the bleak, but beautiful Bodmin Moor; past the creeks and inlets of Daphne du Maurier country in the south, or the breathtaking cliffs of Tintagel and King Arthur country in the north; the more you will be aware that you are entering into the celtic heart of Cornwall. The now ubiquitous black flags with their white cross of St Piran, and the large number of public signs in the Cornish language bear witness to a place that is inceasingly aware of the value of its own culture and history. And if you are now in the heart of Cornwall, travel on westwards, cross the River Hayle into *Penwith*, and you are surely entering its soul.

It's certainly impossible to spend any time here in Cornwall's far western peninsula and not be aware that you are in a very *ancient* place, with overt spiritual overtones. Soon

St Michael's Mount

after crossing the Hayle, the romantic island of St Michael's Mount, topped with its 12th century Benedictine monastery comes into sight, dominating the view seawards. Arriving then at the only town of any size, Penzance, you pass a welcome sign at the rail terminus that proudly declares, by using the original Cornish for its name - '*Pensans*' - that you are now entering the '*holy headland*'. W a l k the lanes, moorland tracks and cliff paths here and as you scan the map the very place names are redolent of the distant past; practically every village and church is named after its own celtic saint and everywhere you look, from natural features like hills and rock formations, to farms and people's homes, there are names in the Cornish language. On the higher ground, the moors are littered with hundreds of remains from the celtic Iron Age - round houses, courtyard settlements and fortified cliff 'castles' -

Pensans - the holy headland - welcomes arrivals at Penzance Station

so many in fact that, despite the best efforts of the local authority and enthusiastic volunteers, only the most significant can be kept in the sort of visitor-friendly trim that similar sites would be if in, say, the home counties of England. Perhaps even more remarkable are the numbers of yet older monuments, like the neolithic and bronze age menhirs, quoits and stone circles. Strange, primeval places that were clearly intended for a ceremonial or religious purpose, they have survived here in large numbers, many for well over four thousand years. For the student of archaeology there is scarcely anywhere else quite like this in western Europe - and all in a small peninsula where you are never more than four miles from the sea.

The Merry Maidens, near Lamorna.

As we have seen, Derek's childhood memories drew him back to Cornwall for their holidays together and they knew instinctively that it was here that they could find what they needed. Although they had a dislike for institutionalised religion, they both had a strong spiritual side to their natures and knew that in Cornwall this would be nourished, rather than chipped away at and eventually destroyed by the selfishness and cynicism they couldn't avoid mixing with in the lifestyle they were living in London.

Derek summed up the atmosphere that pervades the landscape in '*When the Winds Blow*', one of the books that make up The Minack Chronicles: "*There are times in the far west of Cornwall when you can feel yourself enveloped by a mysticism which is not just a word, but an almost tangible communion with those who have been here before.*" He knew that, in their search for a more fulfilling existence, they could scarcely have found anywhere that was more in tune with their needs, or more in contrast to their former lives. Many writers have referred to this concept as the *genius loci*, the idea that certain locations have a 'spirit of place'. The Romans originally coined the phrase to describe the spirit that they thought attached itself to certain shrines and holy places. I firmly believe that what kept Derek and Jeannie Tangye going during some of their really difficult times at Minack was not only their original vision of a working life there, but their awareness of the 'spirit of place' of Cornwall's far western peninsula.

*St Helen's Chapel,
Cape Cornwall*

Penwith has, of course, always been attractive to creative people, and internationally important art colonies were first established over a century ago, starting with the famous 'Newlyn School' of painters who 'discovered' this fishing village in the 1880s. Across on the north coast, St Ives became so synonymous with painting that it is now home to its own Tate Gallery. Writers and poets too, from Virginia Woolf, W.H.Davies and D.H.Lawrence in the last century, to Derek's friend and near neighbour David Cornwell in this, have found Penwith to be fertile ground in which to work. Lamorna, with its mild, verdant valley has for long been a haven to its very own artists' colony - during the first half of the last century, some 40 leading artists lived here, including such illustrious names as Dame Laura Knight and the president of the Royal Academy, Sir Alfred Munnings. The painter, Lamorna Birch, took his very name from the valley and became perhaps the most prolific landscape artist in Britain. That heritage is still strong today - in the autumn of 2009 Lamorna held an arts festival in which 27 artists, sculptors and potters opened their studios to the public to help raise funds for a children's hospice in Cornwall.

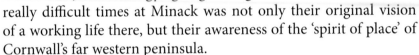

Compared to St Ives and Newlyn though, Lamorna is a tiny place, little more than a short stroll from one side to the other. Turning down the Cove road from the B3315 in the summer the visitor enters a tunnel of greenery with just a few cottages dotted along the road and valley sides. An old chapel by the roadside is now the village hall, and a little further on is the famous Lamorna Wink pub, full of nautical regalia, but changed very little since Derek and Jeannie sat outside and first heard about the

derelict cottage up on the nearby cliffs. In those days there was also a small Post Office and a garage, but they are now long gone. A short

walk away, over a little bridge to the other side of the Lamorna stream is the Mill Gift Shop, run by Estelle Fox, who can proudly trace her family at the mill back to the 13th century. Although no longer a working mill, amongst its moist, dappled greenery and the sound of the nearby stream it isn't difficult to imagine the ancient wheel still turning. The peacocks Estelle keeps there will occasionally wander off into the woods, or sit in the trees behind the Wink and startle the unwary drinker by giving voice with their ethereal call. In the spring the surrounding undergrowth comes alive with daffodils, the legacy of the last war, when farmers grubbed up their daffodil fields to plant vegetables and dumped the bulbs in the woods. Here and there you'll see a cottage with early daffodil bunches for sale. It isn't all bucolic simplicity - a reminder of the comfort and sophistication of the modern world can be found up the lane opposite the Wink, where 'The Cove' hotel looks out imperiously across the valley.

Higher up the lane is 'Chygurno', the house where Robert and Carol Moule have defied their exposure to the winter gales to create a sub-tropical garden, open to the public during the summer, that has surely the most stunning view of any garden in Cornwall.

Back down along the cove road, past the Wink, the valley side falls away to reveal the tumbling stream below as it makes its way towards the sea. Suddenly the vista opens out as the Cove comes into view - and a sea that can be, regardless of the season, a lazy, azure blue, or a spume-flecked, angry grey. Behind it is the dramatic promontory of Carn Dhu, the iconic *black rockpile* that has formed the backdrop to countless paintings and photographs of Lamorna. You'd have to be dull of spirit indeed to watch the sun rise from behind Carn Dhu without feeling uplifted. On the sloping eastern cliffs of the cove a couple of cottages appear to cling perilously, just beneath a massive pile of

View of Carn Dhu from Chygurno Gardens

granite boulders, the spoil from a long abandoned quarry. Below, on the western side, is the small harbour, now worryingly storm-damaged, with its straddle of terraced cottages, a car park, a shop and the 'Cafe at the Cove'.

This then, over sixty years ago now, was the environment that Derek and Jeannie Tangye had instinctively known was worth more to them than all the money and the sophisticated lifestyle they had in London. The things that they may once have enjoyed in the metropolis, a lifestyle that many must have actually envied them for, they eventually felt they were simply enduring. In this far western corner of Penwith they discovered a place whose pulse beat to a different rhythm, and at Minack they found their real home.

ESPITE the fact that Derek and Jeannie hated the jangling intrusiveness of the telephone and refused to have one at Minack, their lives were not lived in complete isolation from the outside world. There were naturally visits from family members and, especially in the early days, the occasional house guest from their former social circle would come and stay. The rigours of Minack's 'facilities' could be relied on to whittle regular visitors down to just their real friends. Although they deliberately avoided replicating a rural version of their former social life, they were inevitably drawn into some of the numerous events on the village social calendar. After all, if you really want to drop under the village radar, it's not a good idea to go out and buy a donkey, let alone one in foal, and that's exactly what Derek describes them doing in *A Donkey in the Meadow*. Donkeys have always been a magnet for children, and when it came to the St Buryan and Lamorna children, the Tangye's donkeys were no exception, inevitably drawing both of them into involvement in various social activities, like birthday parties and opening the annual Lamorna Summer Fete. Their first donkey was called Penny; bred in Ireland and at risk, so Jeannie believed, of being sold for pet food. She soon rewarded her rescuers by presenting them with a foal - a tiny bundle of ears and legs that they named, rather prosaically, 'Fred'. As soon as Fred arrived on the scene, he enjoyed *"a glorious summer of adulation"* and Minack was henceforth guaranteed a regular supply of visitors. From that day, donkeys and Minack became an inseparable partnership, and one that provided an inexhaustible source of anecdotes for Derek's writing.

Fred

Whilst they now had plenty of visitors, especially as the books moved up the best-seller charts, and were increasingly invited to all sorts of social functions in west Cornwall, it has been said that Derek and Jeannie acquired relatively few really close friends. The remoteness of Minack's location, which they had willingly sought, and its spartan nature were hardly conducive to frequent entertaining and the social interaction that helps to create and cement close relationships. It was perhaps only natural that they would gravitate for conversation and friendship to the company of other creative people, especially the artists and fellow writers that shared their love of Cornwall. Living not far away from them was John Miller, an internationally acclaimed artist and, amongst Cornwall's creative community, one of its most loved. A deeply spiritual man, Truro

Cathedral proudly displays a large painting by him that shows the whole of Cornwall, laid out as if viewed from the heavens, showing every church in the Duchy. With his partner, the potter, Michael Truscott, they were often referred to very affectionately by Jeannie as *"the boys"*, and invited to share a special Boxing Day lunch at Minack. John Miller died in 2002 but he can be heard talking about Minack on a DVD that is being published to accompany this book by the photographer, John Coles. Fortunately, he first started recording interviews for this in 1997, so they include one where he meets John Miller in his studio in Penzance. Here he reads eloquently from *A Gull on the Roof* and recalls with affection the *"wonderful feeling of fellowship"* they all shared when meeting together at Minack.

John Miller

Amongst fellow authors they were friends with was Cardiff-born novelist Howard Spring, whose poverty stricken upbringing was so utterly different to Derek's, but who first learnt his craft, like Derek, as a journalist, and had also served in the Intelligence Department in France during the first world war. He'd moved with

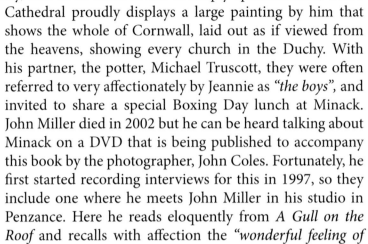

his wife Marion to Cornwall in 1939 and in the early 1960s, towards the end of his hugely successful career, he'd suffered a stroke which incapacitated him for some time. He recovered sufficiently to write another book, *'Winds of the Day'*, but had been very concerned about its quality. Derek and Jeannie had encouraged and reassured him and he wrote an appreciative letter to them in October 1964, looking forward to meeting them again. Howard Spring died just a few months later, on 3rd May 1965, but in the meantime *'Winds of the Day'* had entered the best seller lists.

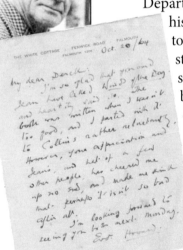

Perhaps the most well known of Derek and Jeannie's friends to the general public is David Cornwell - the writer John le Carré. As one of the most successful British authors of the past fifty years, David could probably choose to live anywhere in the world, but for some forty years now he's made his main home on this same remote part of the Cornish coast. He originally came to west Penwith after his first marriage broke up and he stayed with John Miller, temporarily taking over the top floor of his house in the small village of Sancreed. It was whilst out walking with John that he saw a row of three derelict cottages for sale. The farmer was actually working on the land at the time, so David approached him and virtually sealed the deal to buy them on the spot, along with a large stretch of the cliffs. He converted the cottages into one house, and moved there with his wife Jane, becoming both neighbours and lifelong friends with Derek and Jeannie. It was to be David Cornwell that would give moving tributes at the funerals of first Jeannie in 1986, and then Derek ten years later. He also wrote an obituary for Derek in the Daily Telegraph that was simultaneously generous, critical, perceptive, revealing, affectionate and occasionally very funny.

David Cornwell

David had never warmed to Derek's journalistic tendency towards purple prose, and wrote frankly that it was a mercy he'd never aspired to writing fiction. Living so close, he also loathed the uninvited visitors that would often turn up at his own house, hang around the door or roost in the garden, convinced they'd found Dorminack. Searching for donkeys or the whereabouts of their guru, some would then either mistake him for Derek, or worse, assume he was just one of Derek's acolytes. *"That way"* he would explain patiently, *"about a mile."* Over the years though, he'd developed what he called an 'adversarial' friendship with Derek, which was often cemented over informal lunches and, with Jeannie generously refilling the glasses, the consumption of prodigious quantities of whisky. Although he'd been sceptical at first about the sincerity of Derek's role as a plain man's philosopher, he came to accept that his books were genuinely written from the heart and that *"you could never quite deny the magic"*. As their mutual trust had grown, he would sometimes visit him when his own writing wasn't going well and found that *"within an hour his strength, heart and energy had bounced me back to life"*. Whatever his criticisms about writing style, he conceded that Derek *"gave more comfort and more joy to more readers in his lifetime than most writers dream of "*.

David finished his obituary by describing Derek's absolute determination, throughout his final illness, to stay at Dorminack, where he and Jeannie had created their legend, and concluded that he *"loved him greatly"*, despite the fact that Derek's final words to him were *"bugger off "*.

To Derek and Jeannie's credit the social mix of their friends and acquaintances seems to have been wide and varied - the archive material that survives shows that they kept in touch with many of the people that they'd previously either employed, or first met as visitors seeking out Minack after reading the books. Sometimes this was at the simple level of exchanging Christmas cards and correspondence, but occasionally a deeper personal friendship developed with a reader who'd initially made their way down the 'winding lane' simply to seek the reality behind the books.

One of the most significant of these friendships was with Anne and Malcolm Sutton, both of whom Derek was to eventually name as Trustees in his will. Anne was given the most sensitive task of all, for Derek gave her the specific responsibility of sorting through all of his and Jeannie's private papers, with instructions to sort and destroy all those of a sensitive or intimate nature. Derek and Jeannie had both been prolific writers and correspondents throughout their lives, and the 'papers' turned out to be a Pickfords' van full of some sixty boxes. Diaries and photographs were mixed in with Jeannie's recipe cuttings, shopping lists and various letters from show business personalities and close friends like Gertrude Lawrence and Danny Kaye. Proof copies of books were jumbled up with contracts and general ephemera accumulated from a lifetime together. Over many months Anne sorted these into those that should be destroyed and those that, with legal advice, should be sold as part of Derek's estate. There were also, of course, recent letters from Derek's readers, unanswered during his final weeks of illness, which Anne took upon herself to answer, along with the new post that arrived daily, now redirected by the Post Office. One addressed to *'Derek Tangye, Cottage on a Cliff, Cornwall'* still found its way, courtesy of Penzance postal staff, to Anne. When I visited Anne and Malcolm at their home in west Penwith, Anne told me of many of her memories of Minack, which included an intriguing story about Derek's role in bringing them together.

Malcolm had been the first of them to visit Minack, as early as January 1964. After reading *A Gull on the Roof*, he'd contacted Derek, who had then recommended that he stay at the Lamorna Cove Hotel. Having travelled down from Cheshire by steam train to Penzance, bus to Mousehole and a two hour walk to Lamorna, he checked in at the hotel. It was worth the effort though, because the following day he was to find that Minack was indeed exactly as described in the books, *"almost as if a stage set had been organised for the occasion."* Malcolm had struck up an immediate rapport with both Derek and Jeannie, and returned several times each year, making a number of mutual friends.

Anne then told me how she hadn't found Minack until over twenty years later, but still some years before meeting Malcolm. *"My childhood holidays had always been spent in Cornwall and my mother introduced me to the Minack Chronicles by putting a paperback of 'Lama' in my Christmas stocking."* The following September she'd visited Lamorna with her then husband, Martin, and after initially being too shy to call unannounced, they eventually ventured down the lane. *"Derek and Jeannie emerged from the mist, each leading a donkey. Derek had 'Merlin' and Jeannie was leading 'Fred'. Derek immediately gave me Merlin's rope and we walked together, whilst Martin led Fred and walked with Jeannie. When we left, promising to comply with Derek's invitation to return, we walked up the lane and Martin said to me - 'Jeannie isn't well.' He said he could sense it."* Tragically, Martin was absolutely right and this was to be their only meeting with Jeannie, as she died from cancer the following February.

In 1988 Derek wrote a new will which, after his death, would establish The Minack Chronicles Nature Trust. He chose four Trustees, none of whom at that time had ever met. Anne was one of them and amongst the others was Malcolm Sutton. By coincidence, both their marriages were by then breaking up and each of them had also privately confided in Derek, who was, said Anne, *"kind and supportive"*. She remembered sitting with Derek at Minack and his words when talking about his vision for the Trust: *'When I'm run over by a double-decker bus, my Trustees will have to work together, so I think it would be a really good idea if you all met beforehand.'* Anne had thought Derek was just being sensible, but with hindsight she now realised that he was secretly match-making. Malcolm used to break his journeys to Cornwall near Exeter, which was where Anne lived, so she agreed that Derek could send him her address and telephone number, not realising that he also planned to send her photograph. They met that December and again at a meeting of the Trustees in the Spring of 1989, at which time they realised they had fallen in love. They married in 1994 and when they visited Derek a few days before their marriage, he handed them a copy of his latest book, *The Story of the Minack Chronicles*. They were delighted to find that Derek's dedication, using their new married names read:

'*To Malcolm and Anne Sutton, the Trustees of the Minack Chronicles Trust*'. It was followed by a hand written inscription to say that it came with the '*everlasting love of all at Minack*'.

We talked about what it was in Derek's writing that gave it such a widespread appeal. Anne felt that his real strength stemmed from "*his underlying philosophy that runs throughout his books; essentially that we should care for the environment, and take time to stand and stare.*" They also told me a few anecdotes which helped to shed more light on him as an individual. He was, said Anne, "*A very complex character. He could appear arrogant and was often quite abrasive, but despite his worldwide success, he was actually inherently insecure.*" Malcolm agreed and added "*Once when we were with Derek a friend visited and talked a lot about himself. Derek said suddenly, and not at all in jest, 'Well that's all very interesting, but when are we going to talk about me?' He often seemed to feel somehow at a disadvantage, especially when compared with his brothers, especially Nigel, whom he often told us, 'was always more successful at everything'.*" At first surprising, this residual sibling rivalry is perhaps more understandable when you realise just how hard an act to follow his

Malcolm, Anne & Derek

older brother had been. Nigel Tangye pursued a long, varied and very successful career as a pilot, author, and eventually hotelier at Glendorgal, their childhood home. It also echoed an assessment of Derek's frailties that had been expressed by David Power in his biography, 'Tangye'. As if to balance his comments though, Malcolm added: "*But, you know, Derek could also be expansive and generous, with a great sense of fun.*"

I asked them when they'd last seen Derek. "*A couple of months before he died,*" replied Anne, "*when he was so frail we didn't expect to see him again; but he rallied and we shared some further, rather poignant visits, the last being a couple of weeks before his death. We were honoured and humbled by the trust Derek placed in us, and his faith in our judgement.*"

Anne and Malcolm subsequently served for eight years as Trustees, before pressure of Anne's job forced them reluctantly to resign. They both felt that a personal legacy to them had been the number of close friends, from all over the world, they'd made during those years dealing with Trust correspondence. Anne then confided a final thought - *"Guiding us to our love affair and happy marriage is something for which, over 20 years on, we both every day feel indebted to Derek."*

Soon after this meeting I went to see another of Derek's friends, but this time one that had first come to Minack as an employee. For Derek and Jeannie, the labour intensive nature of the work had originally been one of the attractions of the Minack lifestyle, and they both enjoyed being able to lose themselves in the sheer physical effort of cultivating the land. In practice it meant that it was necessary to employ local people to help, both on the flower farm and domestically, and as the years went by a succession of characters passed through the narrative of the Chronicles. Amongst the first to appear, in *A Drake at the Door*, was a young girl who'd recently moved, with her family, to a cottage above Tregiffian cliff, just a little further to the west. She arrived at Minack one autumn evening, determined to find a job working with plants and flowers. Her name was Jane Wyllie, and she became such a trusted friend that Derek asked her to be one of his Trustees. It was also to be Jane who, some three years after Derek's death, would take over the lease of the empty and rapidly deteriorating Dorminack smallholding and revive it as a working flower farm. Jane had by then far exceeded her original modest aim, having become a well known professional horticulturist, exhibiting and lecturing widely on the subject. For several years after taking on Dorminack she ran it with her partner and fellow horticulturist, Peter Clough, but sadly Peter died in 2008 and Jane now manages the work there alone. We see her quite frequently driving her red van down the lane, and sometimes at her stall selling plants at the St Buryan farmers' market.

When she'd first arrived at Derek and Jeannie's door she was a waif-like girl of fourteen, and Derek admired her sheer unaffected enjoyment at working, often barefoot under the summer sun, amongst the plants she loved. Searching for a descriptive phrase, he wrote that she had something of the pagan about her. Jane is still very much a free spirit and fiercely protective of the tranquillity of Minack and its meadows. I asked her if she would tell me something about her memories of working with Derek and Jeannie on the flower farm. *"It was the magnificent scenery of Tregiffian cliff that made my mind up for me - I decided to give up my planned career, leave school and find work locally, both to contribute to the family income, which we needed because of my father's ill health, and to*

Jane as a teenage prize winner.

immerse myself in the beautiful surroundings. I asked around locally and was directed to 'the young couple who will need someone to work for them in their new glasshouse.' Minack was at that time already a hive of activity, with a strong market for the flowers and the early potatoes." The 'hive of activity' was largely centred around Geoffrey Semmens, a local man who Derek had employed for his professional expertise. *"Geoffrey was the powerhouse"* said Jane, *"with the knowledge and experience of local flower farming, an expert shovel man and extremely fast daffodil picker. Derek was a worrier and quite volatile, but could always be teased into a good humour by Jeannie's infectious giggle and unfailing optimism."*

The Chronicles are full of real life characters like Geoffrey Semmens and over the years a succession of people that worked at Minack pass through the narrative, some with relatively minor walk-on roles, and others that played a more significant part in the ongoing story. Jane especially recalled Shelagh, a young girl who'd joined them at a time when there was a great demand for 'Cornish Posies'. These had been especially developed by the Tangyes to make full use of the very early seasonal flowers, like violets. *"With her nimble fingers, Shelagh became chief violet buncher. We each had our own specialities to care for and prepare for market, but we all pitched in wherever needed, particularly in the daffodil season. We tormented Derek when his bunching failed to meet the standards of perfection we demanded of ourselves. He'd then announce that there were 'too many women here - I'm off to help Geoffrey.' Soon after Shelagh arrived he decided that the staff could now manage the day to day work of the farm and he could take take time out to write. The rest needs no telling!"*

Jane was to leave Minack to develop her career on the Isles of Scilly, but she remained good friends with the Tangyes and they became Godparents to her daughter. She told me that on later visits to Minack she had noticed how the flower business had declined and Minack's original seclusion diminished by the constant arrival of readers with books to be signed, the price that had to be paid for the overwhelming success of the Chronicles. *"After Jeannie died Derek spoke to me often of his agony in having to explain over and over again to visitors why she was not there to greet them with him. He developed strategies to cope, and here the donkeys and the Oliver Land became the focus of the Minack experience, enriching the visit for his readers, whilst deflecting the pressure."*

The books cover several decades starting in the 1950s, so it's quite natural to still meet local people that featured in them, even from the earliest editions. People like Jack Cockram who Derek described as *"a young farmer"* that he'd first met by the stand at the end of the lane, where the milk churns used to be left. Jack is now retired and lives in the nearby fishing village of Newlyn, but I see him regularly on Sunday mornings in St Buryan Church. He told me how he'd originally come here during the last war as a child evacuee from London, staying at Roselucombe, one of the other farms in the lane. He liked it so much that he decided to stay and make his life here. Jack, like Geoffrey Semmens, still refers to Derek as *"Mr. Tangye"* and remembers that first meeting clearly, and how Derek had then put in a good word for him when the lease for the adjacent farm to Minack, Rosemodress, became vacant. As a result Jack had gone into partnership with a well known local farmer, Walter Grose, and subsequently spent many years as Derek's near neighbour.

Then there's Harold Thomas - when the Tangyes originally took on Minack the first thing they needed was a new roof to make it weatherproof and they called in the local carpenter from St. Buryan. This was Ashley Thomas, Harold's father, and between them they represented a family business that had been established in St Buryan since the 18th century. As carpenters they also made coffins, so it was natural in a small village for them to also be the local undertakers. Ashley died in 1967 but Harold, now 90 years old, still lives in the village with his wife Phyllis. Still sharp as a pin, I spent a very enjoyable couple of hours in their cottage being regaled by Harold with stories of working at Minack. Many of these are in David Power's more comprehensive biography *'Tangye'*, so I won't duplicate them in full, but they included a tale about *'croust'* that is a warning to anyone unfamiliar with Cornish cider. 'Croust' is the old Cornish term for a mid morning break and is still very much observed here. Having called Harold in to fix some cupboards in the cottage, the Tangyes had had to travel into Penzance and they told him to help himself to some cider at croust time. Along with Harry Angwin, who'd been working on the garden, Harold, with his apprentice Maurice Hutchins, duly stopped work mid morning. *"Let's try a drop"* said Harry, not realizing there were two casks, and he'd picked up the wrong one. This was a really potent brew, which nevertheless, like most Cornish cider, slipped down the throat with deceptive ease. When lunchtime came up they had some more - *"this is some 'andsome stuff"* said Harold. By 4pm, when the Tangyes were due home, they were practically legless, but Harold somehow finished the cupboards just in time. Fortunately, Derek was in a good mood - *"You're a bloody wonderman, Harold"* he said - the phrase he always used when admiring Harold's carpentry skills.

Over a long, though sometimes volatile working relationship with Derek, Harold and his father Ashley did much of the work that made Minack habitable. And before he died, Derek insisted that, when the time came, he wanted Harold Thomas to handle his funeral.

After Derek's death many of his readers made contact with each other via the Trust and subsequently by joining *The Friends of Minack Society*, usually known now by its acronym, *FOMS*. The Society was established in 1999 by Pauline Ruffles and Tony Finn, two long standing friends of Derek that wanted to provide a focal point for readers to keep in touch with each other, and ensure that the story of Minack would live on. Over the past few years the membership has grown considerably and FOMS now has members all over the country as well as in Europe, the USA, Canada, South Africa and Australia. One member regularly travels from Chicago every year to visit the Tangye archive and attend the AGM in Penzance. The FOMS magazine, 'Wavelength', has a seemingly inexhaustible supply of photographs and stories

Tony Finn, co-founder of FOMS

sent in by its members. Some, like the magazine's indefatigable editor, Patricia Wilnecker, have become so dedicated that they've left their former lives upcountry and moved permanently to west Cornwall. Patricia herself first came to Lamorna as a schoolgirl in the late 1940s, visiting a schoolfriend during the holidays. It was only many years later that she read, by chance, a copy of *A Gull on the Roof'* and decided to make a return visit. *"I was still in touch with my friend Anne and using clues from the books, we eventually found Minack. We approached rather hesitantly, but Derek made us so welcome and we sat chatting in the porch like old friends - we listened to his tales of the local countryside and he was very interested to hear about our escapades in the Lamorna valley as children. Derek was quite elderly by this time and living there alone, but he indicated with a sweep of his arm the fields and cliffs of Minack, inviting us to explore and apologising that he couldn't join us as he had a sore leg."* After Derek's death in 1996, Patricia continued to return every year and now lives at a small cottage in St Buryan, dedicating much of her time to her work

Patricia, Bounty and Derek

for FOMS. She is often to be found in the Lamorna Pottery with fellow FOMS members Gerald and Jennie Murrish, checking out *'Tangye Corner'*. This is a display and information area with books and DVDs that was originally set up with the help of Tony Finn, who knew the owners of the pottery. Jennie has run it since 2003, sourcing and selling hundreds of copies of the Minack Chronicles and recruiting new members.

Jennie was introduced to the books through reading the serialisations in the *Woman's Weekly*. After Jeannie died, she'd written to Derek to express her sympathy, and shortly after, by coincidence, Jennie's step-daughter had moved to Rosemodress Farm, becoming Derek's neighbour. When grandchildren then came along, Jennie would visit and take them down to where they could see the donkeys and jump over the small stream, called *Monty's Leap*, that ran across the lane. The stream had acquired it's unusual name on the night that Derek and Jeannie had first arrived at Minack. When they went exploring with their cat, Monty, he'd refused to be carried across, but having first put out a paw to touch the wet pebbles glistening in the moonlight, he then leapt the stream in a single bound. From then on it was known as 'Monty's Leap' and regarded almost as a moat that separated Minack from the outside world.

Jennie was to visit Minack many times when visiting her grandchildren, and she told me of the occasion, one afternoon in late October 1996, when she went there with her grandson Max. *"It was very quiet, not a breath of wind, no birds singing, the donkeys standing still in the stable meadow close to the cottage. We gave the donkeys their carrots, speaking softly, as the strange atmosphere was*

such that whispering seemed right, and then walked quietly back up the lane. The next morning we heard that Derek had died that very day." Jennie remembers Derek with obvious affection and her work at Tangye Corner has now raised over £7,500 for FOMS. Sadly, founder Tony Finn died in 2007, but he lived long enough to see the popularity of 'Tangye Corner' grow and to know that its fundraising would ensure that this 50th anniversary edition of *A Gull on the Roof* would be published.

Tangye Corner at the Lamorna Pottery Inset: Gerald & Jennie Murrish

The most prolific source of new members in recent years has been the FOMS website, created and run by Linda and Jeff Hartley. Minack has certainly had a profound effect on their lives, although in their case it eventually took them far away from Cornwall. Linda first visited Minack in 1992, having found the books the previous year in her local public library in Brighton, Sussex. She told me how on this first occasion she had stayed at the Cove hotel and made her way to Minack via Carn Barges. *"Derek's greeting was warm and welcoming. That visit was to be the first of many"* she said and went on to describe how she'd met Anne and Malcolm Sutton, and that Derek had added her to his list of Associate Trustees. *"I'd tried finding somewhere like Minack for myself but couldn't really find anything close, for Minack is unique."* Then in 2000 she married her husband Jeff, and he now joined her in a search that took in most of Britain's west coast from Cornwall to Scotland. The quest eventually ended when they arrived, after an exhausting journey, to view a smallholding on a remote Scottish island.

I don't normally like splattering exclamation marks about too liberally, but after listening to Linda enthuse about the day they bumped their way down a winding lane on the Isle of Arran, punctuating her description with mere full stops seemed hopelessly inadequate. *"Travelling down it, half a mile long, it weaved this way and that and crossed a stream - just like Minack! The house was low lying and in the middle of the land - just like Minack! There was a* stable and barns - just like Minack! It had magnificent views of the sea - just like Minack! The mainland could be seen in the distance, lights blinking from the lighthouses - just like the Lizard! This was it - this was my Minack!" And so indeed it was - a few months later, in March 2002, Linda and Jeff Hartley started their own version of Minack, and began to carve out a very special life for themselves in Arran's bleak, but wildly beautiful landscape.

My own first contact with the Minack Chronicles was some thirty years ago during frequent visits to Cornwall on holiday. My wife Mim had been the first to discover the books whilst looking for holiday reading. When I subsequently read some of them it was the central theme of getting out of the rat race and moving to west Cornwall that appealed, helping me to focus on the practicalities of us achieving similar aims, something Mim had long determined we should do. I was no Derek Tangye though. True, my work in London's West End meant I was no stranger to the inside of a number of the hostelries that Derek knew well. We also shared the physical characteristics of being somewhat follicularly challenged - and we'd both somehow contrived to get married to younger, very pretty wives that we probably didn't deserve. I even once took up pipe-smoking. Sadly, I'm struggling to stretch this tenuous list of resemblances any further, not least because, as Mim likes to remind me, she doubts that Derek's grandfather, unlike mine, ever ran a fruit and veg stall. More importantly, stepping out into the unknown with no visible means of support required a courage that Derek possessed, and I didn't. The best I could manage was to set a target that, no matter what, we would be in Cornwall before the millennium was out. And much, I suspect, to Mim's astonishment, I stuck to it. In August 1999, just in time for the total eclipse, we moved into a 300 year old granite agricultural workers' cottage just seventy yards up the same dusty farm lane - the 'Winding Lane' - that leads to Minack.

Before we bought the cottage it had been known as 'Tregurnow Pottery', and was the home of potters George and Margaret Smith. They'd come to Cornwall from London in 1964, searching for a

Blaivoyach Farm, Isle of Arran
Inset: Jeff & Linda Hartley

new life for themselves and their three children, and set up their pottery here in the cottage, which at the time was empty and barely habitable. Derek called by one day asking if they knew of anyone that wanted work picking daffodils and Margaret, needing to supplement the pottery's income, volunteered herself. She soon became a trusted helper and caretaker for the times when Derek and Jeannie had to travel to London on book promotions. Sadly, George died only a few years after they moved to their retirement bungalow at Castallack, a small hamlet on the other side of the Lamorna valley, but we still see Margaret regularly, particularly Mim, as they sing together in the same local choir. We also occasionally meet her two daughters, Jenny and Nina, whose memories of Minack are more from the viewpoint of their childhood. Jenny told me how they used to play with Jack Cockram's children, Susan and Janet, at Rosemodress Farm. *"On one occasion we walked through the fields to the cliffs, and as we were coming back through the daffodils we met*

Jeannie. She took us back and introduced us to the donkeys, Penny and Fred, and also to Derek, who was smoking his pipe. They gave us each a biscuit and said we could visit the donkeys whenever we liked. Later on we were invited to the donkeys' parties, where there was plenty of food for us as well as carrots for the donkeys. When I became a teenager and wanted to earn pocket money, I would go with Mum to help bunch the daffodils in one of the greenhouses. At 11 o'clock Jeannie would bring us a cup of coffee and a piece of fruitcake. Later, when I was about sixteen, I went to work for David Cornwell, looking after his son, and Derek was particularly interested in what went on there, as was David about Derek!" Jenny went on to describe how they saw more of Jeannie than Derek, because he was always busy with his writing, but that he would often give them a lift back down the lane. Derek and Jeannie, along with David Cornwell and his wife Jane also came to her wedding at St Buryan church, and Derek gave her a specially inscribed copy of 'A Cornish Summer' as a present.

Local children with Derek and one of the donkeys. Jenny's sister, Nina, is on the left.

Not everyone, of course, that turned up at Minack was welcomed by Derek with open arms. Jeannie may have been very even tempered, but Derek was well known not to suffer fools gladly. He particularly disliked anyone who seemed overly conscious of their 'rights' and often railed against those that tramped the coastal path as if they were doing a route march from A to B, oblivious to the unspoilt beauty around them, or of their disturbance of the wild creatures that lived there. He could be irritable, especially in the early days when he had money worries and there was so much work to do; he was known then to sometimes make himself scarce in order to avoid unwanted visitors. But he does also seem to have instinctively known when a visitor was on what he called their 'wavelength' and could be genuinely appreciative of the effort they'd taken to find Minack. I've met dozens of people that have told me how, despite arriving as complete strangers, they'd been welcomed at Minack like old friends.

Derek Tangye may not have been Cornwall's greatest writer, but he wrote from the heart and in the pages of the Minack Chronicles you will find many passages of fine, descriptive prose. As a human being he certainly had his flaws, as indeed we all do, but his gentle philosophy of seeking more from life than material things and of care for the natural environment is one that becomes more relevant with each year that passes. It was his great good fortune to meet, in Jeannie, a lifelong companion who, possessing great strengths of her own, brought out the strengths in his own personality. *"You could never quite deny the magic"* wrote his friend, and critic, David Cornwell. That there was a magic at Minack I have no doubt, for although I don't have the words to capture it, I know it touched a great many people, and still does. So read now *A Gull on the Roof*, the first of The Minack Chronicles, and decide for yourself.

DEREK TANGYE

A GULL ON THE ROOF

WITH ORIGINAL SKETCHES
BY JEAN TANGYE

A special edition to commemorate
fifty years since the publication of this,
the first of The Minack Chronicles.

A NOTE ON THIS EDITION

In the years following its original publication, *A Gull on the Roof* was re-issued in many new impressions, but as the 50th anniversary of the first edition approached, it had been out of print for a number of years, and the only copies available were via the second hand market. This special anniversary edition, sponsored by The *Friends of Minack Society*, corrects that omission. Although the typesetting is new, the actual text and Jeannie's illustrations are the same as in the first edition. Having been written in the 1950s, Derek uses references and terminology that, although current at the time, may be unfamiliar to a modern reader - for example his frequent use of the word 'gay' - by which, of course, he simply means 'happy' or 'lighthearted'!

FOMS is grateful to the executors of Derek Tangye's estate for this opportunity to put '*A Gull on the Roof*' before a new audience, for we believe that this is still a story with a genuinely modern resonance that can yet speak to a new generation of readers - a reassuring message of hope, that proves that individuals can, just sometimes, beat the system.

The Friends of Minack Society

INTRODUCTION

I sat down in our house overlooking the Thames at Mortlake and felt a soft, caressing rub against my ankle. Monty was saying in his feline fashion that he sympathised with me over the apprehension that was in my mind.

The humble earth must ever fly (wrote A.P. Herbert).
Round that great orange in the sky;
But, Monty, with devotion due
The home of Tangye turns round you.

An animal, as one grows older, plays the role of the teddy bear in childhood. He stirs those qualities which are best in one's character and is one's patient confessor in periods of distress. So it was with Monty. He was, for both Jeannie and myself, the repository of our secret thoughts.

My apprehension that evening was in reality an ally of the caution I had discarded; for in the morning we had set in motion our decision to leave London in favour of the bath-less, paraffin-lit two-roomed cottage called Minack and six acres of uncultivated land on the coast between Penzance and Land's End. I had completed the settlement of my own affairs and Jeannie had handed in her resignation to the Chairman of the Savoy Hotel. Our livelihood now depended upon the creation of a flower farm from this desolate, beautiful country, aided not by any practical experience, but only by our ignorance as to what lay ahead.

Jeannie's position at the Savoy was the epitome of a career girl's ambition, but it was because she was not career minded that she performed her duties so well. As Public Relations Officer of the Savoy, Claridges, Berkeley and Simpsons, she had a high salary, a large expense account and a multitude of friends. Her salient task had been to promote goodwill, and that was achieved not only by organising efficiently the daily routine of an office, but also by endearing herself to the great variety of people who pass through an international hotel.

'Absolute nonsense!' said the Chairman when she saw him, 'you're obviously tired and want a rest. Take six months holiday with pay'. . . then added: 'When you come back you will want to stay with us for ever.'

I could understand his scepticism for he had no knowledge of the months of reasoning which had brought us to this moment. He could only comprehend the fact she was throwing away a career of distinction in favour of a wild adventure which, after a short while, might appear as a misplaced enthusiasm.

He could not be expected to appreciate the sense of futility which perforce invades the kind of life we had been leading. The glamour and hospitality act as a narcotic, doping the finer instincts of living, and in the grey hours of early morning you lie awake painfully aware that you live in a flashy world where truth and integrity for the most part are despised, where slickness reigns supreme.

We found the pace too fast and any material rewards poor substitutes for the peace of mind which was sacrificed. The world of politics, journalism and entertainment in which we moved requires a ruthless zest for professional survival if you are to do so, and this neither of us now possessed. It is a world in which you cannot live on prestige alone for it is only the present that counts. We had come to distrust both the importance of the objectives and the methods used to achieve them; for it is a world in which acclaim, however transitory and gained at whatever moral cost, is valued in the same currency as the conquest of Everest.

The atmosphere corrodes the individual and it had been corroding Jeannie and me. The moment of self-criticism, the shame we felt for our arid minds, slipped into oblivion as soon as we were in the splash of another party, in a cuckoo land of mutual admiration and sudden rip-roaring friendships.

There was no decisive occasion when we decided to leave. It was a host of occasions mingled into one, so that one day we suddenly realised our life was a spinning top, dizzily circling on one spot. We saw our fate, if we remained, in the men and women around us who had taken no heed of the barrier between youth and middle age, braying prejudiced views, dependent on values that toppled upside down, propping against a future which repeats endlessly the present, resembling worn playing cards. We could either drift on, or start again. We could either suffer the illusion our life was a contented one, remain within the environment we knew too well, or seek a freedom in a strange one.

We had been playing the game of looking for somewhere to settle whenever we had taken our holidays in Cornwall. We wanted a cottage with a wood near by and fields that went down to the sea, distant from any other habitation and remote from a countrified imitation of the life we were wishing to leave. Somewhere where we could earn a living and yet relish the isolation of a South Sea island, be able to think without being told what to think, to have the leisure to study the past, to live the present without interference.

It is a game which is perfectly harmless so long as no place you see fits your ideal. Once the two coincide the moment of decision arrives and it is no longer a game. This is what happened when Jeannie and I found Minack.

1

We had set out, one May morning, from the inn in the Valley of Lamorna to walk westwards along the coast. We were on a week's holiday and as usual the carrot dangling before us on the walk was our imaginary home.

Lamorna was once the centre of quarrying and its beauty was incidental. The great blocks of granite were blasted from the cliff face beside the little harbour, transported in long wooden wagons pulled by teams of horses up and down the hills to Penzance where they were cut into the required shapes and shipped for building purposes all over Britain.

The name means valley by the sea, and it is now a sleepy wooded valley possessing the ethereal beauty, the lush vegetation and shimmering colours, the away from it all atmosphere which tempts people to believe that here is their earthly Nirvana. In the summer, of course, it erupts with a lava of holidaymakers yet, and this is the charm of Lamorna, there is no strident attempt to exploit those visitors. There is the inn, a small hotel, Ernie Walter's filling station and café, Daniel's place down in the Cove; and though a few cottages advertise bed and breakfast in their windows, one feels this is done out of courtesy rather than the desire to earn a living. Lamorna, then, is a pilgrimage of the day tripper and though the narrow road on a summer afternoon is choked with cars, charabancs and dust, the evening comes and the valley is silent again. In the winter it is always silent except for the wind in the trees and the echo of the surf in the cove, and it becomes a valley to cure a cynic. The air is sweet with the scent of the violet plants which climb up the hillsides in neat cultivated rows, and as you walk along you will meet a picker, a basket of violets or anemones in either hand, taking them home to bunch. Or in the early spring when cities are still shivering, you find the valley a factory of flowers with every inhabitant a picker or a buncher, sharing in the hectic race to harvest the daffodils before those 'up along' come into bloom. During the war growers had to surrender a large part of their daffodil ground to the growing of vegetables, and so they threw their bulbs at random in the woods. The effect in spring is as if the constellations had left their places in the sky for Lamorna woods, a myriad yellow lights peeping from the undergrowth, edging the sparkling stream beside moss covered boulders, struggling through twining, unfriendly brambles.

The path we walked along was only a shadow of a path, more like the trodden run of badgers. Here, because there was no sign of habitation, because the land and the boulders and the rocks embraced the sea without interference, we could sense we were part of the beginning of time, the centuries of unceasing waves, the unseen pattern of the wild generations of foxes and badgers, the ageless gales that had lashed the desolate land, exultant and roaring, a giant harbour of sunken ships in their wake. And we came to a point, after a steep climb, where a great Carn stood balanced on a smaller one, upright like a huge man standing on a stool, as if it were a sentinel waiting to hail the ghosts of lost sailors. The track, on the other side, had tired of the undergrowth which blocked its way along the head of the cliff, for it sheered seawards tumbling in a zigzag course to the scarred grey rocks below. We stood on the pinnacle... the curve of Mount's Bay leading to the Lizard Point on the left, the Wolf Rock lighthouse a speck in the distance, a French crabber a mile off-shore, pale blue hull and small green sail aft, chugging through the white speckled sea towards Newlyn, and high above us a buzzard, its wings spread motionless, soaring effortlessly into the sky.

Jeannie suddenly pointed inland. 'Look!' she said, 'there it is!'

There was never any doubt in either of our minds. The small grey cottage a mile away, squat in the lonely landscape, surrounded by trees and edged into the side of a hill, became as if by magic the present and the future. It was as if a magician beside this ancient Carn had cast a spell upon us, so that we could touch the future as we could, at that moment, touch the Carn. There in the distance we could see our figures moving about our daily tasks, a thousand, thousand figures criss-crossing the untamed land, dissolving into each other, leaving a mist of excitement of our times to come.

We stood outside the cottage and stared; a Hans Andersen cottage with the primitive beauty of a crofter's home, sad and neglected as if it were one of the grey boulders in the wild land around. The walls seemed to grow out of the ground, great rocks fingering up the sides until they met the man placed stones, rough faced granite slabs bound together by clay. Once upon a time, it appeared to us, there might have been upstairs rooms and perhaps a roof of thatch; but now the roof was an uncouth corrugated iron jagged with holes, tilting so steeply that it resembled a man's cap pulled over his eyes; and prodding defiantly into the sky above it, as if ashamed of being associated with such ugliness, was a massive lichen-covered chimney. The poky windows peered from the darkness within, three facing the moorland and the sea, and two either side of the battered door which looked upon the unkempt once loved tiny garden. We pushed the door and it was unlocked. Wooden boards peppered with holes gnawed by rats covered the floor, and putting my hand through one of them I touched the wet earth. The walls were mustard yellow with old paper and though the area of the cottage was that of an old fashioned drawingroom it was divided into four rooms, matchbox thick divisions yielding the effect of privacy. At right angles to the door in a cavity of the wall beneath the chimney, an ancient Cornish range seared with rust, droppings of rats dirtying the oven, brandished the memories of forgotten meals. Above, the sagging thin boards of the ceiling drooped in curves, rimmed grey in patches from the rain dripping through the roof. A cupboard faced the door and inside broken crockery lay on the shelves, a brown kettle without a lid, and a mug imprinted with a coloured picture of King George V and Queen Mary side by side. Musty with long absence of an inhabitant, lugubrious with the crush of the toy sized rooms, the cottage seemed yet to shine with welcome; and we felt as if we had entered Aladdin's Cave.

Outside we stood by the corner of the cottage, the battered door facing climbing ground behind us, and looked down upon a shadow of a valley, gentle slopes, heading for the sea. Beyond was the Carn where we had stood, cascading below it a formation of rocks resembling an ancient castle, and in the distance across the blue carpet of sea the thin white line of breakers dashing against the shores of Prah Sands, Porthleven and Mullion. A lane drifted away from the cottage. On its right was a barn with feet thick walls in which were open slits instead of windows and on its left was a tumbled-down stone hedge, holding back the woods we had seen and the jungle-like undergrowth, as policemen try to hold back a bursting throng. The lane led down to a stream, dammed into a pool by the density of the weeds which blocked its outflow, and then, a few yards on, petered out in a tangle of brushwood and gorse bushes. We could see that the cottage was only connected with civilisation by a track through a field.

There was another track which led towards the sea and, as it broke away from the environment of the cottage, we found roofless outbuildings, bramble covered stone walls, with blackthorn growing where once stood men and cattle sheltering from the weather. The track broke into a huge field, or what we could see by the hedges was once a field but now had grown into part of the desolate moorland, then fell downwards to the top of the cliff. It was no ordinary cliff. It did not fall fearsomely sheer to the sea below but dropped, a jungle of thorns, gorse, elderberry trees and waist high cooch grass, in a series of leaps to a rugged teaspoon of a bay; and as we stood there, somnolent gulls sitting on the rocks far below, we saw in our minds a giant knife slicing pocket meadows out of the rampaging vegetation, refashioning the cliff so that it resembled the neat pattern of daffodil and potato gardens that were grouped like hillside Italian vineyards at intervals along the coast. We saw in our minds not only a way of life, but also the means by which to earn a living. It was the sweet moment when the wings of enthusiasm take flight, when victory is untarnished by endeavour, the intoxicating instant when the urge for conquest obliterates the reality of obstacles, dissolving common sense, blanketing the possibilities of failure. We had found our imaginary home. If we were able to possess it the way stretched clear to our contentment.

Details about the cottage were told to us back at the inn. Mrs Emily Bailey who was then the innkeeper, and Tom her son who nursed the adjoining market garden but who now has taken her place – these two listened patiently to our excitement. It was the habit of holidaymakers to lean over the bar expounding their hopes of packing up jobs, seeking an answer as to where they could escape; and these words of good intentions were as familiar to Tom and Mrs Bailey as the good-byes at the end of holidays, a part of the holiday as splits and Cornish cream, a game of make-believe that was played for a fortnight, then forgotten for another year.

The cottage was on the land of a farm which belonged to one of the great Cornish estates. This Estate rented the farm to a large farmer who lived a few miles from Land's End who, in turn, sub-let it out on a dairyman's lease. This lease was a relic of those days when Estates had difficulty in finding tenants for their farms. An established farmer would rent an unwanted farm, stock it with cattle and hire out each cow to a man of his own choosing who would occupy the farmhouse and farm the land. Hence this man, or dairyman as he was called, had no responsibility to the Estate for he was only a cowman. The responsibility of upkeep lay in the hands of the absentee farmer who, in this case, was a man called Harry Laity. As I lay awake that night he loomed like an ogre and, determined to call on him on the morrow, I experienced the same queasiness as I had felt before the interview for my first job.

We took the bus to a hamlet called Poljigga and found ourselves deposited at the end of a drive a mile long; a dusty, pot-ridden drive with the farmhouse eyeing us in the distance. We were absurdly nervous. Jeannie whose success was born from her ease with spangled names, and I whose duty it had been to have a weekly solitary interview with the Secretary of the Cabinet, walked along that drive, nervous as children visiting the headmaster. An over-sophisticated approach, a crude remark, sincerity sounding shallow because of lack of confidence, could batter our hopes for ever.

'What on earth do I say?' I said to Jeannie.

My passport, I thought, could be that I was a Cornishman. My ancestors had come from Brittany at the beginning of the fifteenth century, being descended from the Breton family of Tannegui du Chatel whose ruined castle still exists in the north-west corner of Finisterre. The Tangyes lived in obscurity in various parishes of West Cornwall until my grandfather, Richard, was born at Illogan near Redruth. His parents kept the village shop, and farmed a few acres near by where my great-grandfather followed the plough in Quaker dress and broad-brimmed hat. Richard and his brothers became engineers, and breasting the waves of the industrial revolution their inventiveness quickly brought them fame and fortune. Their success, they used to say, dated from the occasion when Isambard Brunel's huge vessel the *Great Eastern* obstinately refused to be launched from the dock at Millwall where it was built. Its length was nearly seven hundred feet, its breadth more than eighty, the height of the hull sixty, whilst its five funnels were a hundred feet high and six feet in diameter. It was intended to carry four thousand passengers, a crew of four hundred besides a mighty cargo – but there it was wedged high and dry on the stocks. It was then that the Tangye brothers produced their new invention the hydraulic jack, and to the excitement of the watching crowd, the vessel slid into the water. 'We launched the *Great Eastern*,' said Richard, 'and the *Great Eastern* launched us.'

My father was trained as a lawyer and he belonged to that group of men and women who, though without personal ambition, perpetually give their services to the community in unpaid but responsible jobs. He was, among other appointments, Joint Chairman of the Cornwall Quarter Sessions, a Deputy Lieutenant of the County, and organiser of the Cornwall Special Constabulary until he died in 1944. He was easy among people and they could always endear themselves to him by enthusing over the loveliness of Glendorgal. Glendorgal, now a hotel kept by my brother Nigel, was our home on the north coast of Cornwall near Newquay and it has the most beautiful position imaginable; the house is low and rambling and stares up the wild north coast past Watergate Bay and Bedruthan Steps to Trevose Head in the far distance. Below the house, so close that you can throw a stone into it from the dining-room, is a sandy cove which is itself a dent in Porth Beach. Across this beach is Trevelgue Island, historic for its ancient burial grounds, through it is an island only by the length of the footbridge which connects it to the mainland. My father had a great love for this island but just before the war circumstances forced him to sell it. The buyers were the local Town Council and I remember the wrangling which went on during the negotiations. It centred round a public convenience. My father was aware of the Cornish habit of erecting ugly cement blockhouses in the most prominent situations without any regard to the visual effect on the beauty spot concerned. The island had always been open to the public but the Town Council, now that they were buying it, believed they could improve its amenities. They intended to erect a blockhouse on the island which would remain for ever a silhouetted sore against the view beyond. My father was adamant that this should not be done, and though in the end he won his point, it was only by sacrificing a large amount from the sum the Council had been prepared to pay.

My father delighted in affectionate surprises. When I was returning to London by train he would see me off at Newquay station, then race in his old Wolseley car the three miles to Quintrell Downs where he would stand at the railway crossing waving his pipe as the train rushed by. I remember another time, after my twenty-first birthday week-end, I and my friends had said good-bye to him at Glendorgal before returning to London by car and then found him, one hour and a half later, nonchalantly strolling on the Tamar Bridge at Launceston accompanied by Lance his old English sheepdog; by a roundabout route he had raced to the bridge to say good-bye again.

We walked apprehensively along the Laity drive, happily unaware that this was the first of our visits on the same errand. We were nervous, as actors are before a performance, but in our hearts we did not think we could fail. Our zest would smother the awkwardness of the introduction and, because we were accustomed to meeting strange people, we would soon be at our ease. We were wrong.

Harry Laity, whose robust enjoyment of life we were later to appreciate, eyed us as if we had escaped out of Broadmoor. We saw him first in the yard outside the farmhouse watching the cows being brought in to milk; and I began to explain our mission while he stared at the cattle as they passed. I soon became aware that our presence was a nuisance and my confidence ebbed. This was not a situation which either of us had foreseen, and was not one that smooth manners could dissolve. We were out of our depth. The gambits on which we were accustomed to rely were as ineffective as a saddle on a wild pony; and as I stood there awkwardly beside him our plans, which to us seemed so important, became deformed, diminished by their reception into a scatterbrained foolishness.

The cattle disappeared to their milking, and he led us into the house and to the dining-room. Jeannie and I sat down with Harry Laity opposite, the bare dining-table like a frozen lake between us. I sat there and began to describe – defensively, falsely jovial – my Cornish background, our longing for a Cornish home, our plans for Minack. He stared at us, his eyes giving no clue to his thoughts, puffing a cigarette, replying to my leading questions with grunts and monosyllables. His attitude was unnerving. I begun to overstress our case. The more unresponsive he was, the more talkative I became. I slithered into sounding like Uriah Heep. I felt myself acting like a gold prospector who, having found gold, was cunningly pretending he needed the land for another purpose. Handsome Harry as he was known in he neighbourhood was suspicious. He could not be expected to understand why I pleaded as if our lives depended upon his decision. It was beyond his comprehension why two people should wish to leave London for such a derelict, isolated, unwanted place as Minack.

We went away and waited, and visited him again. We wrote carefully worded letters. We enlisted the help of mutual friends to put our case. We sat in our Mortlake home endlessly discussing the tactics which might penetrate the obstinacy of this man who held our future in his hands. We were at the door as soon as the postman knocked. Nothing. The weeks dragged into months. Silence.

And then, one November morning, we had a message to call on Harry Laity the next time we were in Cornwall. Jeannie was in bed with flu, but it was she who proposed we should take the night train to Penzance.

2

The blessing of enthusiasm is its ability to deceive pleasantly. When Harry Laity told us we could live at Minack, it seemed that now the major obstacle had been overcome, our other problems would be solved without effort. And yet, the victory achieved, doubts soon began to enter my mind.

'We're intending to live in a wilderness,' I said to Jeannie, 'we have little in the bank and we haven't a clue as to how to grow anything. The world is littered with people who would *like* to do what we are wanting to do. Common sense stops them.'

We were, for instance, brushing aside the fact that we would have no legal security at Minack. The cottage, and a vaguely defined area of land, had been offered us at a low rent by the tenant of the farm but not by the Estate which owned it; hence we had no lease, yet in our zest to secure occupancy we had promised that all improvements would be at our expense. We convinced ourselves that once we had moved in, no one was likely to turn us out; and that conventional legal niceties, if pursued, might scare Harry Laity away from having anything to do with us. Long afterwards he told us we were right in our guesswork. He let us have Minack because he expected we would stay six months, then creep back to London, leaving a redecorated cottage behind.

The cottage, then, was now nominally ours though it was eighteen months before we were able to set off along the Great West Road to live there; but during this interval, as we continued our rackety life in London, there remained in our minds the picture of Minack, snug, untamed, remote, giving us the same sense of protection as a deep shelter in an air-raid. Whenever we had the time we dashed to its safety.

Our first visit was a week-end in November when we introduced Monty to his new home. When I first met Monty I was allergic to cats, or rather, as we had never kept cats in our family and knew nothing about them, I pretended to be. He had been found, the last of a litter from a tortoiseshell, by Jeannie's mother in a hairdresser's at St Albans, and brought to Jeannie at the Savoy not long after we had been married. One day I walked unsuspectingly into her office and there on the floor, like a miniature foal trying to control its legs, was Monty. It was a few months after the battle of El Alamein.

I feigned my displeasure and as it was to be my task to take him back to our house overlooking the finishing post at Mortlake, I insisted I would drop him over Hammersmith Bridge. But we passed the bridge and he was still in the basket, and though I swore he would only be a kitchen cat, he slept that night on our bed. From that day he shared with us doodle-bugs, rockets, a bomb on the house, wore a light blue ribbon each Boat-race day, sat for hours at night on the window-sill waiting for our returns, made many hours happy with his purrs, and was always universally admired.

To call him a ginger cat would be a mundane description. The postman at Minack, when he first saw him, called him red - after the red cats of Zennor. There is a legend that a woman many years ago came to the village of Zennor, on the North coast of the Land's End peninsular, and announced she was going to breed tigers. The local authorities, not unnaturally, stepped in and forbade her to do so. The woman thereupon declared that if she could not breed tigers she would breed a red cat as fierce as a tiger; and now if you go from St Ives to Zennor it is the strangest fact that nearly every cat has a tinge of red. But Monty was not red. He had a snow white shirt front, magnificent whiskers, white paws except for a front one which had a puddle of orange on it, while the rest of his person was covered with a semi-Persian fur the colour of bracken in autumn. 'Like a fox,' a farmer said, 'and you'll have to be careful when the hounds are around.'

We had left London after lunch on a Friday and in the back of the car were a mattress and blankets, a Valor Stove, other camping equipment, and Monty in a wicker basket specially bought for the occasion. The basket was my idea. I had visions of Monty escaping from the car and disappearing into the countryside; but by the time we reached Andover he was clearly losing his temper, miaowing his head off and clawing at the sides of the basket in fury. 'Perhaps he wants a walk,' I said. We found a quiet spot off the main road, carefully lifted the lid, and fitted him with a blue harness and lead which had also been bought for the occasion. His fury swept the quiet spot like a storm and he would not budge as I pulled at the lead. 'Let him be,' said Jeannie, 'let's get back in the car and let him sit on my lap.' In a few minutes he was purring contentedly and staring with interest out of the window at the passing scene; and the wicker basket and the lead and the harness have now been for years in the attic as a discarded monument to my foolishness in treating him as a cat who did not know how to travel. He came several times by car before staying at Minack for ever, and once by first-class sleeper. I was at Minack on my own and was expecting Jeannie down for the week-end. I was on the platform at Penzance when the night train drew in, and I saw her waving excitedly from a window. I went up to the door of her carriage and she said: 'Come and look what I've got in my sleeper!' I opened the sliding door, and there on the bunk was Monty. She had been dining at the Savoy when she suddenly had the whim of bringing Monty with her. She rushed back to Mortlake, found him by torchlight walking along the garden wall, wrapped him in a rug and carried him to a taxi. At Paddington he behaved like any prudent conspirator as he was smuggled into the train, and Jeannie awoke every now and then during the night to find him purring peacefully beside her. He stayed on with me for a few days after Jeannie returned; then we drove back together to Mortlake.

It was nearly midnight, on that first visit, when the three of us reached Penzance. A gale was blowing in from the sea and as we drove along the front cascades of spray drenched the car as if coming from a giant hose. We crossed Newlyn Bridge, then up steep Paul Hill and along the winding road past the turn to Lamorna Valley; then up another hill, Boleigh Hill, where King Athelstan fought the Cornish ten centuries ago. Rain was whipping the windscreen when we turned off the road along a lane, through the dark shadows of a farm, until it petered out close to the cliff's edge. I got out and opened a gate, then drove bumpily across a field with the headlights swathing a way through a carpet of escaping rabbits. This, the back entrance to Minack, was the way we had to use until the bramble covered lane was opened up again; and after I pulled up beside a stone hedge, we still had two fields to scramble across in the darkness and the rain and the gale before we reached the cottage.

I lit a candle and the light quivered on the peeling, yellow papered walls. Everything was the same as the day we first pushed open the door; the ancient

Cornish range, the pint sized rooms with their matchbox thick divisions, the wooden floor peppered with holes - only it was raining now and above the howl of the gale was the steady drip, drip of water from the leaking roof.

We didn't care. The adventure had begun.

The phase in which daydreams had to be turned into facts had also begun. The romantic, escape-from-it-all atmosphere in which we had battled for the possession of Minack was now dissolving into the uncanny realism of victory. I had the same sense of living in the third dimension as the day when I enlisted in the Army and exchanged emotional patriotism for the discipline of the unknown. We could no longer talk of what we were going to do, we had to act; and the actions increasingly enmeshed us in a condition of living from which there was no turning back. As our first visit was succeeded by others, individuals entered our lives who pushed us forward linking our future with their present, as if they were pylons of a bridge. First we had looked for a bolt-hole from the kind of life we were leading, then we relished the emotion of its discovery, now we met the responsibilities of success. We found ourselves faced with a challenge that defeated our brittle egos, that was only to be accepted by the selves within us who found tranquillity in integrity.

Ashley Thomas was the carpenter in our village of St Buryan. Tubby, twinkling eyes, always wearing a peaked cloth cap to cover his bald head, he reminded Jeannie of Happy in Snow White and the Seven Dwarfs. His family had been carpenters in St Buryan for over two hundred years and craftsmanship was his second nature. And along with his tradition of skill was a quixotic nature akin to the carpenter of a neighbouring village who, after years of never sending out a bill, piled them all in his yard a few weeks before he died - and set them alight. Ashley Thomas never sent out an account within three years of the work being completed; then he would present it most courteously in person while the account itself was a masterpiece of script, a scroll it should be called, in which every nut, nail and inch of wood was meticulously tabulated.

Ashley Thomas looked around the debris of the cottage, notebook in hand with a pencil behind his ear, and promptly provided the assurance that order could soon be created. Our plans were not ambitious. A new roof, that was essential; the thin boards of the ceiling could remain but the matchbox thick divisions had to be ripped away providing us with one large room in which to live and a small one that would be our bedroom. The Cornish range was useless so a modern stove that both cooked and gave warmth would be its substitute. The rat-gnawed planks covering the floor would be torn up and in their place a damp-resisting cement flooring would layer the earth. The mustard yellow paper would be peeled off the walls, and the crater-pitted slabs lime-washed white. The battered front door would be removed, replaced by one divided in half, like that of a stable. There would be no sink or bath and the lavatory would remain an Elsan, posted in a hut like a sentry box thirty yards from the cottage. Water, until we could sink a well, was going to be a tricky affair. We would have to collect the rain from the roof into a water-butt or fill a jug from the stream; but in the summer the stream dried up, and if the water-butt was empty as well, we would have to go three miles to the village tap in St Buryan square. 'Never mind,' said Ashley Thomas looking at Jeannie, 'it's lovely at Minack in summer and lack of water won't worry you . . . but how you'll stand it in winter I just don't know.'

While Ashley Thomas provided the guiding hand within, Tom Bailey from the Inn at Lamorna, acted as adviser without. He arrived at the cottage on a drenching afternoon when the sky seemed to have changed places with the sea. Clad in oilskins and sou'wester he looked as if he had come from a lifeboat. 'Come on,' he said, 'let's walk round' - and he said it as if the sun was shining. Tall and spare, Tom was the man the villagers called on first in times of trouble. He had the dark cadaverous Cornish good looks with a watch in his eyes like that of a sailor, as if much of his life had been spent staring at the signs of the weather in the skies. He had been head gardener of a neighbouring estate before he began his own market garden, and his lifetime experience of growing was at the disposal of anyone who sought it. He was gentle in his manner and never dogmatic, and the advice he gave came hesitantly as if he considered it an insult to correct, however ignorant might be his listener. And he had the gift, despite his knowledge of technical difficulties, of fanning enthusiasm instead of blighting it with past evidence of personal failure.

'That'll make a nice meadow,' he said, looking at the bog which sided the wood below the cottage. It was the second of our brief visits and, despite the rain, we had spent the morning in this bog channelling an escape route for the water using a broken cup and a trowel. I do not know what we expected to achieve except to re-experience the pleasure of bucket and spade on a sea-shore. The task ahead was enormous and though Tom was right, and it did in the end make a nice meadow, it took two years of experimenting and two hundred yards of underground drain pipes before it was dry enough to grow a crop. Then we grew violets and sent away to market five hundred bunches in six months.

'That's yours?' He was looking at the ancient building bordering the lane, half of which was a stable, half a general purpose shed. It was not ours, only the roofless, age-stricken buildings came within our agreement. 'It's John's,' I replied.

John was also a new arrival - as Harry Laity's dairyman he had come to live at the farm at the top of the hill and was our nearest neighbour. The land he worked dove-tailed into ours. We, of course, had accepted the uncultivated land. His consisted of the weirdly shaped, beautiful meadows that bordered the cliff and ran down to the sea's edge, and the green fields which lipped the pocket garden of the cottage. He had called one morning when we were cooking breakfast on the oil stove.

'You're John,' I said, and shook his hand in welcome. He was squat and powerfully built like a miner. He had a round face with skin coarsened by the open air. His eyes were grey and they looked at me as if he was saying to himself: 'I wonder how long these people are going to stick it here.' He wore an old raincoat and a mottled brown cloth cap aslant on the back of his head, showing his black hair tinged with grey; a cigarette hung out of the corner of his mouth and he fiddled a foot with an imaginary stone. And as I talked with him I suddenly became aware of a warning emotion within me for which my town conception of a country life had not prepared me. There was a hint of a challenge in his manner. It was as if I had had a punch on the nose to remind me we were amateurs who had a hazy, paradise notion of country life that had no relation to reality. We did not belong. We were as out of place in the kind of life we were intending to lead as John would have been in the Savoy Grill. I could see him wondering what mystery had brought us here. Why, because we possessed smooth ways, did we think we could exist in a land where skill was the product of generations of struggle? We were typical city dwellers who had the conceit to believe it would be easy. He has seen them come and go before, and we would be no exception. There would be the customary froth of enthusiasm as we put the cottage in order, the showing off to up-a-long friends, the token effort of manual work, the gradual boredom with discomfort. Anyhow *she* won't last. Then, and I could sense the question revolving in his mind: 'Who will get the cottage?' His visit had a salutary effect on us for it promised the stimulus of battle, the realisation that we were going to be watched and judged and expected to fail. He was another pylon of the bridge.

We led Tom Bailey to the little wood, a forest of blackthorn and elm tree saplings with grey boulders heaving up in groups between them. 'Cut them down and dig up their roots,' he said, 'and by dodging them boulders you'll have three, maybe four meadows out of here. They'll be sheltered . . . be all right for daffodils.' And all this time we were pestering him with elementary questions. What varieties of daffodils would be best for us? How do you grow them? What about violets . . . and anemones . . . and potatoes? We left the wood and took the path to the big field and the cliff, into the scrub, the waste-land smothered with gorse and brambles where one day, we hoped, the crops would grow which Tom described to us. 'Mind,' he said, 'everyone will tell you different and no season is ever the same . . . but this is how I find it.'

There are several thousand different varieties of daffodils and narcissi but only a comparative few are recognised in the markets as established commercial successes - such as the yellow trumpet King Alfred, Magnificence, Carlton, Rembrandt, and a hundred or so others. Some of these are early varieties, some middle season, some late, and the aim of the grower is to have a succession of blooms from the end of January to the end of March, usually ending up with the white narcissi such as Cheerfulness, a double white bloom with an exquisite scent. The normal custom is to buy bulbs by weight which means the bulbs will be of different sizes - most will flower the first year but others will take a year or so to reach flowering size. If you buy by numbers you can expect all the bulbs to flower the first year but, quite apart from it being a much more expensive way of doing things, you run the risk of the bulbs taking a rest the following year with the result you pick few flowers. In any case bulbs are expensive. Cornish growers usually buy their bulbs from Holland or the Isles of Scilly and the price, of course, varies according to the variety; normally, standard types such as King Alfred, cost about £150 a ton. The big growers plant bulbs with a plough, placing them two or three inches apart within the rows; the small growers, in their cliff meadows, use a shovel and, when the time comes to dig them out, a special clawed digger. Seven tons average the acre and a good yield per ton is 28,000 flowers.

When you have bought and planted your stock the hazards begin. A gale may blow up during the week the blooms are ready to be harvested, and although they are always picked in bud the damage incurred as the buds rub against each other in the wind may result in all your efforts ending up in the compost heap. Then there is eel worm and the bulb fly, two pests which are as common as household flies and one of which is usually the answer to home gardeners who wonder why their bulbs have disappeared. Eel-worm, microscopic in size, wriggles through the soil attacking a plantation like an invincible army, burrowing into the bulbs and destroying them; and after such an attack, since eel-worm hangs around feeding on certain kinds of weeds, you have to leave the ground empty of bulbs for seven years. 'In fact,' said Tom, 'once you have eel-worm in the soil you seldom get completely rid of it. You can only check it.' Yet if you have the luck not to have eel-worm there is nothing to stop the bulbs being attacked by the bulb-fly for it is on the wing every year. There is a small bulb-fly and a large one but they both look like any other flying insect of the spring. The fly lays its egg in the neck of the bulb and the larvae proceeds to mature within the bulb, feeding on its tissues until it is destroyed into a sticky mess. Hence bulbs should be dug up every three years and given hot water sterilisation treatment before being split from each other and replanted in September; an hour of this treatment will kill the larvae of the fly, three hours the eel-worm. If the bulbs are cared for in this way they will increase considerably in numbers; if they are left as they are generally left in a garden, they will gradually die away and the capital you have invested will be lost. 'The trouble is,' said Tom, 'there always seems something more urgent to do than digging up bulbs and planting them again.'

The flowers are picked when the buds have dropped at right angles to the stem, and they are always brought into the packing shed and put into pails of water. If the weather is cold, there has to be a gentle heat in the shed to help burst the buds open. Then, when their petals are spread they are bunched and sent away to the markets. Every grower has a salesman in each of several markets and he is charged ten per cent on the sales plus a market charge for the handling of each box. Some growers have their own boxes, others hire boxes from the salesmen. In any case the grower pays the railway freight charges to whichever market he sends. In fact a grower has to pay twenty per cent in commission, boxes, market charges and freight, out of any price he receives for his flowers.

Tom said that violets provided his bread and butter. They are a cheap crop to grow because each year's stock consists of the runners pulled off the previous season's plants. They are planted in May and June, fifteen inches apart and about the same distance between the rows. The plants have bushed out by September and have begun flowering by the end of the month, continuing to do so through the winter months to April. There is an average weekly picking of twelve dozen bunches for every thousand plants - twenty violets and two leaves making up a bunch. Up to fifteen thousand plants go to an acre but, Tom warned, such was the time and labour involved in picking and bunching, no small grower could manage such a number. He himself usually had four thousand plants, growing a variety called Governor Herrick which, though it has very little scent, is prolific in flowering and lasts very well once picked. He had no use for the pale-coloured, sweet-scented Princess of Wales because it was difficult to grow, bloomed scantily, and fetched no higher price in the market.

Anemones are more difficult to grow and more expensive, but they are as much part of a Cornish market garden as bacon in a grocer's. The type most in demand in the markets is the De Caen variety, single blooms of multi-colours, and although some growers sow seed, the majority plant corms early in July. Seed is cheaper to buy but this economy is cancelled out by the extra labour involved. Good corms cost around fifteen shillings a thousand and eighty thousand go to an acre - the whole crop being ploughed into the ground at the end of the season. Their flowering period is the same as violets but they are liable to downy mildew which can devastate them, especially in a period of muggy weather when soft misty rain covers the Land's End peninsular - and as the spores of this mildew stay in the soil, anemones must not be grown in the same ground more than once in four years. 'Last year,' said Tom, 'I lost the lot because it was so wet before Christmas.' Frost, of course, sometimes damages them but as Tom explained, a frost hard enough to wipe out the plants seldom strikes West Cornwall. Anemones like a lot of lime in the ground and corms must be planted after the ground has been firmed, only a couple of inches deep and the same distance apart; and you must allow at least twenty inches between rows to enable the pickers to walk up and down without bruising the foliage. Mice sometimes do a great amount of damage. They nip off the buds as they break ground, then carry them off to the hedge where they tear off the petals and eat the heart of the flower. You can find little piles of these petals around every anemone field. The flowers are picked when the bud is just beginning to break. You must on no account send flowers to market which are 'blown' or full open, and this is very difficult to prevent in warm weather. If all goes well you should be able to send throughout the season an average of four dozen bunches a week for every five thousand corms you have planted.

Tom tempered these details with caution. He told us not to accept them as the gospel of the expert because the problems of market gardening were as numerous as a football permutation. Every season provides a different set of circumstances, and there is always an element which no one has ever experienced before. You are at the mercy of gluts and the weather, and they can knock you for six just when you think the season is going to be a good one.

We were now standing in the middle of our big field. It used to be called the cemetery field because at the bottom of it, the old cows and horses of neighbouring farms used to be buried. We were standing at the ridge half-way down - the top half sloped fairly gently, the bottom half suddenly dipped below the ridge until it levelled out just before the cliff. 'That top piece,' said Tom, looking at the upper half, 'that wouldn't take long to break if you had someone to help. Then you can hire a man with a plough and work up the land, then get a few potatoes in by March. Couldn't expect much but it would clean the ground and be a start.'

The growing of new potatoes held a fascination for us. There was past enjoyment of their flavour and the prospect of producing a crop so far ahead of the rest of the country that it had the merits of a delicacy; besides, stories had been told to us of small fortunes being made out of the pocket cliff meadows between Penzance and Land's End - 'the earliest potato land in England' it was called. Potatoes appeared easy to grow. In fact they seemed to be the answer to the amateur's prayers - hard manual work but no specialised skill, the warm climate and high prices ensuring a handsome profit. They would be the first corner stone of our income, so we then thought, as soon as we had the cultivated land in which to grow them. Hence Tom's suggestion suited us well.

Seed potatoes are delivered in the early winter and the varieties have names like Sharpe's Express, Home Guard, Arran Pilot, May Queen. When the seed arrives the potatoes are picked out and carefully placed eye-end up side by side in special wooden trays. They stay like this indoors until planting time, and by then they will have grown shoots a couple of inches long. The larger potatoes are then cut between the shoots so that there are two or even three sections which can grow on into plants. The planting is done in February and early March and, given good weather, the crop will be ready to draw at the beginning of May; and for every ton planted three or four tons should be harvested. The work, because the meadows are steep and small, has to be done by hand labour. Turning the ground in the autumn, planting the seed, digging out the crop - is all achieved by the use of the long-handled Cornish shovel. The seed potatoes are carried down the cliff, the harvest up. Thus every stage is identical to that in use a century ago; but we gladly accepted the prospect of what, in due course, would be our wearisome task, because of the anticipated financial returns. We were assured that whereas a ton of seed potatoes cost £20, the cliff early new potatoes sold at an average of £70 a ton. It seemed to us we had found an El Dorado.

We looked expectantly at the land in which Tom proposed we should grow our first crop. It was late in the year to order the seed so there would not be time to 'shoot' them in the trays, and they would have to be planted 'blind'; but the first step was to find someone to take charge, to prepare the land, plant the potatoes and then look after them. That evening we went up to St Buryan village to seek the advice of Jim Grenfell, a Pickwickian figure who presides at the inn with the slow measured courtesy of the days of coach and horse rather than of motor cars. Jim soon found Harry, a rabbit catcher; and Harry, over seventy, wiry with bright blue eyes and a drooping white moustache, promised that it we left our problems in his hands, all would be well.

That spring as we toiled in London, we thought of our growing potatoes as one might think of a racehorse in training for a great race - and on each visit to Minack we dashed on arrival to stare at their progress. They developed so green and flourishing, five hundred weight had been planted and Home Guard was the variety, that we began contentedly estimating what our profit might be; and when Harry proclaimed the crop would be ready to draw the following week, I promised to come down and help. I left London at three in the morning and reached Penzance at ten - and on arrival I called at the wholesaler who had promised to market the crop.

'I've just driven down from London,' I said, with the rush of the journey still filling my ears, 'and I'm going on now to start digging the crop. You can expect me back this afternoon with a load.'

'Driven down specially from London?'

The man glared at me, and threw the stub of his cigarette viciously on to the pavement outside his shop.

'You must be mad . . . there's a glut of potatoes. They're not worth a penny a pound.'

❃   ❃   ❃

In August Tommy Williams entered our lives and became the last pylon of the bridge. I met him first striding down Market Jew Street in Penzance one Saturday afternoon, wearing a Harris tweed suit, a smart trilby, and smoking a cigar. He looked more like a wealthy farmer than a labourer who had spent his life around a cowshed, and I understood why I had been told I could not fail to recognise him if I saw him. He was very tall with a fine, thin looking face and brown eyes which gazed gently at you except when, and this I later found often to be the case, he became roused; and then they would resemble those of an excited evangelist. He lived alone in a caravan near St Buryan and on the walls hung pictures which he had bought in local curiosity shops. 'I have a Constable,' he said proudly that first day I met him, 'a genuine Constable . . . and a Stradivarius!' His eyes gleamed. 'It's broken but it can be mended!'

Shortly before my encounter with him - after a particularly rowdy argument with his employer - he made it known throughout the district that he would do no more regular work, only casual work and on days which suited him. This attitude admirably coincided with mine as I was looking for a man who would work two or three days a week at Minack throughout the winter so that, when in early spring we came down permanently to live, the foundations of our future endeavours would have been laid.

He was undaunted by what he found he had to do. With eyes of knowledge instead of wishful thinking he mapped the whereabouts of meadows in the undergrowth. He was impatient to slash the saplings and the brambles which blocked the lane. He talked of rebuilding the old roofless buildings and rerouting the course of the stream. He rushed out his plans as if he was drawing zest from the prospect of showing others what he was capable of achieving when left on

24

his own. And then, during the winter, he sent us progress reports:

'I am pleased to inform you that I have trimmed down all the hedges round top and bottom. I have burned the trimmings and been around the field hedges and put back all small stones. I have cut the trees back around the two home meadows and stacked branches around hedges to keep out cattle. The little potato house meadow will be a nice meadow when I've finished breaking it. I have the thorns around the hedges for fences and windbreaks. There is quite sunny weather at Minack between showers. Well, that is all for the present. Tommy Williams.'

Then came the final report at the end of March, a few days before we were due to arrive:

'I have moved the stones in the front garden so that there are four beds instead of two. I have borrowed wallflowers from my cousin. They are in flower and taken well. Also primrose plants from the cliff. Makes the garden cheerful and I hope you will be pleased.'

And we *were* pleased.

3

Jeannie's friends looked out of their own personal windows and judged her decision according to the view they were accustomed to see.

'My dear, what are you going to *do* all day?'

'If *only* I had the same courage!'

'Are you *sure* you're not going to miss all the fun?'

'I'll take a bet you're back in six months!'

Those in the tight little world of parties, American Bars and gossipy sensations, disliked the idea of one of their number deserting – the justice of their lives was being questioned, an end had come into sight when they felt only safe in prolonged beginnings. Hence they interpreted her decision by complicated explanations, and gained satisfaction in their certainty she would soon be back.

Those who had never tasted the flavour of mixing with celebrities found her decision incomprehensible. She led the life of a modern fairy princess yet she was giving it up. She must be out of her mind, and they looked at her as if she were an oddity in a zoo.

There were others who envied her. These, captured by their own success, could only reason that she was showing the courage they believed they lacked themselves. Courage, in their view, was required if you are going to break the routine of butterfly pleasures – whereas Jeannie only saw in her choice a way of escape. We were both, in fact, taking the easy way out towards reaching our personal horizon of living time slowly.

We first met one evening at the Savoy in an air-raid. I had written a travel book called *Time Was Mine* and my first words to her were abrupt: 'You're just the person I have been wanting to meet. Can you manage to get my book on the bookstall?'

I had written in this book of a man called Jeffries, a weird mountain of a man, whom I had met on a Japanese boat sailing from Sydney to the Far East, and who, as it proved, was a link between me and Jeannie. I used to sit on deck till late at night listening to the stories of his nefarious life, leaning over the ship's rail, the soft breeze in our faces, watching the passing shadows of the islands along the Barrier Reef. It was the spring of 1939 and he was on his way to a job in the shipyards of Hong Kong.

'I once studied with Cheiro the astrologist and palmist,' he said on one occasion. 'He told me I would never be any good, but then I was never able to tell him his judgement was wrong . . . you see, I worked out on my own that he would die when he was sixty-eight. And he died on his sixty-eighth birthday.'

As it turned out many of the prophecies Jeffries made to me during the voyage were proved false by events. There would be no war. Chamberlain would be Prime Minister for a further five years and so on. But one evening he asked whether I would be prepared to have my own hand read. I was not very keen because I had always remembered the distress of my mother who, when she was thirty, was told by a palmist that my father would die when she was forty-one. She said it was the most agonising year of her life for she never could get the prophecy out of her mind. However, I agreed and we sat down in a corner of the deck lounge, glasses of saki on the table beside us, and I watched Jeffries study my palm in his ape-like hands. Later I wrote in my diary what he said – among other things that I would marry in 1943, that my wife would be smaller than myself and dark, and that her initials would be J.E. . . . .

Jeannie arranged for my book to be on the bookstall and in celebration I asked her out to dinner. The River Room, with its windows bricked up against bomb blast, was the Savoy restaurant in those days and we sat in a corner while the band of Carroll Gibbons played to a crowded dance floor in the background.

I happened to ask her whether she had any other Christian names beside Jean. And she said; 'The awful name of Everald.' I looked at her across the table. 'Do you mind saying that again?' She appeared puzzled. 'My full name is Jean Everald Nicol.' Two years later in 1943, we were married.

The American *Look* magazine called Jeannie 'the prettiest publicity girl in the world'; and when it was announced she was leaving the Savoy, the newspapers wrote about her as if they were saying good-bye to a star. A columnist in the

Daily Mail described her as slim, colleen-like, with green eyes and dark hair

' . . . who seems so young, innocent and delicately pretty that you couldn't imagine her saying "Boo" to the smallest and silliest goose. But Jean has said "Boo" to all sorts of important people including tough American correspondents.

'For ten years she has been a key woman at that international rendezvous of film stars, politicians, maharajahs, financiers, business men and what have you – the Savoy Hotel.

'She is about to quit the post of publicity boss or public relations officer for the Savoy, Berkeley and Claridge's. Her job consisted not only of keeping those hotels before the public but in stopping indiscreet stories from appearing in the newspapers and sometimes in protecting timid guests from the glare of publicity. Now that is a job requiring tact, intelligence and charm, and Jean has all three qualities.

'Who stopped the story about the colonel (with D.S.O.) who was working in the kitchens of the Savoy from getting into the papers? Jean Nicol. Who arranged Dior's first interview in this country? The same girl. When Ernie Pyle the famous American war correspondent (they made a film about him) was going off to his death in the Pacific he had his last lunch in London with Jean. He told her sadly: 'I'll never see you again. There's been too much luck in my life, and it's exhausted.'

'Close friend of Danny Kaye, Tyrone Power, Gertrude Lawrence, Bob Hope, Bing Crosby . . . there isn't a famous name in the past decade that doesn't know Jean.

'Well, she is going to retire for she thinks that ten years is enough to spend in the glare of London's West End. And she is right.'

We left Mortlake on a sunny April morning when the tide was pushing its way up the river, creeping into the inlets of the riverside like an octopus feeling with its tentacles. On the steps of the Ship, beer mugs in hand, a group stood ready to wave us good-bye. On their right loomed the Brewery, and on their left an empty space, an elm tree, and the house with the roof like a dunce's cap which we were leaving. The act of departure spares only the light hearted, and as I carried out our belongings, sticking them in the Land Rover, I found myself thinking of that ardour seven years before with which we came to this house;

for it was with this ardour, dressed up in new clothes, that we were going away. I looked up at the windows and thought of our happiness which would always live within the rooms; the unfinished sentences of gay conversations, raised glasses, sweet moments when endeavour had met its reward, affection like suffused sunlight warming the company of friends. I saw poised in my mind the fragments of other people's lives, lost perhaps by them, for ever attached to me . . .

Bob Capa, the wayward brilliant photographer, who was killed in Indo China was there, leaning against the door, his sombre face brightened by a stick of bombs falling across Duke's Meadows, cigarette drooping from his lips, quietly, with broken accent calling: 'Coming nearer, coming nearer' . . . a startled A.P. Herbert on a November night, whisky glass in hand, hearing the S.O.S. on the *Water Gypsy's* hooter; the tide had gone out and the crew had awoken when she tilted on her side . . . George Slocombe on a winter's afternoon standing with his back to the fire, red-bearded like an apostle, praising the virtues of France . . . Baron hitching a camera under his withered arm before photographing Monty; 'Come on Monty, give us a smile' . . . Gertrude Lawrence, a cockney again, boisterously shouting the Cambridge crew to victory . . . Carroll Gibbons drawling the song *People will say we're in love* as he played at our small piano . . . Alec Waugh standing on the steps looking at the empty river: 'Your last Boat Race party . . . it was the best.' We had come to this house believing it would be our home for always, yet here we were setting off again, packing away past hopes and ambitions, disappointments and victories, buoyantly confident that we now knew better. 'A chapter of my life was closed,' wrote Somerset Maugham when he left Tahiti, 'and I felt a little nearer to inevitable death.'

We were aware too, that departure meant a crack in the lives of those who cared for us. Jeannie would no longer be calling in to see her parents nor would I be able to have the almost daily, hour long conversations with my mother. I was never unsettled by age difference with either of my parents. My father kept a perpetual eye on his own youth, and so never grew old in his approach to me and my two brothers. My mother's philosophy had been to hold up a mirror to the happiness of the three of us, and gain her own in the reflection. When I was a schoolboy I said proudly to a small friend: '*My* mother would walk five miles with a heavy suitcase if it would help me or my brothers.' The childish boast always remained true.

The canvas hood of the Land Rover bulged like a kitbag . . . an armchair, suitcases, books, pots and pans, blankets, a camp bed, an ironing board. They piled high behind us as we sat ready to start . . . my mother whom we were taking to my aunt's house on the way, Jeannie with Monty on her lap, and myself at the wheel. And as I let out the clutch and slowly moved away, we could only laugh with those who were waving us good-bye.

'I hope you'll get there!' was the last I heard as I turned the corner.

I was on the road to the West again, a road which from my childhood had been part of my life. I used to drive to Glendorgal, our family home, as casually as I drove from Victoria to Kensington. My father saying: 'When in 1903 I drove a car to Cornwall for the first time, a donkey and cart actually passed me on this hill.' My mother: 'Three weeks after my first driving lesson I set off for Glendorgal. We had a puncture at Honiton but there was no garage anywhere near and we had to send to Exeter to find someone to repair it.' And myself: 'Here at Amesbury we had a smash with a Baby Austin . . . on my twenty-first birthday week-end we drove through the night and had breakfast at that café . . . I bought an evening paper at this corner shop and learnt the *Royal Oak* had been sunk . . . the car broke down here and I spent the night in that gateway . . . I was gonged on this stretch . . .' Scores of incidents so vivid in my mind that it seemed to me, as I travelled this road again, that I had 'time regained'.

The full moon was waiting to greet us at Minack, a soft breeze came from the sea and the Lizard light winked every few seconds across Mount's Bay. An owl hooted in the wood and afar off I heard the wheezing bark, like a hyena, of a vixen. A fishing boat chugged by, a mile off shore, its starboard light bright on the mast. It was very still. The boulders, so massive in the day, had become gossamer in the moonlight, and the cottage, so squat and solid, seemed to be floating in the centuries of its past.

I said to Jeannie: "Let's see if Monty will come for a walk.'

He came very slowly down the lane, peering suddenly at dangers in the shadows, sitting down and watching us, then softly stepping forward. His white shirt-front gleamed like a lamp. He sniffed the air, his little nose puzzling the source of scents of water weeds, bluebells and the sea. He found a log and clawed it, arching his back. He heard the rustle of a mouse and he became tense, alert to pounce. I felt as I watched him that he was an adventurer prying his private unknown, relishing the prospect of surprise and of the dangers which would be of his own making. We paused by the little stream, waiting for him to join us; and when he did, he rubbed his head affectionately against my leg, until suddenly he saw the pebbles of moonlight on the water. He put out a paw as if to touch them.

'I'll pick him up and carry him over.'

But when I bent down to do so he struggled free of my grasp – and with the spring of a panther he leapt across, and dashed into the shadows beyond.

'Well done!' we cried, 'well done!'

This little stream where it crosses the lane as if it were the moat of Minack, halting the arrival of strangers, greeting us on our returns, acting as the watch of our adventures, was given a name that night.

Monty's Leap.

We awoke the following morning to the sun streaming through the curtainless windows, to the distant murmur of the sea, to a robin's song hailing another day, and the delicious sensation that there was no frontier to our future.

If our watches stopped what did it matter? An hour, a day, a week could pass . . . there was no barrier to which we were advancing, no date on a calendar which glared at us from a distance. No telephone to shiver us into expectation. No early morning noises, a far off factory hooter, the first rumble of traffic, the relentless roar of a Tube . . . no man made alarms to jerk us into the beginning of another day. No newspaper shoved under the door. No clatter of milk bottles. Time to think, time to read. Go down to the rocks and stare vacantly at the sea. Perform insignificant, slowly achieved tasks – weeding the garden, mending a bolt on the door, sticking photographs in an album – without conscience nagging us with guilt. Take idle walks, observe the flight of a raven, the shifting currents of the sea, the delicate shades of moss. Travel the hours on horseback. Timelessness, isolation and simplicity creating the space which would protect us from the past. The hazy happiness of the present guiding our future.

I got up, collected a jug and went down to the stream. I had invited Monty to come with me but he would not budge. I picked him up and put him down in the garden, but within a second he had rushed indoors again. He behaved in this manner for several days, hating the daylight and only venturing out in the dark, and then if we accompanied him. It was difficult to understand his behaviour for on his previous brief visits, though he had never wandered far, he had always kept his nerve. A week later, however, he gained his self-confidence after meeting a baby rabbit face to face outside the front door. He seized it by the neck, brought it into the cottage while I was having breakfast, and deposited it at my feet – still alive. Henceforth every tuft of grass was a potential rabbit and every capture brought to us for our admiration; and instead of having to lure him outside, we used to spend much of our time searching for his whereabouts.

While I fetched the water Jeannie went up to the patch of ground where we had fixed up a wired run for the chickens. We had always kept chickens at Mortlake where they lived in a disused air-raid shelter and in a run that was messy with mud. Now they had a house of their own and, although the site was open to the four winds of heaven, they had grass to scratch, legions of succulent insects to peck, and farm chicken food to eat instead of the sticky mash which used to be their diet. There were ten of them (I had made a special trip in the Land Rover and they had laid six eggs on the way) and they were delighted with their new home. The eldest was called Queen Mary and although she was too old for egg laying, we had brought her to Minack because we did not have the heart to kill her. But the Cornish air, in due course, worked a miracle and she began laying again; and a year later we gave her a set of thirteen eggs to sit on, from which she proudly hatched one chick. Their devotion to each other was pretty to watch until the chick grew into a cockerel and to its duty of ruling the roost; and then Queen Mary, perhaps exhausted by motherhood, began to ail, and had to be put away.

I stood the jug of water on the table and lit the two valor stoves. The coal stove, in place of the Cornish range, always went out overnight; and so breakfast was cooked with a kettle on one oil stove, a frying pan on the other. Then, while Jeannie got on with the breakfast I walked up to the farm for the milk.

It was not a pretty farm; indeed it was not a single farm but a collection of ancient buildings including three cottages which were allotted to three different farmers. The grey stone buildings were juggled together without any design of convenience for the farmers concerned. A cow-house of one was opposite the tool-shed of another. A barn alongside one cottage belonged to the one opposite. Decrepit buildings, cracked windows, mud and muck on the ground – yet they were a monument to centuries of humble endeavour and this, I found, gave pleasure.

I was looking around for John when an old woman, a battered grey felt hat pressed down over her ears, with a lined face like that of a Rembrandt portrait shouted: 'He's in the shelter, Mister!' Mary Annie lived with her daughter in one of the cottages, and all her life had been spent among these buildings, working a man's day on the land. She was kind, friendly and happy, and if anyone had suggested she would be better off in an old people's home she would have laughed in their face. The spirit of Mary Annie was as indestructible as the boulders in the moorland that she could see from her cottage.

I found John sitting on a stool milking a cow. Farmers are silent and solemn people when they are milking, and as they are likely to be performing this task for two hours every morning and evening they have plenty of time for contemplation. Doubtless their thoughts roam over the crops they are growing but I guess they are thinking of those of their neighbours as well. If they do not wish them ill, they at least derive comfort if the crops are not as good as their own. At any rate some of them do; and I confess I developed the habit myself, when our potatoes were 'cut' by frost, of hastening to look at other people's to discover if they were as damaged as our own.

'Lovely morning,' I said cheerfully.

John replied with a nasal sound like 'urr,' but without any rolling of the r's. It is a sound with which I have become very familiar. It is uttered by any farmer who does not want to make conversation or commit himself to an answer, and it is emitted on various notes of the scale. If, for instance, a tone of surprise is required, the note is high with a slight cadence. If agreement is to be signified but without it being overstressed the note is in the middle; and if it is necessary to make clear that any conversation is unwelcome, the 'urr' becomes a grunt.

'How are your potatoes looking?' I asked. This enquiry, during growing time, is the Cornishman's substitute for enquiring after anyone's health.

A low 'urr'.

I hung about for half a minute, then asked if I could help myself to the milk and I would pay him at the end of the week. The 'urr' came out in the middle of the scale. Then, as I was going through the door, I heard him say, 'Cubs are makin' a mess of them taties down cliff and I be setting traps.' Fearing for Monty, I was immediately on my guard. 'Whereabouts?' There was a pause. 'They won't harm yer cat,' he answered without me having to explain what I was thinking.

In one direction stretched the lane to the main road, nearly a mile long with its surface straddled with cart-made craters; in the other the lane to Minack, rough like the dried-up bed of a river. Tommy Williams had cut away the undergrowth of the last one hundred yards and we could now drive up to the cottage in the Land Rover. Cars could reach the farm buildings but they could not get any further, and in time the lane became known as our chastity belt. We could not be surprised by visitors and, if tempted to go out, so bad was it even for a Land Rover, we usually had second thoughts about going.

I walked happily down the lane carrying the milk in a tin can, marvelling at the way the hedges on either side unfolded the view of the sea like a tape. First a pin point of blue, then stretched as if it were a few inches long, growing longer and longer as I went down the hill until I reached the bottom and the hedges fell away and I looked upon the vastness of Mount's Bay.

I was singing when I came up to the cottage, breakfast ahead of me, and a lovely day at our mercy. Jeannie was waiting at the door, a jug in her hand.

'You clot,' she said, 'when you filled this jug you filled it with tadpoles.'

The tadpole problem remained until they grew into frogs. I used to crouch beside the stream with a jug and a cup, flicking the tadpoles out of one and emptying the water into the other. It was a laborious way of fetching water, and more so when we needed water at night, and then Jeannie would gleam the torch on the swimming black spots while I repeated my methods of the day-time.

We were, in fact, leading the life of two campers, and the prospect of continuing to do so appeared to stretch far ahead. The cottage was sparse of furniture. We had no bed and we slept on a mattress laid on the floor. Our pride was a fitted carpet in the sitting room but with it we had only one armchair, a divan, a table and three kitchen chairs. We saw no reason to grumble. We had left our furniture behind for the very good reason it was earning us money.

The house at Mortlake which we ourselves rented unfurnished, had been let by us to a young Embassy official and his wife. The profit we derived was to be our income at Minack, and we therefore took care to see that our tenants would be satisfied. He was a solemn young man, and neither he nor his wife had been away from their native land before; and when, after a lengthy inspection of the house they expressed their desire to rent it, I proposed that it first should be vetted by the chief of his department. The chief arrived, inspected and gave his blessing both to the house and the rent; and as the young man wanted to move in as quickly as possible, he and I came to a gentleman's agreement that he could take possession without waiting for the formal agreement to be signed.

Hence, although we were now without furniture we did have a small income . . . but not for long. Three months after the young man had moved in, just as the lease was about to be signed, he moved out. I contacted his chief and also the Embassy concerned, but with no result. A gentleman's agreement was not a valid document. Thus Jeannie and I suddenly had our income cut off, had an empty furnished house on our hands, and were three hundred miles away from superintending its reletting. It was a worrying situation until I said to Jeannie: 'Look, we've been compromising by keeping the house. At the back of our minds we've been thinking we *might* want to go back. We won't and we know it. Let's give it up.'

Early one late summer morning we got out the Land Rover and drove up to London; and by the following day we had seen our landlord, given up the lease and sold him the fittings, and had arranged for some of our furniture to be sold, some to be transported to Minack.

The incident was a warning that escape is not an end to itself and it sharply removed from our minds the pleasant reflection of its achievement. London was no longer our home. It was now vital to make a success of the apprenticeship in the way of life we had chosen to follow; and it is the story of this apprenticeship that I am ready to tell.

4

April passed, the potato season drew near and the inhabitants of the district, including ourselves, began to develop the mood of prospectors in a gold rush.

Three and four times a day Jeannie and I inspected the land which Tommy Williams had planted with one and a half tons of seed – the small meadows he had cut out of the top of the cliff, and the upper part of the cemetery field. The sight fascinated us. We stood and stared at the dark green leaves, hypnotised by their coarse texture, greedily calculating the amount of the harvest; then we would bend down and tickle a plant, stirring the earth round it with our hands, and calling out when we found a tiny potato . . .

'Need a nice shower,' Tommy would say, 'and they'll treble in size within a week.' Or in the lane, I would meet John who, in answer to the inevitable question: 'How are the taties looking?' would say gloomily, 'Been known for a gale to come at this stage . . . blast them black and only the weight of seed been lifted.' It was not only the size of the harvest which was at stake, but also its timing. There was a rivalry among growers as to who would be the first to draw, like jockeys at the starting gate; and the information that was circulated was as inspired as that on a race-course. I would go up to Jim Grenfell's pub at St Buryan in the evening and listen to the gossip.

'Bill Strick was cut by frost last night.'

'Over at Mousehole they look handsome.'

'Nothing will be going away until after Buryan Feast.'

'William Henry starts drawing Monday.'

These rumours and false alarms increased as the pace of excitement grew faster every day, and by the end of the month the inevitable question had become: 'Started drawing yet?' The disinterested – the postman, the man at the garage, the proprietor of our St Buryan grocers, put the question as a matter of politeness; our fellow growers, whether neighbours or others living a few miles away, jerked it out as if they were apprehensive we might spring a surprise. Our land, having never grown potatoes before, might upset the balance of prestige . . . supposing Tangye was first to draw? Of course, we caught the fever ourselves and went staring jealously at meadows other than our own, and asked repeatedly: 'Started drawing yet?'

The mounting tension had an effect similar to the concern of a general who feels he is being pushed into battle before he is ready. There was the pressure of local prestige on the one hand, hard economics on the other, and the economics were very confusing.

Supposing the price on a certain day at the beginning of the season was 1s. a pound but a week later it dropped to 8d. a pound. In that week the crop may have doubled in size and you would therefore be receiving 1s.4d. a pound. On the other hand the increase in weight would cost more labour and more in freight, and require twice as many chip baskets; and in any case the price might have dropped to 6d. a pound and the crop failed to increase as expected. Moreover for the early potato growers like ourselves whose crop is grown in the cliffs, there was always the shadow of the farmers. We had to hand dig our crop with a shovel, while they careered through their fields with tractors towing spinners. These spinners threw out the potatoes so fast that with sufficient labour a farmer could send away ten tons in a day; and so our economic survival depended on clearing our crops before they began.

There was the bewildering problem of marketing. No difficulty existed about finding a salesman, the problem was which salesman to choose. Several had visited us representing different firms and different markets but their methods of approach were the same; they smiled winningly, talked jovially, and then offered us identical terms. We had to pay 9d. for each chip basket (chips were used at the beginning of the season), pay the freight charges and ten per cent commission on the gross sales, and had to trust to luck for the price obtained on the morning our consignment arrived in the market. With this information I was able to calculate approximately how much each ton of potatoes we sent away would cost us. One hundred and sixty chips were required for a ton – £6. Each chip was scheduled to contain 14lbs. of potatoes but another 1lb. was required to allow for shrinkage in transit; if the price, then, was 8d. a pound, we would give away £5. The charge for freight to the Midlands or London (and it had to be a passenger train in order to travel overnight) was another £10 a ton. There was paper to put in the chips, string with which to tie them, and the cost of taking them to Penzance station – another £5.

Thus we had to pay £26 a ton, or about 3d. a pound out of the price we received in the market – in addition to the ten per cent commission. Then there was the cost of the seed, fertilisers and labour involved, all of which had to be covered before we made any profit ourselves. From the purist's point of view all new potatoes should be in chips because they travel and keep much better than when they are in sacks; but the 56lb. sacks cost only a shilling, the shrinkage required for each sack is only an extra 2lbs. and these are despatched by freight train instead of by passenger train. Hence there would be a stage during the season when the potatoes had begun to arrive in the market in bulk with the consequent drop in prices, when sacks would replace the chips.

One Monday morning Tommy Williams came striding up the lane while we were sitting on a rock sipping cups of coffee, idly watching Monty stalk a mouse in the grass. Tommy was now working the first three days of the week for us, another two days for John ; and thus his loyalty to the potato meadows was divided. On this particular morning he had an evangelist look, his chin thrust out, and his tall figure in ragged working clothes like a prophet on the warpath. 'John's told me he's starting to draw this morning,' he rushed out as if he had brought news that war had been declared, 'we must go down the cliff at once and see what ours are like. You bring the chips and I'll take the shovel.'

We swallowed our coffee and off we went, Tommy with the shovel over his shoulder, I with a bundle of chips, and Jeannie walking hopefully behind. The weather was perfect. The sea was smooth as a pool and flecked with gulls swimming nonchalantly like ducks; and as we trudged down the cliff the old steamship *Scillonian* sailed past outward bound to the Scilly Isles, cutting through the water as gently as a yacht. Tommy brought out the telescope he always carried with him. 'Got a car on board,' he said importantly. In the summer she sailed to and fro to the islands every day, and in the winter every other day in each direction except when the Scilly flower season was at its height. She was a friendly sight and she became, as her successor has also become, a timepiece. 'Has the *Scillonian* gone past?' I would call out, or Tommy or Jeannie.

Her course took her parallel to our meadows a half mile out, a sea green painted hull and a yellow funnel; and sometimes in a storm when the sea was running mountainous waves we would watch with our hearts in our mouths as she lurched toy-sized among them. Then Tommy – brutally – would roar with laughter, 'I bet them passengers are feeling bad.' In fair weather she berthed at Penzance, in bad she made for Newlyn and as she was the link between the Scilly flower growers and the mainland markets, her skipper sailed her in seas when she might have been expected to remain in harbour. There was one occasion when, after leaving the islands, a gale so fierce blew up that when she reached Mount's Bay she was three hours late and it was dark. The skipper, a Scillonian, unexpectedly decided it was too dangerous to enter Newlyn harbour, and chose to spend the night steaming to and fro across the Bay, sailing out the gale. There was wry laughter in the Scillies when this was known. The Government, a few weeks before, had announced that the Scillonians were to be liable for income tax – and off the boat the following morning stepped two sick-looking Inland Revenue Inspectors.

We reached a meadow at the top of the cliff and I cut the string of a bundle and singled out a chip while Tommy banged the edge of the shovel on his boot in the manner of an acrobat calling attention to a special trick. Then, with Jeannie and me standing expectantly beside him he stabbed under a plant and turned it upside down. Several little white potatoes connected together as if by a string lay in the soil. Tommy said nothing and moved to another part of the meadow and stabbed again. The same thing happened.

'Look's like we're going to be disappointed,' he murmured, 'we'll try the May Queen over there. They should be ready.' We walked over to the meadow which was steep and fringed with bluebells. Tommy turned over one plant, then another, picked up the stems and shook them, and ran his hands through the soil. We were out of luck. The May Queen were no better than the Pilot we had tried first. 'Marbles!' Tommy snorted with disgust, 'just marbles!' We gathered up the little white things for ourselves, cross and disappointed and trooped back silently, disconsolately to the cottage. As Tommy put away his shovel he looked at me, his eyes no longer blazing, and grunted: 'Don't say a word to anyone in the village about this. Keep your affairs to yourselves. Some of them are a mean lot and they'll be pleased.' I nodded solemnly in agreement.

Our village of St Buryan stands on high ground three miles from the coast on the road to Land's End, and the church spire is a beacon to ships far out to sea. It is a sturdy village of neat granite cottages with grey slate roofs and no pretensions about being quaint. It is a business-like village and makes you feel that it prides in brawn and courage rather than in brain and guile, in the basic virtues rather than those which are acquired. Until a year or so ago there was no main water and the village supply was tapped from a spring in the square opposite the inn; so that when you stood in the bar looking out of the window, you watched the inhabitants filling their pails of water as their ancestors had done patiently for centuries before them. It is a village which challenges the sensibilities and yet soothes them, as if it were an integral part of the gales which lash it and the calm which follows. It is not a village in which to live and be idle, for work conscientiously performed is the yardstick of value. It is generous both in spirits and in pocket, for no worthy cause fails to meet with success; but if it is willing to like, it is also quick to distrust, and slow to forgive. It is, in fact, a village of character.

The name comes from that of an Irish girl saint and is pronounced Berian. How she came to the Land's End peninsular is obscure, but in ancient days Irish pilgrims used to travel to the continent by way of Padstow and Mousehole. The object was to avoid the stormy passage around the 'corner' of England by landing at Padstow, travelling overland to Mousehole and embarking in another ship for France. It is believed that in the sixth century she was one of these pilgrims. In any case the shrine of St Buryan existed in the tenth century when King Athelstan swept into Cornwall to drive out the Danes who garrisoned the county and the Isles of Scilly. His final great battle in Cornwall was at Boleigh Hill, two miles from Minack, and he afterwards rested his troops at St Buryan before setting out from the beaches of Sennen near Land's End to invade the Isles of Scilly. On the day before he sailed he worshipped before the shrine and vowed, if the expedition was successful, that he would as a thank-offering build and endow a church.

The original church decayed into rubble during the fifteenth century and at the beginning of the sixteenth the present one was built. It is a beautiful old barn of a building, and in a village whose limited number of inhabitants are divided between Methodists and members of the Church of England, it has the effect of a cathedral. In a corner of the church is a collection of ancient finds that have been made in the district and which were gathered together by a remarkable old man named Croft who was Vicar of St Buryan when we came to Minack. It seemed that Croft was as much interested in the past as he was in his parishioners and he spent much of his time seeking the history of the parish from ancient documents and in leading groups of earnest archaeologists in excavating from the soil the traces of Stone Age settlements.

A few months after our arrival, a mason repairing a wall in the cottage had discovered a cavity, neatly roofed with small stones, which he explained was an old oven dating back some five hundred years. A few days later I looked out of the window and saw an old man struggling slowly up the steep path to the door. 'The Vicar's come to call!' I cried out to Jeannie, and Jeannie in those few split seconds between the sight of an unexpected visitor and his arrival, rushed round the room picking up papers and hiding unwashed plates. 'Why didn't he warn us?' she moaned, while I wondered how I was going to explain why I never went to his church. I ushered him into the room and he sat down on the sofa, panting from the exertions of his walk. He sat silent until he had recovered himself then, with a gleam of excitement in his eyes, looked at me and said, 'I've come to see the oven!'

The trail of archaeologists used to irk the inhabitants of St Buryan and there was one old man, many years ago, who became a hero to the village for the trick he played on a group. He was a specialist in stories about Athelstan's Battle of Boleigh which, he declared, had been handed down from father to son in his family from generation to generation; and so sincere was his note of authenticity that historians never failed to bring out their notebooks in excited belief. The fields where the battle is supposed to have been fought are known as Gul Reeve which is the old Cornish for 'red field'; and as neither the soil nor anything else in the neighbourhood is red, it has always been presumed that the name is derived from the blood which flowed. Near by is a farm and the old man declared one day to a group of believers that the dead of the battle were buried in a long trench in a field adjacent to the farm buildings. He knew the exact position having carried in his head the number of paces from each corner of the field that led to the trench, details which had been told to him by his father. A score of men dug for two days and not a bone was found. The archaeologists were angry, the men who had done the digging happily pocketed their pay, and the old man grinned. 'If mistake there be,' he said, 'it be due to father.'

On these same Gul Reeve fields stand, some distance apart, two massive upright stones which are known as the Pipers. They are, in fact, Peace Stones, representing the Conqueror and the Conquered, erected presumably after the Battle of Boleigh. But during the centuries in between they acquired the name of the Pipers so that they might dovetail into the story that the elders of St Buryan told their children about the circle of nineteen stones known as the Merry Maidens which stand in a field a few hundred yards away on the other side of the road. The elders told the story as a warning against playing on Sundays. The nineteen stones were nineteen maidens of the parish who were lured by two young men to dance on a Sunday afternoon; and while the girls tripped daintily hand in hand, the young men played their flutes – until there was a flash of lightning and they were all turned to stone.

Our post came from St Buryan, and the telegrams from a sub-post office at Lamorna. Our first postman had an eccentric sense of delivery and his route to the cottage across fields and over hedges was to him an unwelcome steeplechase. Letters, therefore, sometimes reached us two days late, sometimes three, sometimes not at all. This waywardness fitted our mood until one morning I received a writ for an unpaid account without ever having seen the letter of warning which preceded it. The telegrams also came across the fields, and the authorities awarded the sub-postmaster with a special bonus of sevenpence for each delivery. Usually they were from Americans who had arrived at the Savoy to find Jeannie had left, and a telegram would arrive asking us to lunch the following day as if the distance between Minack and the Strand was that between Chelsea and Kensington; or else it would be a request for us to telephone at some inconvenient hour as if the charge was a fourpenny call and the call-box in our front garden.

After a sequence of such requests I made enquiries about installing a telephone, half-hearted enquiries which were more of a gesture to conventionality than a desire to have one; and made in the confident belief that the cost of installation with its half mile of wire and poles would in any case be prohibitive. I was surprised when the Post Office informed me that the cost would be twelve shillings and sixpence and the installation immediate; and the Post Office was surprised when it received my letter explaining I had changed my mind and did not want one after all. We still have no telephone and although it is sometimes irritating to drive two miles to the nearest call-box, we are spared the far greater irritation of a menacing ringing bell.

A month after our arrival, and when the tension of the impending potato season was reaching its climax, we received a telegram, 'Expect me tomorrow night' and signed 'Uncle B,' – the nickname by which many knew Baron, the photographer. He was to be our first visitor and the first to pose a problem difficult to solve. If you earn your living from the land you have to work regular hours like anyone who goes to an office, but unlike the office worker, you do not have the security of an office building to shelter you from your friends. A further difficulty is that most people who visit Cornwall are on holiday with time to spare and an inclination to look up old friends or to stay with them for a night or two at the same pressure of gaiety as in the days of their former acquaintance. On our part although we usually quailed at the prospect of visitors, we surrendered when they arrived and suffered penitence for the lost hours after they had departed. Our real difficulty arose when such visitors arrived in sequence throughout a summer, each an old friend regained from the past, each deserving the full attention of a merry reunion. It was on such occasions, and those when we paid rare visits to London, that our ego of sophistication reasserted itself leaving that of the peasant to provide the remorse.

The gusto of Baron was that of a roaring gale which eventually exhausts itself into stillness. He pounded every twenty-four hours like a punchball, working, playing, loving, talking, drinking, dazzling his friends with his wit, kindness and a great gentleness. His behaviour was often outrageous. He once asked me to introduce him to Mike Cowles, proprietor of the American magazine, *Look*, and I arranged that we should all meet at Claridge's for drinks. After an hour and there was no Baron, Jeannie suddenly turned to me, 'Heavens,' she said, 'its Thursday!' Thursday was a notoriously unreliable day for Baron as it was the day of his weekly Thursday Club luncheon. Another half hour and we saw him beaming smiles at surprised strangers as he weaved his way towards us, 'Jeannie, Jeannie,' he cried, 'forgive me, forgive me!' And he thereupon knelt down in the dignified foyer, clasping his hands together in mock prayer. A few days later I was with him in the Savoy bar when Mike Cowles passed by and

I waved. 'Who's that?' asked Baron. I told him. 'That's the very man I want to meet,' he replied, 'do introduce me.' I put down my drink and looked at him, 'I have done so already . . . we all spent an hour together the other evening at Claridge's!'

Our spare room at Minack was a chicken house which we had bought and converted. We had erected it adjacent to the cottage with its floor lifted clear of the soil by pylons of stones, and the windows looked out on the croft and Mount's Bay. On the floor was a rug, and the furniture consisted of a camp bed and chest of drawers. We had painted the walls white and there was little sign of the hut's original purpose except a small hatch door at ground level where the chickens should have come in and out. Baron was delighted. 'Just the place for an old rooster like me,' he said. He stayed with us on that occasion for twenty-four hours and during that period we visited every pub in the district. We ended the first evening at the Tolcarne in Newlyn where Gracie Thomas rules tough seamen of many nationalities in the manner of a kind headmistress. We had been there ten minutes when I saw Baron was the centre of a group of French fishermen who were roaring with laughter. 'En avance à bateau,' he called out when he caught my eye, and off we all went to the French crabber in the harbour and spent two hours of drinking from a demi-john of wine.

We waved Baron good-bye and felt no nostalgia for the life he represented. We were enjoying a honeymoon with the primitive and tasks that could become monotonous – fetching the water from the stream, filling the paraffin lamp, cooking, cleaning, lighting the stove – possessed the brisk pleasure of the unusual. When I first knew Jeannie she could not even boil potatoes, and the first meal she gave me consisted of cinder-burnt chops due to the fact that she was unaware that frying required fat. She now had a file bulky with recipes and it was not long before she added two more – those for Cornish cream and home-made bread. She collected four pints of milk from the farm, poured it into a bowl and allowed it to settle for a few hours. Then she put the bowl on the edge of the stove where there was a gentle warmth and left it overnight. On the first occasion she tried this out I watched her, as excited as a girl going to a first night, skim off a thick layer of yellowy cream and then, with the confident air of a farmer's wife, serve me with thunder and lightning - treacle and Cornish cream on slices of bread. A few weeks later I had a pain in my side and I said the Jeannie, 'I believe I've got appendicitis.' I was nervous of going to the doctor and put off doing so until the pain or 'feeling' became so persistent that I had no alternative but to make an appointment. As I entered the surgery I visioned the hospital, the operation, the convalescence which would keep me incapacitated throughout the potato season. The doctor examined me and poked my side, then asked, 'Have you been eating a lot of Cornish cream since you came here?' And with his question the pain disappeared.

Jeannie's mother sent the recipe for the bread and it was such a success that we never bought a shop loaf again. She makes four one pound loaves out of three pounds of wholemeal flour and three teaspoonfuls of dried yeast. While the yeast is dissolving in a cup of warm water, she mixes half the flour, a tablespoonful of brown sugar and one of coarse salt in a warmed basin. To this she adds the dissolved yeast, about one and a half pints of warm water, mixes it all into a batter and leaves it on the back of the stove for fifteen minutes. The rest of the flour is then emptied into the mixture and kneaded for five or ten minutes – after which the dough is cut into four sections, put into warmed, greased bread tins and left to rise on the back of the stove until the dough has doubled in size. Finally the tins go into a piping hot oven for about three-quarters of an hour, and the sweet smell of baking fills the room.

My mother had arrived to stay when we dug our first potatoes. She came loaded with gifts for the cottage including dust cloths, saucepans, detergents, a pair of sheets, and a water filter. My mother was never thrusting either with her views or with her presents, and when out of a packing case she produced the water filter, she very softly said, 'I was thinking of the tadpoles, dear.'

It was on the first evening of her stay that she saw the square figure of John leading his horse and cart, piled high with potato chips, past the cottage. She was irritated that he should be meeting with potato success while we were sitting back and waiting, and she urged that we were not showing enough confidence in our meadows. I explained that we had planted our seed later than he had done, that our meadows in potato parlance were considered later than his, and that in any case Tommy had warned us to wait another week. My mother, however, had the gambling instinct inherent within her and she insisted that no harm would be done if I collected the shovel and the three of us went down the cliff to try a few plants.

The bright light of the day had gone from the cliff when we reached it and the sun was dipping to the sea on the other side of the Penwith peninsula. The shadows of the rocks were enjoying their brief passage of life before dark, and the sea was dotted with the waking lights of the pilchard fleet. I poised the long-handled shovel and cumbersomely jabbed it under a plant, lifting the bundle of earth and tossing it to where Jeannie was standing. She stopped, shook the sturdy leaves, and ran her hand through the soil. And there, gleaming bright in the dusk were six potatoes, each the comfortable size of a baby's fist.

Jeannie and I were up at dawn the following morning and I drove the Land Rover over the shoulder of the cemetery field and down to the top of the cliff. It was a heavenly morning with a haze hiding the horizon, the first swallows skimming the landscape, the white parasols of the may trees pluming from the green bracken, and the scent of the bluebells mingling with the salt air of the sea. In the back of the car we had a spring balance weighing machine and a tripod on which to hang it, a bundle of chips and a ball of binder twine with which to tie the cardboard tops when the chips were full, a pair of scissors, the shovel, a box full of salesman's labels with printed addresses of different markets. It was a lush moment of hope blissfully blinded from the realities the years would see.

5

During the days that followed, smoothly dressed salesmen appeared on the cliff, watching me dig and ache my way through a meadow, bantering me with news of prices better than their rivals.

'We paid 8½d. home at Bristol,' one would say, and then another two hours later would announce; 'Manchester is strong. We expect 9d. tomorrow.' They served too as the errand boys of news from other potato areas and I would clutter my worries over the prices with the threats that these areas, so much larger than our own, would soon be in production. These threats became progressively worse in their nature, beginning gently with: 'Marazion starts next week,' edging dangerously to 'Gulval are opening up their fields,' or the generalised black news that 'the farmers begin Tuesday': and growing to a climax with 'Jersey are at their peak' or 'Pembroke has a bumper crop,' and then, most disastrous of all: 'Lincoln has begun.' If you have not cleared the cliff by the time Lincoln stream their potato lorries to the markets, you might as well tip your potatoes in the sea. Nowadays these threats have become internationalised and one goes dizzy with the news that Covent Garden is flooded with Morocco, Birmingham with Cyprus, Liverpool with Malta; and it is only when you hear that France has Colorado beetle and has stopped sending that you have a glimmer of hope.

Tommy Williams, during the three days of the week he worked for us, dug in one meadow while I struggled in another; and at the end of the day he would have forty full chips to my fifteen. The Cornish shovel has a long handle like that of a rake and, until one becomes accustomed to it, is a most unwieldy instrument to use. You do not dig as if it were a spade, but scoop under the potato plant using your leg just above the knee as a lever, the left if you are right handed, on which you poise a section of the long handle. As I lunged away my mind rattled with the absurd game of guessing how many potatoes would be under each plant. A meadow of potato plants is seldom uniform, some have squat stems, some thin, some elongated as if they were trying to reach the sky instead of making potatoes among their roots. The ideal plant has a tall firm stem with the shine off the top leaves while the bottom ones are yellow – these are called 'going back' and the fattest, most numerous potatoes should be under them. But, as usual, the dogma of experts was frequently at fault, and I dug plants with squat foliage which had many fine potatoes, some with copy-book stems which had few, and some with green leaves and plenty of shine which had plenty. Sometimes I would be digging a meadow where the crop was light and it seemed to take an age to fill a chip. In another, where the crop was good, the chips seemed to fill on their own and I would shout: 'Lovely samples here, Tommy!'

Tommy's mood varied according to the meadow he was in. If it were large enough for Jeannie to follow behind him, she in blue shorts thrusting her hands in the soil and dropping the very small ones in one chip, the rest in another, and he shirtless in patched brown trousers and wearing a sun-drenched Panama hat, he would treat her to endless dissertations on the problems of the world and his theories on their solution: and from the meadow I was in I would hear the drone of his talk with the gentle voice of Jeannie interrupting every now and again. If he were happy and in a meadow by himself I would suddenly hear the roar of his bass voice, startling the placid cliff with the fragment of a hymn. 'When I start singing in Chapel,' he once told me, 'the congregation stops singing so that they can listen to me solo.' The *Scillonian* was always subjected to close scrutiny. 'Got a tractor on board,' he would say severely, as if it had no right to be there. Or he would spy through his telescope a group in the stern: 'Look to me like Indian students.' And this remark would provide the excuse for a monologue on British policy in India.

Sometimes this telescope annoyed me, for there were days when it seemed more a part of him that his shovel. 'Every time I look at Tommy,' I would say to Jeannie, 'he's staring out to sea.' And Tommy, unaware of my annoyance, would call out: 'That's a Frenchy coming in,' or 'Never seen that white crabber before,' or, if there was a liner on the horizon, 'That's the Mauretania bound for Cherbourg.' His diet came from tins and when Jeannie, sickened by the jellified mess of meat he ate for dinner day after day, offered to warm the tin in the oven, he replied 'It's proper as it is, thanks very much.' There were occasions when he would work for nothing. 'I know what your expenses are,' he would say to me, 'but I want to break the back of this meadow and I won't charge you .'

He did not seem to be happy working for John. 'Mark my words,' he warned, 'I don't think I'll be with him for long.' And sure enough a couple of weeks later Tommy came raging into the cottage. 'It's all over between me and him,' he shouted, and poured out a torrent of detail which was difficult to follow. From then on he worked for us full time, but the row which parted him from John seemed to irritate. He proceeded to carry on a pin-pricking feud with John, sometimes to my embarrassment. One morning I found him planting a clump of lilies in a piece of ground in front of the cottage. 'Where on earth did you get those from Tommy?' I asked. 'They came from the wood,' he replied without looking up, 'and they belonged to my sister.' Tommy's sister had been married to the man who had the farm before John – and he had been killed in his barn by a falling bale of straw. 'I like to think they are hers.' This same line of reasoning governed a later occasion at the time of the flower season when I saw Tommy climb over our boundary hedge and pick a bunch of wild daffodils on the other side. 'You can't do that,' I shouted.; 'Oh, yes, I can,' he shouted back – and then I caught sight of John a little way off, silently watching, his cloth cap on the back of his head, a grass stalk in the corner of his mouth like a pipe. I strolled up the field to him, anxious to disclaim any part in the affair. 'I'm very sorry about this, John,' I said, 'Tommy was over the hedge before I could stop him . . . here,' I began to fumble in the pocket, 'here, you'd better have 1s. 6d. for the bunch.' I held out the money and John, like a magistrate's clerk accepting a fine, thrust it in his pocket. 'As you like,' he said, and then turned away.

Tommy's roughness was balanced by his tenderness for birds and animals, and I have seen his eyes soften in wonderment at the sight of a young robin being fed by its parents. Once I saw him half-way up a tall elm, climbing with one hand while the other held a tiny object. 'A baby owl,' he shouted down at me, 'I won't be a minute before I put it back in its nest. You look at the bottom and you'll see two mice its mother must have brought it during the night.' There was the incident of the fox cubs who chose one of our potato meadows as a playground, gambolling at night among the green plants and crushing flat the leaves and stalks. It was the custom in the neighbourhood when this sort of thing happened for the farmer to set traps; and I have seen of an early May morning four cubs each in a corner of a meadow with a leg caught in a gin. I remember how curious it seemed to me that they did not appear frightened, as if it were still part of the game they had started to play in the night; and they waited there as the sun rose until the farmer, in his own good time, arrived to knock them one by one on the head. We, however, were prepared to leave the playground as it was, losing the potatoes to the cubs, but Tommy, on the other hand, was more practical. 'We can't afford to lose the taties,' said he, 'and we mustn't hurt the cubs. I know a way of persuading the vixen to move them to another earth. You leave it to me.' He never told us what he did though I can guess. In any case the meadow was never used as a playground again.

An hour before Tommy was due to go home, he and I used to begin carrying the chips up the cliff. We carried them one in either hand, a hateful, exhausting, back-breaking task, forgivable when the price was high, but when it began to dip I used to mutter curses, as I climbed, against the city dwellers who had no notion of the endeavour that lay behind the potatoes on their plates. Jeannie and I were too tired to weigh them in the evening, and we would have a meal and go immediately to bed, falling into a revolving kaleidoscope of dreams – potatoes with human faces, crushed haulms served for lunch at the Savoy, the *Scillonian* in the guise of a whale, stinging nettles dancing like a chorus, running a cross-country race on a magic carpet which never moved, Tommy looming out of the sky like Mephistopheles. We awoke as tired as when we went to bed, limbs aching, our minds fogged by our dreams and the prospect of another day of chain gang labour. I would get up and put the kettle on the paraffin stove and when it had boiled replace it with a saucepan for the eggs. Then, breakfast over, we would walk along the path to the top of the cliffs where the chips in neat rows awaited their weighing, and suddenly, as if an icepack had melted miraculously before our eyes, we became aware of the glory of the early morning. We looked down on to the sea, glittering from the sun which rose above the Lizard, spattered with fishing boats hurrying to the Newlyn fish market like office workers scurrying to town. A cuckoo flew past, topping the undergrowth, calling as she went. A cormorant perched on the rock that is called Gazell, its black wings extended, drying them against the softness of the breeze. High in the sky a wood pigeon courted another, clapping its wings, then swooping silently and up again, and another clap as sharp as a pistol shot. Around us bluebells brimmed the green grass and foxgloves pointed to the sky like sentinels. Meadow sweet and may blossom clung the air with their scent. A woodpecker laughed. And the sea, sweeping its cool tranquillity to the horizon, lapped its murmur against the rocks below us. Here was the heightened moment when the early morning, unspoilt like a child, is secure from passing time; and when a human being, sour with man-made pleasures, awakes to the sweet grace of freedom.

I weighed, while Jeannie tied the cardboard tops to the chips with binder twine, and while we worked we worried where we would send them. 'I think Birmingham,' I would say, and then, a few minutes later: 'Of course that Scots salesman did say Bristol was very good.' Jeannie would suggest Covent Garden. 'After all,' she reasoned, 'the West End restaurants surely want Cornish new potatoes and should be ready to pay a decent price.' But a few moments later: 'What about Glasgow – the man with one arm said it topped all the other markets last week.' 'All right,' I would reply, 'We'll send to Glasgow.' There would be a pause while I hooked another chip on the crook of the spring balance. 'Of course there's all that extra freight to think of,' Jeannie would murmur. 'Oh hell,' I would answer, 'let's send to Birmingham.' We would pack the chips into the Land Rover, make out the invoice and despatch note, and I would drive to Penzance station. And there, as I waited my turn to unload, doubts would arise again for I would see some farmer of great experience and ask him where he was sending. 'Liverpool – I always send north at this time of the season.'

Our indecision could be blamed on inexperience, but as the years passed the guesswork has continued. Growers despatch their produce to the market, and then, like punters, hope for the best, and storm with irritation when they back the wrong town. There is no way of gauging the see-saw of demand. A salesman said to me once: 'Cardiff is going to be very strong at the beginning of next week. I'll take all that you can dig.' We hired extra labour and sweated through the week-end until we had one ton of potatoes to despatch on Monday and off they went to Cardiff. Three days went by and I received no sales returns – and when sales returns are delayed, it is usually an ominous sign. They came a week later and the price, as by then I had expected, was disastrous. I did not see the salesman again till the end of the season when he appeared at the door to ask for seven chips, the balance of those his firm had sold me and for which I had not paid the price of 9d. each. 'They're broken,' I said truthfully, but grimly, remembering Cardiff. 'Well,' he said, 'you'll have to show them to me or pay.'

That was enough. I burst. Jeannie and I had worked for a month in the manner of peasants of a hundred years ago, and we were exhausted both with potatoes and salesmen. 'Get out of my sight,' I yelled, 'go down the cliff and find them yourself.' I have never seen him again.

There are the same lottery selling methods for flowers. Except on special occasions such as Christmas, Easter and Mothering Sunday, no one seems to have a clue when flowers will or will not be wanted. I have had a telegram from a salesman at 10 a.m. saying, 'Market is glutted,' and another two hours later from from the same man saying, 'send all you can.' There was one February week when the weather in Cornwall reminded one of the Alps. The St Buryan road was impassable with drift snow, no buses could climb the hill out of Newlyn, and the flowers, of course, were unpickable. Yet we ourselves did have a meadow of Magnificence daffodils growing close to the sea which were bravely coming into flower although the ground was white around them. 'We ought to get five shillings a bunch for these,' I said to Jeannie. We proudly picked, bunched and packed them, two boxes with fifteen bunches in each, and then set about thinking how we were going to get to Penzance. We had been cut off from the main road for five days but, propelled by the excitement of our achievement, we spent five hours digging away a track for the Land Rover; and when we reached the station we were greeted as conquering heroes by the porters. 'Nothing going away at all,' said Owen, who was head porter on the flower train platform, 'nothing at all.' Three days later we received our sales returns and scribbled across the bottom were the words: 'Sorry, it's too cold for the buyers.' The price was sixpence a bunch.

There are, too, the hazards provided by British Railways. I have known a consignment of our potatoes take a week to reach Newcastle by freight train and three days to Bristol. During a period when the price is swiftly falling day by day, such delays mean financial loss for which we can claim no recompense. It is, however, when our flowers are delayed that Jeannie and I are most enraged, and the fury is the more violent because one is impotent to do anything about it. We have pursued the arduous task of growing the flowers, then picked, bunched and admired their exquisite freshness in the packed box – only to learn later that they never reached the market in time for sale. There was the time, on a Tuesday, when we sent forty boxes of Wedgewood iris by the special flower train to Hull. The engine of this train broke down, the truck containing our flowers was put in a siding, and none were sold till the Thursday when a shipload of Guernsey iris swamped the market and brought the Wednesday price of twenty-five shillings a box down to five shillings. Thus we had lost £40 through no fault of our own and, as usual, we could claim no compensation – for British Railways absolve themselves from blame provided the flower boxes reach the station of destination within thirty-six hours of the original arrival time. The fact that the scheduled service has failed to delivery them for the next day's market is immaterial.

Such frustrations, however, lay ahead, for during that first summer we had beginner's luck; and when the potato season was all over and the meadows were strewn with the withering tops of the plants which a month previously had looked so green, with a broken chip lying here and there, an unused sack and the crows poking in the soil among the untidy desolation for the potatoes which had been left behind, we estimated we had made over £200 profit. This figure, minute against the background of a year, inflated our expectations owing to the comparative ease with which it had been gathered. If, with so little land yet under cultivation, with only thirty hundredweight of seed, we could make that sum of money, surely in another year we would have room for four times the seed and make four times as much.

My mother, who had rejoined us for the last week of the potato season, was delighted with these calculations: she had spent most of each day standing in the field holding open the sacks for us to fill, making the professionals smile by her ardour, but saving time and temper for Jeannie and myself who had not yet mastered the knack of tipping a basket without spilling the potatoes. Her gaiety, however, was tempered by increasing concern over our water supply.

There had been no rain for a month, the water butt was empty, a pencil-sized trickle was all that was left of the stream, and Jeannie had been forced to discover that soap does not really lather in sea water. My mother, naturally, was unable to adjust herself to the situation, and I used to drive to the village tap in St Buryan, fill up a milk churn I had bought and bring it back for her use. It was inevitable that sooner or later we would have to sink a well, and in view of the drought it seemed best not to waste any time.

'Tommy,' I said one morning, 'we're going to dig a well. What do we do?' Tommy, of course, rejoiced in a question which gave an opportunity for a display of his knowledge and he proceeded to inform me of his personal theory that all spring water in the Land's End peninsular came from Switzerland, that the snow in the Alps melted through the crevices to deep underground, and then slowly crept during the course of hundreds of years across Europe and under the Channel to Cornwall. As often happened, he spiced his imaginative discourse with a practical point. 'You can get a subsidy for sinking a well, I fancy,' and so, at his suggestion, Jeannie and I paid a call at the dingy Penzance offices of the local branch of the Ministry of Agriculture. We had been there once before.

It was shortly before we came to live at Minack and we wanted to seek the advice of the then Agricultural Adviser as to how we should grow potatoes and whether he could arrange for a soil analysis of our land. We were ebullient with enthusiasm and naïve with our questions, but the grizzled-faced man greeted our fervour with: 'We don't want anyone else growing potatoes down here. . . you'll be wasting your time and your money.' Incensed at such a reaction to our zest, I said to Jeannie, 'Come on, let's go, we don't want to spend any more time with this moron.' We went back to Minack and the next morning as we were sipping coffee on a rock outside the door, a neat Homburg-hatted gentleman, dressed in a double breasted black suit and wearing shiny black shoes, suddenly appeared. 'I have come to test your soil,' he said solemnly, in the manner of a doctor who might say, 'Let's hear how your chest sounds.' We were delighted, and as I led the gentleman to a meadow we required tested, I found myself feeling ashamed that I had left the dingy office so abruptly. We came to the chosen meadow and our friend bent down, ran his fingers through the soil, then heaped some into a little canvas bag. 'Oh,' he said, 'this *is* a kindly soil . . . I should say this is a *very* kindly soil.' There was a note in his voice which made me suspicious, and a few minutes later I asked him how long he had been with the Ministry of Agriculture. He smiled at me blandly. 'Only three days,' he said, 'I've just been transferred from the Ministry of Labour. They change us around a lot, you know.'

I was sceptical when I arrived at the dingy office once again and I was thus prepared for the Alice in Wonderland conversation which followed. 'The Ministry,' said the girl clerk, 'cannot grant a subsidy unless a sample of the water has been passed by the County analyst, and you may not start work on the well until an analysis has been approved.' I looked at her limply. 'How can I have a sample of the waster analysed if I have not got the water?' She smiled primly. 'That's what we wonder too.'

Our next step was to find the source of water on our land and this could only be done by a water diviner or dowser. The mysterious gift of dowsing defies scientific explanation and if you are not born with it, it can never be acquired. Its use is of immemorial antiquity, but not until Elizabethan times is there any record of its first practical use in Britain; and then some merchant adventurers finding the Germans using it in the Harz Mountains for the prospecting of minerals, introduced its use into the tin mining industry of Cornwall. Scientific instruments can now, of course, trace minerals underground but they still cannot trace water; and whether you live in a cottage or belong to a great oil company planning a reservoir in the desert, you have to pin your faith on the man who communes with water. He has to have the sixth sense to gauge the depth underground of the spring, its strength, and its course within a foot or two. There are many stories of dowsers who have judged wrong, of wells that have been sunk at great expense only to produce no water, and my own particular sixth sense on this occasion warned me that unless we were very careful we too might be unlucky.

Our first dowser charged five guineas and displayed such showmanship that he made us feel like natives witnessing black magic. He was a Londoner who had come to Cornwall a few years before and he had, so he told us, made a lifetime study of water divining. 'I've developed a method,' he said proudly, 'that has made water divining almost scientifically accurate.' We gaped in belief as, opening his suitcase, he produced numerous gaily coloured little flags, and a dozen or so forked hazel sticks. 'Now leave me alone,' he said, 'I need to get in the mood.'

We left him and promptly went inside the cottage to watch from a window; and in a few minutes he rose from his prayer-like position and began to shuffle down the lane, his head bent, his hands holding the hazel stick. Suddenly he stopped, stood a flag from his pocket, dropped it and then shuffled on. He stopped again, dropped another flag, then came back to the point where he had started and went off in another direction. It was an hour before he called us to join him, and then he proceeded to give us a lecture as to why, under a pink flag forty feet from the cottage, we would find a spring strong enough to flood St Buryan. 'But how,' asked Jeannie meekly, 'are we to sink a well so near the cottage when there are rocks to dynamite?' 'Ah,' said the man, 'that's not my problem.'

It was not only for this reason that we decided to seek the advice of a second dowser. That evening we were in Jim Grenfell's pub when someone said: 'That fellow may be wrong . . . now the man you want is old John Henry. He's never been wrong in his life and he's nearly seventy . . . he'll find you a spring if anyone can.' I was still cautious and during the following few days I asked other people in the district. 'Oh yes,' everyone said, 'John Henry is the dowser you're looking for.' The Cornish, like the Irish, are adept at providing those remarks which, they sense, will bolster your personal hopes; and in this case no one wished to tell me that old John had given up regular professional dowsing and that, as he himself later put it: 'I be afraid my sticks have lost their sap.' It was so apparent I wanted our dowsing to be a success that to cast a doubt on my hopes would have been an offence.

The old man had kindly blue eyes wrinkling from his gnarled, weather-beaten face, a character who was so much the countryman that the mind, in his company, was blind to any conversation other than that which concerned the open air. I told him about the other dowser and pointed out the spot where the spring was supposed to be. 'The trouble is,' I said, 'it's so near the cottage that I don't see how we could sink a well.' The old man stared at the soil deep in thought, then pulled his forked hazel twig from his pocket, steadied himself as if he were trying to anchor his feet on the ground, and began to dowse. I looked at Jeannie and smiled. I felt I knew what was going to happen; and a moment later the old man swung round to me crossly. 'Minerals,' he snorted, 'not water.' For the next hour he wandered about while we followed as if we were in the wake of a sleepwalker. Sometimes he would stop and the stick would dip, but never, it seemed, in a way that satisfied him. 'Look,' I would cry out hopefully, 'it's dipping!' But the old man only replied by smiling mysteriously. And then we went up to the crest of the hill above the cottage to a point a few yards from the wire netting of the chicken run. Once again he steadied himself, held out the stick horizontally, gripping it as if he were afraid it might catapult from him. It dipped . . . quickly, strongly as if it were making a smart bow. The old man broke into smiles. 'Here's your spring!' he cried out triumphantly, 'come and feel for yourselves!' I first held the twig by myself and nothing happened; but when he clasped my wrists a power went into that stick as if it were a flake of metal being sucked by a magnet. 'Now there's a strong spring,' said John

Henry, 'and you won't have to go more than fourteen or fifteen feet to find it. You can be sure of that.'

Fourteen or fifteen feet. It seemed simple. Jeannie gaily waved good-bye to the old man expecting the water to be gushing into a kitchen sink within a month.

Within a month – the chickens having been moved to a place of safety – there was a hole in the ground seventeen feet deep, eight feet square, and the bottom was as dry as soil in a drought. Its creators were two miners from the Geevor tin mines at St Just, Jack Tregear and Maurice Thomas, and they were as distressed as we were; while old John hastily called in again by me when the fifteen feet limit was reached, nervously scratched his head and said: 'If you go another foot there's sure to be water.'

It was all very well for him to lure us downwards, but for how long were we to pour money down a hole chasing a spring which might not be there? And yet we had gone so far that the tantalising prospect existed of a spout of water waiting to be released within a few inches of where we might stop. We were, of course, given plenty of advice. 'Ah', said a neighbour, 'you should have had Visicks the bore-hole drilling people. They reckon you have to bore one hundred feet to get a good supply. They charge thirty shillings a foot, but' – looking lugubriously down our hole – 'they do get results.'

One hundred feet! And here we were at seventeen feet wondering whether to call a halt. The miners had hoped to complete the work within their fortnight's holiday and at their charge of £2 a foot I had expected the well to cost £30. But from the beginning the plans went awry. Instead of being able to dig the first few feet with pick-axe and shovel, the miners came across solid rock within a foot of the surface. Dynamite had to be used and dynamite meant the laborious hammering of the hand drills to make the holes in which to place the charges. Three or four times a day Jack and Maurice would shout 'Fire!' – and scamper a hundred yards to the shelter of a hedge while we ourselves waited anxiously in the cottage for the bangs. One, two, three, four, five, six . . . sometimes a charge would fail to explode and after waiting a few minutes the miners returned to the well to find out the reason; and there was one scaring occasion when Jack, at the bottom of the shaft, lit a fuse which began to burn too quickly. He started scrambling up the sides, pulling himself by the rope which Maurice held at the top. These events added to our distress. The well was a danger besides being a dry one.

I was now paying them by the hour instead of by the foot and the account had reached £50 without value for money except the sight of a splendid hole. It was a hole that taunted us. It laughed at us. It forced us to lean over the top peering down into its depths for hours everyday. 'Now let's go and see how our hole's getting on,' Tommy Williams would say as often as he felt I would not mind him dropping the work he was doing. The miners had carved a rectangle and the point where John Henry's stick had dipped was its centre; the sides were sheer, the slabs of granite cut as if by a knife. We would stare downwards and when our eyes had grown accustomed to the dark we would gaze at the veins which coursed between the dynamited rocks; the veins through which, if a spring was near, the water would flow.

The miners would make hopeful comments and Jack would shout up from the depths: 'The rab here feels damp.' By now the hole had become a talking point in the district and monotonously I would be asked, 'Any luck yet?' It became, too, the reason for a walk and in the evening or at the week-end neighbours and far neighbours would lope towards it and add their opinions as to its future. 'Now I reckon you'll have to go thirty feet before you strike water,' said one. 'My cousin Enoch found plenty at twenty,' said another. 'In Sancreed parish,' said a third, 'there are two wells within a mile of each other forty feet deep and never a drop of water from either.' Tommy Williams would comment about these remarks with acid sharpness. 'That fellow,' said he about one who prophesied we were wasting out time, 'is worried about his own water, he's frightened we might drain his.'

We were down twenty feet, then twenty-two, then twenty-five. By now, made frantic by the tortoise pace of the hand-drills, we had hired a compressor and the drills to drive into the rock. It speeded the blasting but there was still no sign of a thimbleful of water. Twenty-six feet. Our money was falling into that hole with the abandon of a backer doubling up on losing favourites; and sooner or later we would have to stop. But when? We now had planks across the top and a winch to pull up the debris after each blast; and back we brought old John Henry to stand on the planks so that we could see again the reaction of his hazel stick. Down it dipped, relentlessly, a powerful character staunch to its original opinion. 'If you go another foot . . .' said John.

It was that evening I met the manager of the Newlyn Quarry to whom I described the nightmare in which we were involved. He was a young, Rugby three-quarter type of man who considered my story as a challenge to himself and his organisation. 'I have some compressor equipment and some new drills I want to try out,' he said with a light in his eye, 'we'll bring them out next week-end and we'll have a helluva bang.' The following Saturday a caravan from Newlyn wormed its way through gates and across fields to within a few yards of the hole. A shiny new compressor with a tractor to power it, the manager and his foreman, two quarry men in snow white overalls and polished black helmets who moved speedily about arranging the equipment with the expectant air of conjurers before a children's party. By Monday, I said to myself, we will have water. By Monday the hole was thirty feet deep and my friend had offered to return the following week-end.

Down the hole the next Saturday went a quarry man, the compressor started up its whining roar, the drill spat like a machine-gun, and the dust began to rise, blanketing the bottom. I hung around with the others bemusedly chatting, dazed like a boxer after a fight. 'When I was a child,' I was saying to the foreman, 'I started to dig my way to Australia . . .'

Suddenly from the murk below us was a shout. 'Water! I've struck water!' We let out a cheer which may have been heard across Mount's Bay and I ran around shaking everyone by the hand like a successful politician after an election. Water! It was as if I had won a football pool. I ran down to the cottage where Jeannie was patiently kneading dough on the kitchen table. 'They've found it! I cried. 'Water! . . . old John Henry was right!'

But Jeannie was going to wait a year for her bath and her indoor wash-basin. For one thing our money had gone down the hole. For another, the water turned out to be a 'weeper' which seeped into the well at a gallon or two an hour. And the third reason was that the rains had come. The water butt was full.

6

onty hated the proceedings of the well, and the bangs frightened him into remembering the bombs, flying bombs and rockets which were the companions of his youth; and into remembering the night when, the dust of the ceiling in his fur, he hid terrified in the airing cupboard at Mortlake while Jeannie and I frantically searched the neighbourhood believing he had bolted after a bomb had blown the roof off the house. Thus Jeannie, as soon as the miners shouted 'Fire!' always sat beside him, stroking him, until the bangs were over.

But his contentment, these events apart, was a delight to watch and as the months went by he quietly eased himself into the comfortable ways of a country gentleman. He hunted, slept, ate; then hunted, slept ate. He never roamed any distance from the cottage, but sometimes he would disappear for hours at a time and we would walk around calling for him in vain. He was, of course, curled up in some grassy haunt of his own and he would reappear wondering what all the fuss was about; and although the reason for our searches was mainly due to the simple curiosity of wanting to discover the whereabouts of his hiding places, we also possessed secret fears for his safety. He was, after all, a London cat and therefore could not be expected to have the intuition of a countryman; and we were prepared to appear thoroughly foolish in any efforts we made to protect him. Our concern was due to three reasons – the fact that the colour of his fur made him look, from a distance, like a fox; rabbit traps; and because we knew that sometimes foxes kill cats. And if, by our behaviour, it looked as if we possessed neurotic imaginations, the future proved our fears were justified.

There was, for instance, the young man with an airgun whom I saw emerge from our wood and begin to stalk, the airgun at the ready up the field at the top of which Monty was poised beside a hole in the hedge. 'What are you doing?'

I yelled, running towards him; and the young man who, in any case, had no right to be there, halted for a moment, looking in my direction and began to make grimaces as if he were trying to tell me to shut up. Then crouching, he began to move forward again. 'Stop!' I shouted again,' what the hell are you up to?'

I reached him panting, and he stared oafishly at me. 'Have you any chickens?' he said bellicosely. 'I have . . . but what's that got to do with it? You've no right to be here.' He looked at me with disdain. 'I was doing you a favour. I saw a cub at the top of this field and if it hadn't been for you I could have shot it.' At that moment Monty sauntered down the field towards me. 'A cub?' I said. The young man went red in the face. 'It looked like a cub!'

Monty was given the freedom of the window at night and paradoxically, though our fears for him were bright during the day, they were dulled at night. We were deluded, I suppose, by the convention that cats go out in the dark and that a kind of St Christopher guards them from danger. Then one day a neighbour told us he had found the skeletons of three cats outside a fox's earth not half a mile from the cottage. 'There's a rogue fox about,' he said, 'so you'd better look out for your Monty.' A rogue, by its definition being something which does not pursue normal habits, earns odium for its whole species. Badgers for instance, are generally supposed to be chicken killers but there is unchallengeable evidence that they are not; it is the rogue badger who has brought them their bad name. So it is with foxes – only the rogues kill cats; but once a rogue gets a taste for cats a district will not be safe until the fox is killed. But even after this warning we did not interfere with Monty's nocturnal wanderings. We were aware of the rebellion we would have to face if we tried to stop him, and so we preferred to take the easy way out and do nothing at all. He was agile, he could climb a tree if attacked and, as he never went far, he could always make a dash for the window.

Then one night Jeannie was woken by a fox barking seemingly just a few yards from the cottage, and this was followed by a figure flying through the window and on to the bed. The following night we were determined he should stay indoors, and we gave him a cinder box and shut the bedroom door; and a battle of character began. He clawed, battered and cried at the door while Jeannie and I, trying to sleep, grimly held to our decision that he should *not* go out. At dawn we surrendered. 'After all,' argued Jeannie, as if cats cannot see in the dark, 'it is light enough for him to see a fox if one is about.' Our bed lay against the wall which contained the window, and the window was so placed that with my head on the pillow I could watch the lamps of the pilchard fleet as it operated in Mount's Bay; while beyond, every few seconds, there was the wink of the Lizard light. Three feet below the window was the rockery garden and the patch of trodden earth on which Monty jumped when he went out on his adventures – one moment he could be on our bed, the next outside.

On the night after our attempt to keep him indoors, he was curled asleep on the bed and the window was open. Jeannie too was asleep and I was dozing, when suddenly through my haziness I heard Monty growl like a dog. Instinctively I put out my hand but he was on the windowsill before I grasped him. I fumbled for the torch and switched it on. 'What's the matter Monty?' I murmured, 'what's outside?' I leant forward so that I was half out of the window with my torch shining downwards . . . on to the head of a fox. There he was so close to the wall that he was touching it, so large that in the first startled moment I thought he was an Alsatian dog. 'Quick!' I shouted irrationally, 'a fox is after Monty!'

But before Jeannie was aware of what was happening the fox was away, gliding down the lane like a ghost, only pausing a second to look back, its eyes meeting the beam of my torch like two phosphorescent pin-points. Monty was still growling and struggled to free himself from my hold. 'What's happened? What's happened?' Jeannie called sleepily. 'Only this,' I replied, 'Monty has seen for himself why he can never go out again at night.' And he never did unless we accompanied him. As for our method of keeping him in, we had a carpenter make a frame of wire netting which we fixed to the open window at night. Thus we had our fresh air and Monty could continue to sleep on the bed. He was perfectly satisfied.

A dividing line between a townsman and a countryman is the attitude to rabbit traps; a townsman abhors them and a countryman considers them a necessity. Today the gin trap is banned by law and only a specially designed trap can be used legally which fits in the entrance of a rabbit hole and kills the rabbit instantly as soon as it comes out. But since myxomatosis rabbits have changed their habits and instead of using the burrows they lie out in the undergrowth of the open ground; hence gin traps are still in use, illegal though they may be. Our district is still free of rabbits and we hope we may never see them again;

but one day they probably will come back and we may live again the summer nights when, with the background of the murmuring sea, we would lie awake waiting, waiting, for the curdling screams that inevitably would pursue the hours until the trapper arrived to collect his harvest.

And yet I found myself, possessing as I did, the intellect of a townsman and the way of life of a countryman, in a quandary. The rabbits showed no appreciation of our efforts to be nice to them, and they ate our anemones, violets and lettuces with the same abandon as they ate those of our neighbours. We bought hundreds of yards of wire netting, but I found they used it as a rope ladder, climbing up it and into the meadow on the other side; or sometimes I would find a hole in the wire neatly made as if by wire cutters, and then I believed the story I had been told that cliff rabbits had teeth as hard as steel, and the intelligence of monkeys. As a townsman I admired their cleverness, but as a countryman I became infuriated by their destruction of my livelihood; and so I reluctantly began to trap.

I used to set the traps at dusk, go round to see them with a torch at midnight, and again soon after dawn. The object of these tactics was, of course, to curtail the sufferings of my victims, but the result was hideous to witness; for the brief period of their pain had not sapped their strength, and when the light of the torch announced my coming they darted crazily this way and that within the circumference of the chain which joined the trap to its anchor in the ground. Each time they rushed to escape, winnowing their terror, the gin bit deeper, while I myself, the amateur executioner, fumbled in my attempts to take a firm hold so that with a jerk I could break their necks. Such incidents, etched into the grotesque by the shadows cast by my torch or turned into a Wagnerian Valhalla in the still soft scent of the dawn, gobbled the zest I had to protect our crops.

Then one night I forgot to set my alarm clock and slept peacefully until within an hour of the time Tommy was due to arrive for his day's work. I jumped with horror from my bed and hurried in my pyjamas to the eight traps I had set the night before. Five were undisturbed, in two others were full-grown rabbits each of which must have struggled hard through the night because their trapped feet were gouged red by the gin's fangs, and in the eighth was a sight I will never forget. By some horrible chance two baby rabbits had been trapped together, and as I approached they were knocking each other as they tried to escape, giving the appearance – had I not known what had happened – that they were playing. I killed them and went silently back to the cottage. 'Jeannie,' I said, without telling her what I had seen, 'Hell to the crops, I'm never going to set a trap again.'

The incident was still vivid in my mind when a week later, as we were finishing supper, we heard the tap, tap, tap of the trapper's hammer in John's field above the cottage which ran towards the sea. It was a May evening and although John and I were still on speaking terms, there was a simmering friction between us that seemed certain sooner or later to erupt. 'I do think he might have warned us,' I grumbled, 'we might easily have been out for the evening and then what would have happened to Monty?'

The custom of a trapper was to ring a field with traps two or three days running, leaving them open during the day and setting them afresh in the late afternoon or early evening. Sometimes, however, a trapper was not so conscientious and I remember an occasion when traps on a neighbouring land were set at midday on Sunday and were not visited again until breakfast time on Monday. I was waiting when the trapper came down the lane in his car.

'Good morning,' I said, and then without wasting any time: 'I believe you went to Church yesterday evening.' The man looked at me doubtfully. 'I went to Chapel . . . I'm a Chapel man.' 'Well wherever you went,' I replied, my voice rising, 'your aim was to give thanks to God and yet . . . at that very time you were allowing His creatures to suffer agony at your hands.' The man stared at the ground. 'Come here,' I ordered, and led him to a rabbit which was hanging head downwards from a trap set on top of a hedge. 'That rabbit was caught at one o'clock yesterday afternoon,' I said, 'and had I not heard its cry it would have taken several hours to die in agony . . . and you were in Chapel!' My anger, of course, made me pompous but it had an effect. A few months later I saw the man again. He had given up trapping.

Passion, therefore, was always waiting to come to the surface when traps were set – that of Jeannie was born of imagination, mine of experience. And so when we heard the tap of the hammer in John's field there was the growl of anger within us, the dread of the coming night with its screams, the nag of knowing Monty was in danger. On the second evening, a couple of hours before sunset, Monty was sitting in the front garden, sphinx like, eyes half closed, his burnished fur glossy in the light of the ending day. There was no hint he aimed to wander. His white whiskers sprayed his lion cub head, his tail curled round his body so that its tip gently flicked his front paw. He was at peace, utterly secure in the small world we had found for him. Then I looked through the open door and he was not there.

'Where's Monty? He was outside five minutes ago.' We had panicked often enough before, and been calmed, and made ourselves feel foolish that love should exaggerate fear; and yet the instant of warning repeated itself each time with the same spasm of fright. I ran up to the field and stood on a bank.

The young green corn was brushing the soil, and far our to sea aslant to the Lizard a liner was making for Cherbourg. A raven grunted overhead, flying heavily westward towards the sun, and a charm of goldfinches fluttered chirruping before me, then dived out of sight behind the hedge on my right. A buzzard lazily glided, and silent in the heavens a jet traced its plume. It was very still and only the sea whispered. Suddenly across the field a hundred yards away near the gap pencilled by barbed wire which led to John's cliff, I saw Monty's tail flapping in prisoned puzzlement, as if a hand at ground level was feebly motioning a welcome. 'Jeannie,' I shouted, 'Monty is in a trap!'

I led the way across the field yelling: 'Monty, we're coming!' . . . absurdly frightened, my mind racing with stories of trapped cats. 'It's easier to kill 'em,' a trapper once told us, 'than to get 'em out of a trap. That wild they be.' And I felt enraged that a threat guarded against had yet materialised, that even with all our care Monty could still be trapped. Irrational thoughts, I know, but such are often the companions of distress.

He was lying quietly on his side, his little front paw with the white smudge on it squeezed in the gin; and his yellow eyes gazing up at me as if my presence alone was enough to make him believe the trap would release him. Then, when in those first few second I did nothing, he uttered a little cry, a querulous cry as if he were cross.

'You'll hold him firmer than I can,' Jeannie said when she reached us, 'I know how to open the trap.' I grasped his soft body, limp as a fur stole while Jeannie, her knees in the green corn, put her hands on the gin. It would not budge. 'It's rusty,' I said, 'look, its coated with rust.'

It was as if Monty understood the significance of my remark because he began to cry and struggle and scratch, and try to bite his paw free. 'Hold him! For goodness sake hold him, or he'll pull his paw apart!' At that instant he slipped from my hands, lashed out with his three free legs, tugging at the trap with his fourth, claws like knives ready to rip anything within reach. There was blood on Jeannie's wrist.

'Something's wrong with the trap and we'd better get him back to the cottage.' I had the crazy idea that once there I could rush up to the farm for help. 'Pull the peg out of the ground,' I said, 'then take the weight of the trap with the chain while I hold him.' He had become exhausted and was still again, except for his panting which made his body heave like bellows.

We began to walk, a miserable trio, across the field . . . Jeannie with the chain, I holding him in front of me like a tray, the paw and the gin between us.

'What about your wrist?'

'It's only a scratch. Nothing deep.'

We were nearly there. The lump of the chimney bulged at eye level, the height of the field parallel with the roof, the open door now below us waiting. Suddenly Monty gave a twist with such vicious strength that he caught me unawares. He slipped from my hold, and like a macabre juggler I went this way and that in an effort to regain him. 'Keep the chain up!' Miraculously Jeannie succeeded so that the weight of the gin went along with his paw. He had his terror and pain but she saved him from the awful wrench of the weight, and in those few seconds of success I had grasped him firmly again and he was still limp in my hands.

'I'm going to put him on the ground.' His little pink tongue frothed as he panted and sweat damped his fur and he lay on his side so quietly that he might have been asleep. The next instant I seized the trap, gave it the wrench of a maniac – and it opened. He stretched in the green corn for a minute shuddering with exhaustion; and then Jeannie picked him up and gently carried him home.

Our sweet relief very soon turned into unreasonable anger. Unreasonable because it was nothing to do with us what people did on land under their control. Unreasonable because we had learnt to our cost that rabbits steal with the same effect as a thief putting his hand in the till. Unreasonable because trapping, however much we might disapprove, was the main method of checking the rabbit plague. Our tempers, however, were flaring and only action could bring abatement.

'I'm going to throw that horrible trap in the sea!' Jeannie had bandaged her arm and Monty was still lying exhausted on the sofa.

'All right,' I said, 'and I'm going to find John.' I tramped up across the fields to the farm and the breeze cooled me and told me to be calm – Monty was safe and there was no point in adding to distress. And then I thought of the scratch on Jeannie's arm, and Monty's panting little body and the sound of the screams of the rabbits at night – and when I reached the farmhouse door I was angry again.

Only John's wife was there, peeling potatoes in the kitchen, and his small son who eyed me silently, suspiciously from a chair by the window as I told my story. 'I know nothing about it, Mr Tangye,' said John's wife, 'nothing at all. You speak to John about it.'

I returned to the cottage to find Jeannie had completed her mission. 'I didn't throw it in the sea,' she said doubtfully, 'I threw it over the hedge into the brush . . . we can always get it back if we *have* to.' My own interview had damped my temper, and I was now wishing it had never taken place. I had fired a shot without the compensation of seeing it land on the target – and John was warned. I was now in any case not sure of my ground; and it seemed to me on reflection that inner forces were at work within us to use the incident as a tilt at John and the attitude he represented. If we were desiring a peaceful life and to be left on our own, this was not the way to go about it. I awaited John's coming.

He came thundering up the lane soon after breakfast the following morning. Cap askew, his face red as a beetroot, squat and powerful as a gorilla, he advanced on me with arms swinging as if his intention was to knock me down.

'What right had the cat to be on my land?' he shouted at me when he was still twenty yards off. 'What right had you to trespass on my land to let him out?'

He was now ten yards away.

'What right had Mrs Tangye to throw my trap away?'

He was now five yards away and he had scored a point.

'I tell you what, mate,' and he had now stopped, thrusting his face at mine, 'from now on you go your way, I go mine. When I come down here I won't speak to you.'

He swung round and stamped away.

7

The winds curl Minack in winter. In the beginning while we sat snug in the cottage a sense of security acted as a narcotic against the roar outside. A book, a pipe, the scent of a wood fire, Monty on my lap, there was comfort in joining the ghosts who had listened to the same rage, in sheltering within the walls that withstood centuries of siege. Then as we passed through the shoals of first enthusiasm, facing the reality of the task we had undertaken, tension replaced comfort as the winds blew.

I am afraid now when the westerly comes galloping over the hill behind the cottage and charges with thundering hoofs into the elms that edge the wood; when the northerly steps aloofly along the valley, chilling its visit with frost; when the easterly bites from the Lizard, mouthing the sea and ripping our cliff which puts up a hand to stop it; when the southerly brings the rain and the storm which binds the sea and the land in gloom. For all are our enemies. Those from the east and the south carry salt as they blow, salt which films over flower petals and leaves and burns them papery white. That from the west savages the crops like a madman, that from the north shivers black the plants in its way. I have learnt now the wisdom of Tommy's advice when, at the start, he said to me one day: 'We'll have to have good hedges if we're going to save our crops, and the sooner we start planting them the better.'

I remember at the time that I was grateful to Tommy for looking ahead. The evening before, a man in a pub had asked whether we had yet packed our bags. 'Everyone roundabouts,' said he facetiously, 'is sure you'll never stay. You won't stand Minack in winter . . . oh no! Minack's all right in summer. But winter . . . !' Only the seasons could prove to those who were watching us that we were not flirting with the life we had chosen, and that we belonged to the land they loved; like recruits to a battle-proved battalion we had to wait to earn respect. Meanwhile our ways were sure to be smiled at, and our failures seized upon as evidence of coming surrender; and so when Tommy countered the prophecies of our departure by discussing the planning of hedges for the future, his unconscious gesture gave us unreasonable pleasure. But the advice itself made me apprehensive.

There were so many other tasks to perform, so many other things on which to spend our limited capital that it seemed a dreary prospect to lay out time and money on hedges which would take years before they became effective. I know now that my attitude was that of an amateur who is unable to believe that the conquest of the land is only achieved by monumental patience. I was in a hurry. My chief concern was to earn sufficient money from immediate crops to secure our survival. I had no time for the laying of foundations and my faith depended on the years ahead looking after themselves; and yet my instinct conflicted with my inclination and I knew that I should listen to Tommy. 'All right,' I said to him half-heartedly, 'I'll find out what we ought to do.' I proceeded to find out, then discarded my findings, and compromised with a plan of my own; and the result is that even today I am ashamed of my hedges.

Hedge planting is in effect the mapping of a market garden, and that was another reason why I was shy of it. What kind of a map did I want? I did not know. I was not a man sitting at a desk drawing up a blueprint with skilled experience behind him. I could see no further ahead of me than potatoes and more potatoes, interspersed with daffodils, violets and anemones, and I possessed a sublime faith that a vague number of these would provide our living. What number, I had no idea. Nor the ground space which would represent an economic unit. Costs in relation to turnover were a mystery to me and thus prospective profits, if any, were a blank figure. True I tried to find out, but the growers I talked to were loquacious about their contradictory methods of growing yet dumb on finance. They looked prosperous in their fashion and I was not to know that at this particular time they had passed the peak of the war and post-war years and their profits had begun a diminishing slide. The Horticultural Advisory Service of the Ministry of Agriculture were helpful on the techniques of growing but they too were silent on how to make a market garden pay. I suppose I was expecting too much of them because Minack, in the eyes of an expert, was a folly, and no professional market gardener would ever consider embarking on the task Jeannie and I had set ourselves. We were aiming to make a market garden out of a home, instead of a home out of a market garden.

It was a coincidence that the Ministry of Agriculture itself was establishing a vast experimental horticultural station from one hundred acres of farm land thirty miles away at Camborne at the same time as we were scratching our heads over our own few acres. Rosewarne, as it is called, is now a showplace of planning achievement and there is not an aspect of horticulture – except how to make it pay – that is not investigated. Similar experimental stations, including those maintained by large private firms, exist all over the country, and in the past few years they have developed into being an industry within an industry. Vast sums of money are spent, hordes of scientists and manual workers employed, bevies of reports are issued – while the humble grower who provides the purpose for all this effort remains in the earthy reality of shortage of capital, higher costs and falling prices.

Progress is the scientist's justification, and in the horticultural sphere this means the conquest of the soil and plant diseases, and the production of larger and better crops. This praiseworthy aim is pursued without any thought of likely economic results and thus a scientist's howl of success may be the grower's toll of doom. Daffodil bulbs have in the past been checked from over-production by the fly which lays its eggs within them in the spring, the larvae of which eats and destroys them. Today there is a chemical which, if the bulbs are dipped in it before planting, will secure them from fly attack for at least two years; and this is resulting in a staggering increase of daffodils for sale in a market which is already overloaded. Glasshouse lettuce, unless very skilfully grown, has in the past suffered much from botrytis, a fungus which rots the leaves and stem; now a dust has been produced which can result in a 100 per cent cut of a crop instead of, perhaps, 70 per cent. Rosewarne, among its other activities, is engaged on the conquest of downy mildew on anemones, a disease which attacks large quantities of plants every season and which prevents anemones, as a precautionary measure, being grown in the same ground more than once in every seven years. From the scientist's point of view this would be a conquest worth achieving and hence a mammoth effort is being made to do so; but here again a victory for the scientist means a bell tolling for the grower. 'You know,' said a backroom boy to me gleefully, 'when we succeed . . . anemones won't be worth growing in Cornwall, they'll be so easy!'

Of course, the claims of the scientists do not always prosper in practice, and this adds to the grower's bewilderment. The trade papers bellow with wares of hybrid names promising myself and my colleagues a grower's paradise, luring us to buy concoctions that are found wanting within the year, leaving us with half-filled tins. During the battle of the bulb fly the scientists produced a smelly dust which, they assured us in extravagant language, would kill the menace if dusted over the bulb meadows at fortnightly intervals during April and May, making five applications in all. I bought the dust together with an expensive dusting machine which hitched weightily on my back and was operated by my hand pumping a lever, energetically as if I were a boxer pommeling an opponent. April and May was potato time so I had to be up at dawn marching over the dew filled meadows with the smelly dust spoiling the sweet scented air, exhausted by the energy involved and in any case sceptical whether the effort would be worth the result. It was not. I conscientiously performed my duties for two seasons, then discovered the whole idea had been discarded as worthless by the scientists, leaving me with memories of ruined early mornings, a dusting machine which is now rusted with disuse, and a sack of the smelly dust which seems too expensive to throw away.

Growers, like punters, are gullible and are only too anxious to believe that these dangling promises will provide the profits which are so elusive; hence the chain of scientists, manufacturers and horticultural merchants exercise the same hypnotism as Littlewoods. One autumn I decided to grow spring onions and I had gone through the preliminaries of preparing the ground and sowing the expensive seed when I was advised to use a pre-emergence weed killer. This tempting concoction would spare me the task of weeding throughout the winter and assure a bumper crop at harvest time; and all I had to do, so I was told, was to spray the ground a couple of days before the spring onions were likely to emerge. The timing was important and so was the weather. By leaving the spraying to the last possible moment, I would kill the maximum number of weed seedlings which had grown faster than the spring onions; on the other hand, according to my directions, the weather had to be dry and the sun hot – as if I were able to arrange these factors as easily as opening the week killer tin. I scratched the ground daily until I saw the seeds had germinated, then looked up at the sky, decided it was going to be fine, and brought out the sprayer. Unfortunately the weather took no heed of the manufacturer's directions and within a few hours there was a sharp heavy shower; and the spray instead of staying on the surface was washed into the ground – and that was the end of my spring onions.

Some sprays are so dangerous that the operator must wear a spaceman's suit when using them. Some, drifting on the wind from a neighbour's field, creep through the open windows of the greenhouses and destroy the tomato plants. I have used a spray to kill greenfly on lettuce, and have killed both the lettuce and the greenfly. A spray to kill aphis on brussel sprouts was being spread from an aeroplane when some of it wafted into a country lane bordered with blackberries – police set up road blocks at each end of the lane while the blackberry bushes were forthwith cut down, carted away and burnt. I have never used slug pellets since a friend's dog, finding them scattered in his garden, ate them as if they were biscuits, and died. One season we had a plague of mice eating the anemone buds and, bemoaning the fact to a merchant, I was recommended a liquid which, when sprayed on the ground, killed the mice when they walked on it. 'What about other animals?' I asked, 'cats or dogs I mean.' 'Oh them,' said the merchant, as if nothing else mattered so long as the mice were killed, 'it wouldn't do them any good either.'

A time came when we had a greenhouse at Minack and the first crop we grew were April sweet peas which had to be dusted with a special powder throughout the winter as a protection against mildew. Sweet pea plants need endless attention, and during the countless days we spent in the greenhouse Monty used to be our companion. We were amused by his presence and innocent that he ran any risk; and indeed we considered the greenhouse his playground so that when the weather was stormy we put him inside so that he could exercise in comfort. One March day we had driven over to Newquay and did not return until seven in the evening when, as so often happened, the tiger-like face of Monty staring from the bedroom window welcomed the lights of the car as we came up the lane to the cottage.

Inside we gave him the usual vociferous greeting and Jeannie, anxious to appease the long absence, doled out the boiled fish on his plate. He made to go towards it, halted, began to stagger, then fell down. Jeannie's back was turned and I alone was the witness. 'Jeannie!' I shouted as if I were calling against the wind, 'what's happened to Monty? He's had a stroke!' Panic can easily seize me and as quickly be defeated, just as my temper can flare and fade. Here seemed the threatened instant of finality, the wink of the eyelid that makes the past unreal, love silenced, the agony of leaning on memories threaded like gossamer. And then, quite suddenly, I was calm again. Monty had got to his feet and was weaving towards the bedroom door, crying, and I bent down to hold him, then picked him up in my arms and saw that his eyes were glazed, unseeing and circling in their sockets, control abandoned. 'I'll get the vet,' I said firmly, 'if he's in he'll be here inside the hour. I'll get the Land Rover out and go up to the farm and telephone. I'll put Monty on the bed and you do what you can to keep him quiet.'

Within the hour the vet was leaning over Monty, sounding him, taking his temperature, talking to him in a quiet Scots accent, and by his presence alone making us feel the worst was over. 'His heart's sound,' he said puzzled, 'and I don't see any sign that he's had a stroke and yet . . .' I suddenly thought of the sweet peas and the mildew powder, and I ran out to fetch the tin. There was no mention of poison on the label but when the vet read the analysis he put out his hand and stroked Monty. 'Here's the trouble, old chap,' he said, 'you've been going into the greenhouse and the dust has been brushing off the plants into your fur, and after all these months you've absorbed it into your body. You've got a bad dose of slow poisoning . . . that's what's wrong with you!'

The treatment was bicarbonate of soda every four hours for the next forty-eight and Jeannie and I took it in turns to watch throughout the night. On the second night, it was shortly before dawn, Jeannie, who was in charge of the difficult task of emptying the spoonful of bicarbonate down his throat, was just about to go off to sleep after giving him his dose, leaving me awake in a chair beside him, when there was a noise from the bed on which Monty was lying. We looked at each other. The crisis was over. The noise from the bed was a purr.

I am, then, suspicious of those who feed from the struggles of growers. Conventionality provides them with a mask of altruism towards us, but it is a thin mask. So vast is the industry that now exists on the perimeter of the once basic one of growing, so many are the ramifications of the subsidised bodies that thrive on horticultural research, so huge is the number of men and women whose salaries depend on these sources, that the role of the grower has become that of the guinea pig – the purpose of his existence belongs to others.

I once pinned one of these highly paid gentlemen in a corner in an effort to extract from him a practical programme for a mythical market garden. He was well qualified to give me the advice and I had a simpleton's belief that he would provide an answer. 'Supposing,' I said earnestly, ' you were offered £5,000 on condition you gave up your job and spent it on planning a market garden in Cornwall. How would you set about it?' The man looked at me in astonishment, then roared with laughter, 'Good heavens,' he said, 'I'd forget the condition and put the money in Consols!'

Of course, like all who are prejudiced, I am being unfair, expecting too much, forgetting the occasions when those whom I attack have helped. I rely, for instance, on John Davies, Horticultural Advisory Officer for West Cornwall in the same way that in the old days one relied on the family doctor. If a plant shows signs of a mystery disease, if I want soil samples taken, if I want bulbs tested for eelworm or basal rot, if I just want him to walk round Minack and to listen to his comments, then John Davies will be at my service. And Rosewarne has helped me personally, though it seems to me the expenditure lavished on it far outweighs its usefulness to the ordinary grower.

It is like a wonderful department store where none of the goods are for sale; packing sheds, bulb stores, machinery buildings, heave into the sky like jet liner hangars; an elaborate oil heating apparatus pipes heat to the greenhouses and offices; pedigree cattle and pigs are kept solely for the manure they produce; tractors of the latest design fuss over the land, labourers swarm like bees where mechanisation is impotent; dutch lights and cloches of various shapes and sizes cover an area like a frozen lake. The whole is laid out with the vision of a Capability Brown – avenues and cross sections, myriads of plots where groups of similar flowers or vegetables are grown under different conditions, their progress of growth meticulously noted. It is a vast laboratory, like the site of a space rocket where no expense is spared yet it would be a shambles without a master mind of organisation. One is envious. One feels if one could hitch a particle of the skill and money expended to one's own particular programme, the cares would dissipate. I look at the hedges, thousands of yards of them running sturdy and thick across the open land and marvel at the shelter belts of trees now twenty feet high; and then I come home and stare at the wispy things which represent our hedges, the long gaps between them, the trees which have remained obstinately stunted, tangible evidence of disappointment.

I can plead the excuse of expense, I found that escallonia, the type of hedge planted at Rosewarne, cost £160 for every thousand eighteen inch plants, that other suitable hedge varieties were around the same price; and so, as I was unable to afford rooted plants I had to use my initiative to take their place. There were already around Minack patches of elder and privet, and at my old home of Glendorgal there were hedgerows of tamarisk. All three stand up to salt winds but, compared to escallonia, they have disadvantages; privet sucks the ground of its goodness and nothing will grow satisfactorily within a few feet of it; elder, when full grown, is often attacked by woodworm and decays into a petrified hedge; while tamarisk usually leaves an unwelcome gap of two feet, through which the wind rushes, before the feathery foliage branches out. But they were free. That was the point which appealed to us, and we gaily treated the difference between cuttings and rooted plants as of no importance whatsoever.

I asked for advice and the advice I received was of the kind I wanted to hear. 'Just stick 'em in the ground,' said an old gardener, 'no need to concern yourself. They'll take.' Tommy, too, was our ally, and for an encouraging reason; he had pushed elder branches into the ground where, the year before, he had dug the meadows in the cliff and now each was a vigorous little plant of its own. It seemed, therefore, that the success was limited to the labour involved, and so we proceeded to collect a load of tamarisk branches from Glendorgal, and added hundreds of privet and elder from Minack. It was autumn. It took a week to stick them in the ground, and the winter to find that only a hundred or so had taken. Rabbits were partly to blame for they used the thin cuttings to test out their teeth, nipping them neatly like secateurs, even ignoring the stinking paste I smeared on the bark to check them. Yet the cuttings which escaped their interest fared no better and when in the spring, in irritation, I began pulling them up to see what had happened, the few inches that had been stuck in the soil were as dead as a walking stick. 'Let's put some more in now,' said Tommy, 'they might grow on through the summer.'

We painstakingly collected a further pile of cuttings and once more laboriously stuck them in the ground; and as a gesture to conventional methods I bought a hundred rooted plants called New Zealand Ollearia. Our defeat, on this occasion, was caused by a hot dry summer; there was not enough moisture to excite the cuttings nor to satisfy the Ollearia, and when autumn came round again Ollearia had been cut by half and the cuttings had gone the way of the winter ones.

I was beginning to lose patience. At this point, however, I learnt of a chemical solution in which the cuttings could be soaked, which would hasten the growth of the roots. I decided to give it a chance, and off we went collecting cuttings again. We tied them in bundles, dropped them in the tin bath specially bought for the purpose, and waited the required time for the chemical solution to perform its magic. Then, instead of sticking the cuttings haphazardly in an embryo hedge, we arranged them a few inches apart in a meadow. Now, I said to myself, I have at last done the right thing and by the spring we will have several hundred rooted cuttings to transplant. Unfortunately it was the coldest Cornish winter of the century and for a month the ground was frozen like cement. None of the cuttings survived.

This tale of misfortune, I now realise, need not have happened had I been more methodical. The soil does not accept impatience, short cuts, or the attitude of take it or leave it; and it rewards only the careful. The weather is a market gardener's standby excuse but it also covers a multitude of his sins. Hedge plants, like roses, need weeding and watering and the fact that there may be hundreds of them does not hide this necessity. I now know that it is my fault that hedges do not ring Minack. They bored me. There were so many other things to do. They grew too slowly to capture my imagination; and once I stuck them in the ground I forgot them. They could look after themselves.

Jeannie spent the first winter locked in the chicken house we used as a spare bedroom, writing 'Meet Me At The Savoy'. There was the camp bed used by her father in the 1914 war and now strewn with her papers, the rug, a second-hand kitchen table with her typewriter, an upturned box as a chair, another box where a paraffin lamp hissed at night, except when the winds blew and then it was silent against the roar outside. 'Where's Jeannie?' some friends who had called would ask. 'In the chicken house,' I would answer, 'here's the key. Go and see if she wants to be let out.'

This apparent brutality, I say in self-defence, was at her suggestion because she was aware that incarceration was the shortest way to completing her book. She had no one to help her in the cottage, and though it was small and though I did what I could, the eyes of a woman saw work to do; and so if she had freedom of movement the mind would fuss and time be wasted. Thus I would clean and light the stove, make a gesture of dusting the two rooms, do the shopping, provide a snack lunch and endless cups of tea; and then in the evening, Jeannie would emerge to cook the dinner.

She performed this tiresome task quite unconcerned that the world she had left on her typewriter was a gay and glamorous one, while reality was that of a peasant. The essence of marriage is ease of companionship and this the two of us shared. Our professions had forced us to mix with people as a duty, and it was a duty which we often enjoyed; but neither of us were ever dependent on mass companionship, the sickness of being afraid of being alone. And now that time was ours we saw no virtue in leaning on conventionality; attending gatherings whose purpose was to hide the boredom of those who gave them. We kept to ourselves. We did not have to escape to pleasure, for pleasure was watching Monty jumping Monty's Leap or noting the time the woodpecker went to bed in the hole of the elm twenty yards from the cottage, or wondering what bird called a piping cry at dusk, or opening a parcel from the London Library, or becoming aware of the colours of lichen, or that of old stones, or rejoicing that we were both so lucky. We would have dinner with the candlelight flickering the white walls, and discuss what she had written and what she planned to write on the morrow, and I would give an account of what I had been doing during the day. And then we would clear the table and cover it with newspaper, for there was still work to do.

Violets waited to be bunched.

8

We had planted the violet runners in June – six thousand Governor Herrick in the top half of the field, the cemetery field where we had cropped potatoes; and two thousand Princess of Wales in the meadow walled by elms near the cottage which we whimsically called 'Gee's Meadow' at the request of Gertrude Lawrence. 'It would give me a nice warm feeling,' she wrote to us from New York, 'if I knew there was a corner of England which was for ever me.' Sentimental, loyal, enchanting, provocative Gertie – what compelling force made me go into that meadow one August evening and be quietly standing there when Jeannie came running, calling: 'Gee's dead! . . . a cable from Richard . . . !'

Death can bring anger as well as grief. The old die creeping gently into our sorrow but those with uncompleted lives, promise unfulfilled, gifts unspent, savage the placid sweetness of our memories, thrusting frustrated yearnings into our hands, bruising the tears with cries of what might have been. 'Rage, rage against the dying of the sun!' said Dylan Thomas.

Gertie's life – or Gee or Gertrude – although she herself preferred Gee, belonged to the age when talent of the arts was leisurely matured so that the future was always more enrichening than the past. Time hovered instead of rushing, yielding the opportunity to delve into the secret self, extracting from its recesses the uncorrupted truth. Temptation was not always at the elbow to offer the illusion that sudden fame was permanent success because the arbiters of achievement – the Charlots and the Cochrans – were governed by standards that did not admit false values. Thus Gertie, steered in her youth by their guidance, was able to find as she grew older the gifts deep within her which earned the homage that dipped the lights of Broadway and Shaftesbury Avenue on the August evening that she died.

Gertie had an irrepressible ebullience which enabled the sleek or the humble to rejoice in her company – an audience of 'Private Lives' or that of troops in a concert hall. She had no conceit and beneath the gloss was a perennial wonderment that the little girl who once danced to the barrel organ outside Kensington Oval had become a star in two continents. She preferred to remember her childhood rather than to forget it, and this was the strength of her sympathy for those who were struggling. Danny Kaye made his debut on Broadway in 'Lady in the Dark' of which Gertie was the star, and on the first night he brought down the house with a song he sang just before her own big number. Danny, instead of being delighted, was terrified. How would Gertie react? He could not believe that she would be pleased – but of course she was and insisted that he be promoted to star billing. A few years later Danny came to London to repeat his first big triumph at the Palladium, and at the same time Gertie had a great success in Daphne du Maurier's 'September Tide.'

'How's Gee?' he asked Jeannie on the morning of his first night. Jeannie replied that she thought she was rather lonely. 'You see,' Jeannie said to Danny, 'here she is with London at her feet but she is so famous and glamorous that people hesitate to ask her out thinking she would never come anyway, and the result is she often gets left out.' Danny picked up the telephone and asked for Gertie's room. Jeannie heard her tinkling voice reply, then Danny saying: 'Will you be my girl tonight Gee? The American Ambassador is giving a party after the show.' And there was another day when Danny came rushing into Jeannie's office. 'Do you know what day it is?' 'Yes, of course,' she answered, 'its Independence Day.' 'No, not that . . . it's Gee's birthday! Here's a card, get someone to send her masses of flowers, and they mustn't cost less than ten pounds.'

I was in San Francisco before the war when Gertie was playing 'Susan and God' at the Curran Theatre, and one evening we decided to make a tour of Chinatown. The Chief of Police offered to be our guide and off we went along the dark alleyways and up rickety staircases, pretending all the time we were risking the dangers that had not existed in years. A British warship happened to be on a courtesy visit to 'Frisco, and towards two in the morning we saw three able seamen swaying slightly in the middle of Grant Avenue. They affected both of us with nostalgia for home, and so we went up to make their acquaintance. By way of introduction, Gertie, in her delightful confident way, with the words going up and down the scale, said: 'I am Gertie Lawrence!' We waited in suspense for their reaction 'I am Gertie Lawrence,' repeated Gertie, 'you know . . . the actress!' They looked at her a little unsteadily; then one of them mumbled: 'Well . . . if you are . . . sshow ush where we can get shome women!' Gertie pulled three ten dollar bills from her handbag and gave one to each bewildered, weaving seaman. Then she turned to the Chief of Police: 'I think these boys are looking for trouble . . . couldn't you arrange to get them back to the ship . . . gently?' And he did.

Gertie had a passionate love for England and during the war she was the driving force behind a transatlantic parcels service; then later, before and after the Normandy landings, she served in ENSA. One evening, after she had said goodbye at Drury Lane, ENSA headquarters, before returning to America, Jeannie and I were sitting with her in the Grill Bar of the Savoy. 'You know,' she said firmly, 'I have one ambition I am absolutely determined to fulfil.' Gertie was always able to wrap her ambitions in a rich canopy of sentiment, and this was no exception. Her voice changed, a hint of drama.

'That wonderful old theatre,' she went on, 'with all its traditions and glamour and triumphs . . . just think of the emotions in holds within its walls. I was thinking as I walked over here . . . I must play there!'

A few years later there was a memorable first night on Broadway at which Gertie triumphed as Anna in Rodgers and Hammerstein's 'The King and I'; and soon afterwards she wrote us a letter in which there was this line: 'Anna's staying two years on Broadway . . . and then THE first night at Drury Lane!' She was not to be there at that first night, for she died a few months after writing to us; but when the night came, Jeannie and I far away at Minack, thought of the gay audience making their way to their seats, the lights going down, the orchestra beginning to lilt the melodies she loved so much, and of the secret wish she never saw fulfilled.

We spent our last New Year's Eve in London with her and her husband Richard Aldrich, and I remember the gusto with which she led the Conga that threaded through the Savoy, boisterously enjoying herself; and I remember the toast she gave us that night after the trumpeters had blared their welcome to the New Year. 'Good luck to you escapists from the rat-race!'

Alas, the Princess of Wales violets in Gee's meadow did not prosper. Our wish to grow the particular variety had been dominated by the whim that we preferred it to any other, and that, of course, is no way to run a commercial flower farm; and the reason we liked it was because, unlike any other commercial variety, the blooms had an exquisite scent. We had been warned it was difficult to grow, that it bloomed sparsely, that the price obtained for the bunches did not recompense these disadvantages – and yet we had obstinately clung to the supreme confidence that in our case the results would be different. The runners bushed into plants and for a few brief weeks we thought our green fingers were going to succeed where others had failed – and then the plants collapsed. We hastily sought advice and the adviser diagnosed the microscopic red spider as the cause of the sickness, but here was a puzzle – red spiders thrive in dry conditions and yet the weather at the time was rain day after day, so wet that it was useless to spray the plants with the concoction which was recommended. Tommy too, was at a loss. 'I've always heard,' he said solemnly, 'that red spiders were bad sailors – yet here they be awash and living.'

Whatever the sickness the plants died and we have never grown Princess of Wales again; but we do now grow a few scented violets of a variety called Ascania. We found it by chance growing wild in a hedgerow, a pale green leaf with a tiny bloom a soft purple in colour and with a scent so sweet and strong that a single small bunch perfumes a room. It is, I believe, the original Cornish violet which was discarded by growers long ago when the hybrid commercial varieties were introduced. It is still useless for sale on its own, but when we have time we add a bloom or two to the bunches we are sending to market and imagine the delight of those who receive them.

While Jeannie worked at her book, I picked the Governor Herrick in the big field. We have now at Minack certain jobs we call lady's jobs and others called gentleman's jobs; and of these, violet picking and bunching are clearly a lady's job. They are fiddling tasks requiring the deft fingers of a seamstress rather than the clumsy hand of a man; and whereas I plod along picking perhaps three dozen bunches an hour, Jeannie picks twice that number. A market bunch consists usually of twenty blooms and two leaves, so when we are picking we count the blooms until we have sixty odd, then collect the six leaves and slip a rubber band over the stalks of the lot; this in violet jargon is a field bunch, a bunch which is not too big to hold and a bunch that, at the end of the day's picking, enables you to know exactly the number of market bunches available.

The stalks are brittle and can easily be snapped off too short; and the blooms, if the plants are big ones, hide among the foliage so that unless you are painstakingly careful you can easily leave a bloom or two behind. You have to examine every bloom to see if it is marked – for there is nothing so irritating to a buncher as having to pick and choose between good and bad blooms; and the secret of speedy bunching is to be free of the responsibility of bloom choice. Normally the marked blooms you have to watch for are those whose petals have been nipped by tiny slugs and snails, insignificant holes but enough to spoil the whole bunch. But there are also the occasions when wind or frost or hail sweep through the plants leaving no bloom undamaged; and then you have the nightmare task of picking not for the market, but just to have the useless blooms off the plant.

Leaves are equally liable to damage and there is also a period during the season when they are often in short supply, and then we use ivy leaves in their place. This shortage, except when frost has done its harm, is due to a natural pause in the life of the plant, and it will occur once, or perhaps twice, during the October to April flowering season; the leaves go small like buttons, and yellow, and the crown of the plant is bared to the sky and for a week or two it seems as if the plant is dead; and then miraculously, little green shoots thrust upwards followed by the pin points of the buds, and soon the plants are in bloom again.

In the beginning I used to help Jeannie with the bunching but my laborious efforts, my groans as I fumbled with the stalks which swivelled this way and that in my fingers, became a handicap to her enthusiasm. She was so fast and I was so slow that I was like a runner who is lapped several times in a race; and her bunches were so much better than mind. I have seen professional violet bunchers who work at great speed show no regard as to the final look of the bunches; they gather the required number of blooms, add the leaves, slip on the rubber bands, and that, as far as they are concerned, is another bunch ready for market. Jeannie works as fast but she arranges every bloom to face the same way, so that when you hold up the bunch all the violets are looking at you, wide open like miniature pansies.

There is an art, too, in packing them in the flower boxes. First, however, after being bunched, their heads are dipped in water and the bunches are left overnight in jars filled to the brim with water; violets revel in wet and, as they drink through their petals, they will survive for days if they are dipped regularly. The bunches are packed tightly in the boxes but the number depends on whether they have short or long stalks, which in turn depends on whether it is cold or mild weather; when they are short Jeannie packs forty-two bunches, when long, thirty bunches; and she lays them on white tissue paper, the ends of which are folded over to cover the blooms before putting on the top. Then off the boxes go in the Land Rover to Penzance station and from there on the flower train to whichever market we have decided on; and in two or three days the price returns arrive through the post and we open the envelope in excitement. 'Sixpence!' I shout with delight. Or gloomily I murmur: 'Only threepence.'

It is a depressing experience, an experience which sets the mood for the day, when a box of flowers we have admired, which has caused Jeannie to shout from the flower house: 'You must come and see these before I put the top on... they're so beautiful!' – when such a box fetches a poor price. We feel cheated and angry, and we curse the salesman, and I scribble a note of complaint. Or we say stoutly: 'We won't send to *that* market again.' Just like the potatoes, just like anything else a market gardener grows . . . once a product is away from the packing shed it becomes a ticket in a lottery. Yet, as there is no alternative, as it is far too complicated a business to sell direct to retailers, one has to learn, like growing old, to accept the situation. We now accept it by sending our flowers regularly to the same salesman season after season. We send to Clifford Cowling at Leeds, the Dan Wuille Group, a firm in Birmingham and to Carlo Naef, the Italian born doyen of Covent Garden salesmen. They receive between them the whole range of our present day output – violets, anemones, daffodils, freesias, wallflowers, forget-me-nots, calendulas, polyanthus, Christmas flowering stocks; and if sometimes their price returns disappoint, enraging us, we have to admit to ourselves that they too are at the mercy of the same flighty mistress; the mysterious, intangible, elusive 'supply and demand.'

The first winter I cared not a rap for such economic factors because my imagination did not wish to grasp the prospect that they would ever beset me. I was doped by the sheer pleasure of being a peasant; by the plodding work that did not require mental activity; by day-end exhaustion that did not repay with worried, sleepless nights; by the pleasure of achievement after I had defeated the wind and the rain, and the baskets were filled with violets.

Physical effort is so much more gentle than that of the mind and, being new to it, I found it more rewarding. Mine was the pleasure of the mountaineer, the Channel swimmer or the marathon runner – enthusiasm allied with determination that brought victory which is sweet to the senses and provided tangible conquest in a personal battle. I was blessed at the time by the simple belief that flower growing was determined by obeying certain well defined rules, and success was automatic for him who did so; manure the ground, for instance, see there is enough lime, stick the plants in at the right time, and so on. I had, of course, to work hard and be ready to accept advice from experienced growers whenever I was in doubt, and pick their brains whenever I had the chance. I had, in fact, to behave like any intelligent man with initiative, and my reward would be flowers in abundance. I had not the slightest conception of the savage surprises ahead of me, nor of the bewildering contradictions that growing provides. Quite early on, during that first winter, however, my education was to begin.

The Princess of Wales had already disappeared and now the Governor Herrick started to look anaemic; and instead of lush green plants cascading violet blooms like those of my neighbours, they resembled row upon row of pale faced schoolboys in need of a holiday. The stalks were short, the length of my thumb; the blooms were like pin-points and the petals unwilling to open; and the leaves were grey-green and crinkly.

I am giving the wrong impression. They never at any time looked bursting with life, but a philosophy of wishful thinking convinced me they were certain to improve; and only the departure of autumn forced me to admit that something was radically wrong. My best week's picking had been twenty-four dozen bunches; and in view of the number of plants we had it should have been three times that number. 'What's wrong with the violets?' I said at last to Tommy. I was often to be amazed how Tommy, who was so intelligent on many subjects, was so ignorant on matters that directly concerned his profession; or perhaps his profession was to make use of his strength, leaving questions of skill to his boss. 'They look sick,' was all the answer he could give me.

I had, I now realise, a child-like faith in the wisdom of those who lived close to the soil; and it never seemed possible to me that nature often defeated them. However, it never occurred to me, until experience proved it, that growers, like all experts, frequently offered advice that was diametrically opposite in its content. There was another occasion in another year when our violet runners failed from the beginning to take a grip with their roots; and I travelled the district, samples of dead runners in my hand, seeking an answer to the mystery.

Surely, I said to myself, these people who have been growing violets all their lives will be able to give me the answer; and yet each advanced a different theory none of which, as I learnt later, was the right one. I found out on my own that the damage had been inflicted by myself; in an effort to provide special food for each runner, I had dropped a handful of blood and bone mixture in each hole as I planted them, and this had burnt and killed the fibre roots.

As for the Governor Herrick, one man said the runners must have come from stock which had become exhausted, another that I could not have put any manure in the ground (I had put plenty of fish manure), and another that the wind had stunted the plants. Jeannie and I came to the conclusion that the latter explanation was the most likely one and we decided, after much discussion, to invest £30 in coconut netting and posts. The gesture, however had a feeble result. It was too late. If a winter flowering plant of any kind has not become firmly established by early autumn, there is nothing you can do afterwards to bring it to life.

I have learnt now – and how costly the lessons have been – that you must anticipate trouble if you are to be a successful grower; you must be an optimist in the long term, a pessimist in the short, and you must be perpetually on guard against sudden attack by the elements, insects and diseases which are always in waiting to catch you off your guard.

Along the bank above the Governor Herrick we had planted an assortment of daffodils which had come from Gordon Gibson, a famous grower in the Scilly Islands who was an old friend of Jeannie's family. It was not an ideal position for they faced the full blast of a Lizard wind, but we were short of space and the prize position in the wood had been given to 5 cwt. of King Alfred and 2cwt. of Soleil d'Or. Nor for that matter were they fashionable daffodils; for daffodils like everything else can outlive popularity. We were, however, only too pleased to have them because we could not afford a stock of up-to-date bulbs, and any bulbs were better than none.

Each variety had arrived in the autumn with meticulous explanations from Gibson as to how they would look when the time came to bloom; Hospodar, for instance, coloured best when grown slowly in an open cool situation and would then have a deep orange red centre, in a warm season the colour would be poor; Campernelle, according to Gibson, was a dainty yellow scented jonquil, a lot of which could be packed in a box; Bernardino was white with a heavily frilled cup edged with apricot; Croesus was a mid-season variety with an orange red cup; Coverack Glory was a strong growing scented daffodil with a yellow trumpet. We were bewitched by these descriptions. We forgave the failure of the Governor Herrick in anticipation of this harvest of daffodils.

The first to bloom were the Soleil d'Or in the wood, and the first Sol in any year is a breath-taking moment that lifts the soul on a pinnacle, leaving it there high in the air to contemplate in exultation the wonder of the coming spring. This particular Sol appeared on a late January day, after a harassing morning during which, in our ignorance, we thought we had lost both the Soleil d'Or and all the King Alfred. During the night there had been a hard frost and when we went into the wood after breakfast we found the leaves and the stems quite flat – as if a roller had been driven over the meadow. It was a bitter moment. 'Well,' I said, 'that looks like the end of our daffodil crop.' But I was wrong and it took only a few hours for me to know it; for as the day brightened so did the leaves and stems recover, and then suddenly we saw among the beds of the Soleil d'Or that solitary bloom; a button of yellow too beautiful to pick, its delicate scent touching the cold air like a feather.

Sols, like the early scented Scilly Whites, do not bloom uniformly, so unless you grow a large quantity you can never at one time send away in great numbers; their season protracts over weeks. King Alfreds, on the other hand, once a few blooms have heralded the way, rush in together crowding the meadow with buds. That first year they took us by surprise.

One day at the end of February we had picked a handful, the next I was lugging two baskets back to the cottage. 'Heavens,' I said to Jeannie, 'look at all these . . . and we haven't done a bunch in our lives!'

The remedy was to fetch our old friend Tom Bailey from Lamorna; here was a man who would not laugh at our enthusiasm nor our innocence. 'Tom,' I said, 'we've grown the flowers and now we haven't the slightest idea how to send them away!' I had found him bunching his own daffodils but he showed no irritation at the interruption. 'We'll soon put that right,' he grinned, 'come on, take me up to Minack and I'll show you.'

He was a good teacher because he had a high standard. There are many daffodil growers who seem to have no standards at all, no pride in a beautifully packed box; who bunch blooms however badly marked, jamming them into old cardboard boxes and wrapping them in newspapers if paper at all; farmers, for instance, who during the war and afterwards cashed in on the shortage of daffodils, growing them as if they were a field of turnips.

I once called on a farmer who showed me an outhouse filled with a white variety of daffodil standing in jars on the shelves with the petals stained the colour of autumn leaves. 'Caught the wind,' I said sympathetically, knowing that if they were mine they would all be thrown away. 'Damn nuisance,' he replied, adding blandly, 'I'm afraid it may affect the price.'

The reward for maintaining a high standard comes usually when the markets are glutted with daffodils; and then buyers will ignore the rag and bobtail senders and stick to those whose standards are known. Our own aim is to send every box away from Minack as if it were going to an exhibition; and it is an aim that can only be achieved by having, at times, to dump large quantities of daffodils on the compost heap.

We ran into no trouble with those first King Alfreds, the weather was brisk but there were no strong winds to break the barrage of the wood and hurt them: and we picked when the buds had dipped at right angles to the stems and had begun to open, the yellow just showing. We brought them into the spare bedroom which Jeannie and her typewriter now vacated, and stood them in galvanised flower pails, perhaps for two days, until the bud had formed its full beauty. Then we bunched them in twelves, finding the long firm stems easy to hold and arrange, boxed them in a bed of white paper a dozen bunches at a time, and then sent them off to Honor Bannerman, the head florist at the Savoy, who paid us a price far above anything we would have received in an ordinary market.

This, we said to each other, was a fine way of earning a living; and we had the further satisfaction of hearing of a man who so admired a bunch he bought at the stand in the Savoy's front hall, that he enquired where they came from, then ordered ten dozen to be sent to his friends. Pride, therefore, was mingled with the pleasure of profit; for we had found that in a fortnight's hectic activity we had earned enough to cover the capital outlay of the bulbs, and the bulbs were still there for many seasons to come. 'Just think,' I said to Jeannie with the gambler's aptitude to tot up prospective wins, 'we have taken £56 from 5cwt. of bulbs . . . seven tons fill an acre, so if we could raise the capital to have that amount, we could earn over £1,500 a year!'

There was the beauty of the work as well. Tiredness, as known in other spheres, had no chance to conquer when the senses were being constantly refreshed by the tangible evidence of spring. Each morning we would enter the wood, then stop and marvel before we began to pick. Overnight buds had dropped, opened and were peering their golden yellow over the green foliage, each with a destiny to provide delight. It was like a ballroom of child dancers, innocent and exquisite, brimmed with an ethereal happiness, laughing, loving, blind to passing time; and yet, almost unnoticed, day by day the flowers were leaving, then gathering speed, until suddenly there was only a floor of green, flecked here and there by a bloom that had stayed behind. The dance was over.

Along the bank in the field the Campernelle were flowering and beside them the Hospodar were thick with buds. Campernelle, Hospodar, Coverack Glory, Bernardino, Croesus . . . they would flower in that order, the poor relations of the King Alfred. We would not dare to despatch them to the Savoy, and we would take the luck of the markets; and yet we still had the advantage of being so far west that each variety would flower early, earlier than Lamorna, earlier than Coverack, earlier than Falmouth.

We were well satisfied with the shilling a bunch the Campernelle were fetching as thirty-six bunches were packed in a box; and then followed the Hospodar, first an odd bloom or two and suddenly a rush, stems clawing the air with nodding buds, a concourse of faces crowding the bank; and no sooner had these appeared than the Coverack Glory a little further down the field nearer the sea began drooping their yellow heads, demanding the attention we were giving to the others.

Up to then – it was the second week of March – the weather had been soft and warm, so gentle the wind one could not believe the gales of winter had ever existed, or could ever come again. Our only concern was to pick, bunch and send away. We had no time to anticipate trouble. We listened to the weather forecast but day after day it was so monotonously the same that there came an evening when we did not bother to turn on the wireless. The sky was clear, the sea still, and there was a pleasant security in the quietness, lulling us early to bed and quickly to sleep.

Suddenly I was wakened by a crash, and in the dimness I saw the curtains billowing before the open window like a sail torn from the mast. I fumbled for my torch and at the same time Jeannie cried out: 'My face cream! That was my new bottle of Dorothy Gray I left by the window!'

I had time neither to sympathise, laugh nor investigate the damage. It was the Lizard wind hissing through the trees, tearing into the daffodils that were scheduled to be picked in the morning.

'Hurry,' I said, 'we must get down to the field . . .' and we pulled on our clothes and in a few minutes were fighting, heads down, against a gale that was to roar across Mount's Bay without pause for thirty-six hours. Our task was absurd, but ignorance at first made it appear feasible, the comfortable optimism at the beginning of a battle, the sheer stupidity of believing we could conquer the elements.

We had one torch which Jeannie held as I grabbed at the waving stems, and unable to stand in the screaming wind we crawled on our hands and knees up and down the paths between the beds. For ten minutes we fought with the Hospodar and then, only a handful picked, I yelled at Jeannie: 'It's hopeless here . . . let's try the Coverack Glory!' Down we staggered to the lower part of the field and the beam of the torch shone on a sight which resembled a herd of terrified miniature animals tethered to the ground. Spray was now sticking to our faces and our hands, and a sense of doom was enveloping our hearts. We could not win. Nothing we could do would save our harvest.

9

Fishermen call the Lizard wind the starving wind, for the fish hide from it on the bed of the sea and the boats return empty to port. Landsmen solemnly call it the gizzard wind as it bites into the body and leaves you tired when the day is still young. It is a hateful wind, no good to anybody, drying the soil into powdery dust, blackening the grass like a film of oil, punching the daffodils with the blows of a bully. It is seldom a savage wind as it was on the night it destroyed the Hospodar and Coverack Glory; if it were, if it spat its venom then recoiled into quiet, you could cry over the damage and forget. Instead it simmers its fury like a man with a grudge, moaning its grievance on and on, day after day, remorselessly wearying its victims into defeat.

The wasted stems of the Hospodar and the Coverack Glory were piled high on the compost heap and now the Bernardino and Croesus hastened to join them. Nothing dramatic in their destruction, no sudden obliteration to grieve over; the wind bit at each bud as it unfurled from the calex, flapping the edge of a petal until it turned brown; or it maliciously made the stems dance to its tune so that they swayed together hither and thither, the buds rubbing and chafing, bruising each other to an inevitable end.

We watched and did nothing. As strangers to the wind we bargained that any hour, any moment it might shift to another quarter – hence we refused to buy coconut netting. We considered moving that which surrounded the Governor Herrick, but perversely the plants were now hinting at signs of growth; and, having waited so long, surely it would be foolish to remove the protection that might at last ensure us a reward? Thus we dithered, and hoped, and grew edgy. Our income was blowing away before our eyes, and a little of our confidence too; and when at last the wind moved round to the south it was too late. The Bernardino and the Croesus had enriched the compost heap while the violets, having demanded our loyalty, proved in due course their promised growth was a mirage.

The flowers were behind us and the potatoes ahead, and spring comes to Minack when people begin to ask: 'Are the taties covering the rows?' Lobstermen were dropping their pots and I had excitedly told Jeannie I had seen the first swallow skimming the coast line from its landfall near Land's End. The green woodpeckers were laughing again in the wood at hilarious jokes of their own and I would lie abed in the morning listening to the tap-tap-tap of one carving a hole in an elm. Sea pinks plumed from fat green cushions. A bat fluttered briefly as dusk fell. Robins pounced on worms and hurried off to an early brood. Foxes were bold, appearing casually in daylight in places where winter saw only a shadow. Wrens flighted with feathers bigger than themselves. A male mistlethrush wooed his lady by absurdly building a nest ten yards from our door. Monty looked gorgeous, his fur glistening titian, as he stalked through the lush green grass. Bluebells abounded. Primroses lit the banks with their soft yellow beckoning you to bury your face in their fragrance. These were the regular signs repeated year after year, bringing centuries together and denying the passage of time, shining security in a brittle present, taunting the desperation of beehive cities. If a man could not be at peace among them his shadow must be the enemy.

John again was the first to draw his potatoes and as the cart lumbered up from his cliff, I saw the glint in Tommy's eye. 'Better try ours tomorrow,' he grunted. The same old envy ricocheting down the coast – Tregiffian, Boscawen, St Loy, Penberth; all the way shovels were poised, eyes watching neighbours, silver tongued salesmen angling for custom, neat little meadows falling down the cliffs grinning at the sea and green with hope.

'Started drawing yet?' . . . 'Samples any good?' . . . 'Joe's digging two hundredweight a lace' . . . 'Where are you sending?' . . . 'Manchester is strong, Birmingham is weak' . . . 'A shower won't do any harm' . . . 'Farmers will be early this year.'

John's meadows were round a shoulder of the cliff, facing due south and gaining an hour of sun over our meadows which fell into shadow in the late afternoon. That hour's sun meant a week in earliness, and nothing Tommy could do would alter the fact. Thus the ceremony of trying out stems was doomed to failure.

'We'll wait a few days,' I said to Tommy, 'no use murdering them.'

I was not, however, as calm as I appeared, for I too was gripped with potato fever. It was a deliciously buoyant sensation. Here we were on the edge of retrieving our misfortunes of the flower season. The precious prospect of hitting the jackpot lay ahead, and if I did not wish to appear anxious to Tommy, it certainly did not matter how I appeared to Jeannie. 'Come on,' I said after Tommy had gone home, 'let's go and explore on our own.' It was a gesture of curiosity, not of expectation and we completed the formality without disappointment. 'Another week,' I said, 'at least another week.' And in that week Jeannie, Monty and I gained a companion who, when I started to dig, followed me up and down the row wagging his tail. His name was Gold Bounty.

Gold Bounty was a friendly black greyhound, and his arrival at Minack occurred in this way. A few years before, the White City had offered Jeannie a greyhound to run in her name, and invited us down to the kennels at Barnet to meet it. We were introduced to Gold Bounty who greeted us with such affection, so trustingly muzzled his face in Jeannie's hand, that she wanted to take him back to Mortlake immediately. We were limited, however, to occasional visits to the kennels, but there came a time when he knew us so well that he began to whimper and yelp in excitement as soon as he heard our voices in the corridor.

One day the manager said to us laughingly: 'Well, I can see that Bounty's going to have a good home when he retires.' We, too, laughed in reply. It was a long time off before such a thing would happen. Horizons away, and in the meantime he had races to win. This public side of his life began in sensational fashion; sensational at any rate, and delightful, for Jeannie and myself. When Gold Bounty made his début, we were having dinner in the glass-fronted terrace of the stadium with Don Iddon, the outspoken columnist of the *Daily Mail*, and A.P. Herbert, whose devotion to greyhound racing and football pools has brought him much frustration; and Jeannie was relaxing in the glow of being an owner whose dog was about to race, a situation which has its hazards, as she was later to find out.

For instance, the most unlikely people would sidle up to her: 'See Bounty's running tonight. What's his chances?' The craving for inside knowledge nurtured the delusion that the owner possessed that knowledge. Thus if Jeannie appeared in a mood of optimism, that mood would be responsible for a flow of whispers: 'Bounty's going to win tonight.' If she shrugged her shoulders and said she did not know, the converse was concluded. Unfortunately, she never possessed any secret information, and thus she deserved neither the smiles nor the black looks which followed her imaginary tips.

Indeed as Gold Bounty pursued his career he became a source of embarrassment to ourselves, for loyalty demanded we should back him but circumstances often made us forget; and the times we forgot were those when it seemed he most often won. But there was one awful occasion when he and another greyhound which had been presented to Jeannie called Corporal Mackay, both won on the same night, at combined odds of one hundred and fifty to one. We had not a penny on either. The trainer had told us before racing began that neither had the ghost of a chance.

Gold Bounty's first appearance resulted in a win by a short head after a photo finish. He came up round the last bend from fourth place in the red jacket of Trap Number One, and pipped the favourites on the post. We were hysterical. Alan Herbert shouted like a busker, Don Iddon filled our glasses with champagne, Jeannie stood on a chair yelling: 'Bounty! Bounty! Well done Bounty!' and I shook the hands of everyone at the next table, all of whom were strangers. The custom is for the greyhounds filling the first three places to be walked round the arena after each race; and Jeannie and I ran down to the rails to see Gold Bounty as he passed. He was a beautiful looking greyhound, not very big, and he walked as if on springs. 'Well done, Bounty!' we called. For a moment he looked in our direction, then barked. 'Oh what a good dog am I,' he seemed to be saying. He raced at White City for four years; always genuine and intelligent, he was loved by the crowd, and many a night I have heard the arena filled with the roar: 'Bounty! Bounty! Come on Bounty!'

Then came the letter from the manager of one of the kennels saying it was time for Bounty to retire. Would we have him? Otherwise he would have to be put to sleep since he was not of high enough class to be of use at stud. Of course we agreed immediately to do so. At the same time we realised we were heading for trouble. Track greyhounds, being trained all their lives to chase the electric hare, had also the habit of chasing any other small animal on four legs. How could we keep Bounty and Monty apart?

We shut our minds to this problem in the excitement of his impending arrival, and when one late afternoon he was led from the guard's van of the

Cornish Riviera we were waiting on the Penzance platform to give him a hero's welcome. He greeted us as old friends, barking excitedly and leaping up on his hind legs. He was home. We had not let him down. He was going to have a wonderful time!

But as soon as we returned to the cottage we were faced with the reality of the problem with which we had landed ourselves. Monty, whom we had left shut up indoors, met us with an enraged glare from the window; Bounty saw him and started to bark furiously.

'Look,' I said to Jeannie, 'I'll take Bounty for a walk while you try and make peace with Monty.'

Monty never took any notice of a dog if it passed by him when he was on his own; but if we were about his back would arch, his fur rise, and then wham! . . . he would attack. In his own mind I suppose he was protecting us, but his ferocious behaviour was certainly startling to his victims. Jeannie's cousin once called unexpectedly and arrived at the door holding a terrier in her arms. In an instant Monty was at it, and five minutes later the wretched girl herself was having first-aid in the bathroom. The same kind of episode happened time and time again, and the odd thing was this . . . whenever we rushed out to warn any visitor with a dog, we were always greeted with the same lofty remark: 'Our dog never goes for cats . . . you don't have to worry.'

We, therefore, knew from the beginning that Bounty would never be able to stay with us, although in the moment of welcome we had conveniently forgotten the fact. Our idea was to keep him at Minack for a few days and then to find him a permanent home; sensible but unwise, because every minute he spent with us our hearts became more emotionally involved. He was my shadow. He trotted trustingly at my heels when I took him for long walks, and when I started to shovel out the potatoes he followed me up the meadow, foot by foot, as if he thought his presence was essential. I would return to the cottage with him gambolling beside me, there to find poor old Monty sitting as usual in the window with fire in his eyes.

The nights were chaotic. Our intention had been for Bounty to use the potato hut as a kennel while Monty continued his custom of sleeping on the bed. But Bounty tore at the door and the walls and howled like a hyena until we were driven to silencing him by despatching Monty into the sitting-room, and bringing Bounty into the bedroom. A sliding door divided the enemies and rather than risk one of them slipping through when we opened it, we hopped in and out of the windows. Such a strain could hardly last and its end was sudden.

Jeannie had gone up to the farm to fetch the milk and had taken Bounty with her, and I had stayed behind to weed the garden. Suddenly I saw her running towards me up the lane. She was alone. 'What's happened?' I said, and saw her anguish.

'Bounty's killed a cat and he let out that awful howl as they do when they catch the hare!'

It's a blood curdling sound, a siren of the jungle. 'He must go! He must go!' It was an old cat, a dying one at that, and the farmer who owned it eased our minds by saying he would have had to kill it in any case. But we could not keep Bounty any longer. The honeymoon of his retirement was over.

That afternoon we put him in the back of the Land Rover and set off to find him a home. He thought it great fun. He put his paws on the back of my seat and pushed a wet nose in my neck; and he barked out of the sheer joy of barking. As for ourselves, we were remembering the roars of the White City crowds; 'Bounty! Bounty! Come on Bounty!' – and comparing this memory with the incongruous present; and as happens when one deceives an animal we felt humiliated.

Yet we knew we could find him a good home in St Buryan parish, for it has an ancient tradition of coursing and of breeding greyhound champions of the show ring. And we did. Trethewey looked at Gold Bounty with a grin on his face, and scratched his head in wonderment that such a beautiful dog was being given to him. He had three other greyhounds on his farm, and five minutes was enough to see that he was gentle with them; so we said good-bye to old Bounty feeling assured that he had many years of happiness before him. And it seemed we were right when, a few weeks later, we called and found Bounty curled up in the best armchair by the fire.

The next time I saw Trethewey was three months later when he knocked at the door of the cottage. 'Hello Mr Trethewey,' I said cheerfully, 'how's Bounty?' He looked at me quietly for a moment. 'He's dead,' he said, 'he died last night of a heart attack.'

We ached our way once again through the potato harvest, and when it was all over and we had counted our takings, we were pleased by the immediate present, but disturbed by the future. We had had a good crop and fair prices, but viewed with dispassion we had to admit the outgoings were proving greater than the income. The bliss of the first excursion was being tempered by the knowledge that we had embroiled ourselves in a business that had a considerable appetite. The element of wage paying demanded capital expenditure in order to provide it; thus experience at Minack was beginning to teach us the truth of Parkinson's Law.

If, for instance, you have an acre of land, you may be able to crop it yourself but the work is so exacting and returns so limited that you are certain to decide that you must increase your turnover by cropping more land; and this means you must have labour to help you. More land means more fertilisers, seeds, equipment and general overhead expenses all of which, added to the wage you now have to pay, cancel out the value of the increased turnover. An itch thereupon gets in your mind which worries you into believing that yet more capital expenditure is the answer. If you buy a motor hoe and so lessen the use of the hand hoe, if you buy a motor scythe and dispense with the old-fashioned hand one, if you buy a rotovator and give up digging the ground, if you buy . . . all these purchases, you say, will increase efficiency, spare labour for extra work, and thus bring nearer the elusive margin of profit.

You find the magic result does not materialise, yet the nagging thought develops that you have not been bold enough. What about a greenhouse? And if one greenhouse does not earn what you expect, what about two? Perhaps on the other hand you ought to increase your stock of bulbs, or have a new packing shed, or would it be better to invest in cloches? The ideas for expenditure roll out of your mind as if on a conveyor belt, and you lie awake at night and pace your room in the morning, tussling as to which idea to put into practice.

Funds meanwhile are falling low and instalment commitments increasing. A compelling force drives you to give up your intention of having a new suit in favour of the fertilisers the advisory officer urges you to spread over the bulb ground. Fertilisers, you argue, will increase next year's turnover while a new suit will rest most of the time in the cupboard. You realise by now that you are the victim of your own enthusiasm. So much money has been spent, so much energy expended, that retreat means disaster, and you are drawn by a magnet into a future which is grey with doubt. If the daffodils bloom in profusion, if they do not coincide with a glut, if the violets or anemones are not killed by frost, if it is not a bumper year for everyone else's tomatoes, if the potato plants are not blackened by gales, if their harvest does not have to compete with shiploads of foreign imports . . . then you may expect the year's endeavour to earn you a living.

Market garden efficiency cannot be classified in the same way as a factory. For one thing there is no roof to protect you from the weather; for another you cannot put your goods in a stockroom until there is a demand for their sale because your goods begin to die after they are gathered; and you cannot possibly draw up an accurate budget as you have little idea of what your output may be, and not the faintest notion what price your goods will fetch. Placid looking market gardeners, therefore, are inveterate gamblers and their life is not, as it appears, a plodding one. It dwells in high excitement, and the charm of it is that the grey doubts of the future are invariably quelled by titillating prospects of a new season.

Meanwhile we divised means to live cheaply, and in such efforts the countryman has the advantage over the townsman. Appearances, unless you leave the compound, do not matter and thus old clothes which, in a city, would have been pushed into retirement, continue in rough service for year after year. Rents are a fraction in comparison and nagging bills such as those for warming the house in winter can be tempered by a walk and collecting your own logs. You can have your own fresh eggs and by growing vegetables you can spend the townsman's contribution to the greengrocer on something else.

Jeannie and I now began to wonder whether we could catch our own fish in some manner which would not necessitate my dangling a rod for hour after hour when I should be doing something else. I considered the merits of the kite which is used by off-shore lighthouse keepers. This kite with a baited hook attached is set off before the wind until it is far enough away to be pulled down into the sea, and then is reeled into the rocks beneath the lighthouse. Such a kite is independent of which way the wind is blowing but obviously, if I were to use a kite, I would only be able to launch it when the wind was blowing off the land.

I then had the idea of a toy clockwork motor-boat sailing out to sea from our rocks attached to a line which I would hold, and towing a short second line with a swivel hook attached. This swivel hood would provide the same effect as one being pulled by a fishing boat, luring perhaps mackerel which are rarely caught within casting distance of the rocks – pollock being the normal catch. I found, however, that clockwork did not have the power to face the sea, and any other model was far too expensive. I thereupon settled for a lobster pot.

But a lobster pot still did not provide the answer. We had an ideal spot to drop it, a rock which jutted out into the small bay then fell sheer to the water so that even at low tide it was thirty feet deep. Our method of operation was to weight the pot with stones, bait it with gurnet which we collected from Newlyn fish market, and thow it with a splash into the sea, watching it gurgle its way to the depths. The connecting rope was fastened to a ring we had cemented in a hole in the rocks – one of several holes each a few inches wide which obviously had been man-made for some mysterious reason in the distant past.

Then we left the pot for twenty-four hours in hopeful expectation that lobsters and crabs would crawl to their doom. We had good reason for hopefulness because the lobstermen themselves dropped their pots out in the cove within a stone's throw of our rocks; and so what was likely to go into their pots had only to travel a few yards to go into our particular one. They did not bother to do so. Our total catch in eight weeks consisted of several useless spider crabs, one lobster, and a three-foot conger eel who fang-like teeth gave me the fright of my life as I fought for half an hour to extract it from the pot. I was proud of this conger eel and I carried it up the cliff to the cottage as if I were Monty boasting of the catch of a mouse. 'Look!' I said to Jeannie, 'look what I've caught!' The dead eyes leered at her, the grey elongated body was slimy in my hands. Quickly I realised my pride was misplaced. 'It's horrible,' she said, 'take it away out of my sight!'

Then one evening in the Mousehole pub we met a fisherman called Ned who described a trammel net to us; and he made it sound so alluring that we concluded we would be able to catch enough fish to supply not only ourselves but our neighbours as well. The technicalities were these.

The trammel net was fifty yards long, six feet deep and had a two-inch mesh. Weights were fastened at intervals along one length of the net and corks along the other, specially balanced so that the net floated six feet deep from the surface of the sea. Normally the net was used by either end being attached to two boats, so that they swept the fishing ground like a minesweeper; but Ned's proposal was that we should adjust this principle to our particular conditions which demanded, of course, that we should 'shoot' the net from the rocks and use a buoy anchored in the cove with a pulley attached. The net had long ropes at either end and one of these was threaded through the pulley, then brought back to the rocks; so that when we 'shot' the net we would haul one rope to send it out to sea, and haul the other when we brought it ashore, both ropes of course being at other times securely tied to the rings we had cemented in the holes in the rocks.

One morning, therefore, when the sea in the cove appeared as quiet and innocent as a cow musing in a meadow, Ned nosed in his boat and dropped overboard a 56lb weight with the buoy attached about sixty yards out from where Jeannie and I were standing on the rocks. He had with him the net and the ropes, one of which he threaded through the pulley; then, feeding the net over the side of the boat into the sea, he edged his way towards us until he was near enough to throw the rope-ends which we promptly fastened to the rings. Thus the trap was set and we could see the shadow of the net stretching half-way across the cove; all we had to do was to go away and think of the fish swimming into it.

For a couple of weeks they obliged to such an extent that we had fish for breakfast, lunch and dinner while Monty stuffed himself with plateful after plateful. The snag was, however, that it was always the same fish – pollock – and we grew sick of the sight of it. True we also caught the bony, many coloured, uneatable rass, but these were thrown back into the sea; there was never a sign of the fish of the fishmonger's slab, the mullet, bass and mackerel. The hope they would come remained. Every day at low tide we went down to the rocks and pulled in the net, picked out the fish, then 'shot' the net once again. The weather was fine and the task was simple except for one aspect; and this was to prove our undoing. There was no clear run between the buoy and where I stood pulling in the net. I had to stand in such a position that the net had to be dragged on a jagged channel of rocks close to the water line, and where in fact we picked out the fish. Inevitably I stood the risk of tearing the net but, heavy and cumbersome as it was to control, there was little danger of doing this while the weather was calm; and if it were rough Ned had already warned us to untie it from the ropes and hoist it far out of danger on to the upper part of the rocks – for if the net was out in the cove when a gale blew up, it would certainly be lost.

The first gale caught us prepared, or so we thought. We heard the warning on the six o'clock shipping forecast, and raced down to the cliff, pulled in the net and carried it high and dry above the rocks. As I have said, the net was heavy and when just out of the water, felt like a ten ton weight; so it took time to get it to safety, and the effort brought a sense of satisfaction.

Around midnight I was wakened by such a convulsion of wind roaring round the cottage that I began to worry whether we had taken the net high enough up the rocks. The old nagging worry of the wind which chased us always at Minack; lying cosily in bed with a sound outside like tube trains rushing; as if the cottage had angered a madman who was jabbing at it with a madman's venom. Hate in the wind. Merciless with a bully's power. Wedging a stick of conscience as I lie in bed and listen and fear. Was I careful enough? Or did I only pay court to care? Was I lazy because the day was still, my imagination dull? The seasons lie behind me and the wreckage of the wind cuts into my memory like a general remembering the dying in a lost battle.

At one a.m. Jeannie and I got up and dressed and lit a hurricane lamp, and with heads down against the wind, the light spangling the dancing grasses at our feet, we struggled down the cliff. The seas were enormous. Spray wetted our faces like a sponge and the white crests of the waves ribboned the rocks; and it did not take an instant for us to realise that the net had been dragged from its safety.

'It's my fault,' I shouted, 'I should have taken it further up!' So easy to self-blame when the exception had occurred; such admission softens, too, the disappointment. And yet that night the waves were lunging at the rocks, high above the water line we had never seen wet before; where wayward seeds had fertilised, like meadow sweet and sea pinks and wild alyssum, in crevices of wind-blown soil. We staggered forward oblivious of the danger, enraged that care in our fashion had been rewarded by the cheat of the sea. Then, as we stood amid the shower of the waves with the lamp swinging in my hand, I suddenly saw the net stretched like a straddled whale along the rocks; for one instant in black relief in the lamp-light, the next lost in the mouth-wash of the sea.

I gave Jeannie the lamp and she held it above her head, the light shining on her salt-wet face, feebly acting as sentinel, eyeing the gush of water as it recoiled from the rocks, reflecting the quiet pause, flickering a warning as a white mass gathered momentum then crashed in a thousand fragments splintering the night with spray. At each pause I dashed forward and tugged at the net. I loosened it first from one crevice, then another, and above the thunderous noise Jeannie would shout: 'Quick! Come back! Another one coming!' I struggled as if with an octopus, bit by bit, further and further from the water line until the waves no longer grasped with hands but clawed with fingers instead, becoming weaker, strength in spasms, until impotent and defeated they could only stretch at the net as if to caress.

The next morning we looked at the damage, and it was not as bad as expected. We laboured up the cliff and took the net to the fisherman's store in Newlyn where we had bought it. It remained there for three weeks during which time an old salt patiently repaired it. By now the net had cost us over £20, and the fish it had so far produced had been highly expensive; but the summer was still young and the lesson to take greater care well learnt. We listened to the forecasts and whenever there was a suggestion of wind we pulled in the net and piled it high up on the rocks. Such methodical caution was admirable provided the forecasts were correct, but one Sunday evening when the net was stretched across the cove, the sea as still as a saucer of milk, the sky clear, the forecast promised the same quiet weather would continue for the next twenty-four hours – yet within twelve the sea was a cauldron.

As dawn broke behind the hills on the other side of Mount's Bay, I was straining with all my might to bring in the net, but just as part of it reached the channel of rocks where it lay when we picked out the fish, the pulley jammed on the buoy that was bobbing like a cork out in the cove. I was in any case in danger and Jeannie was yelling to me to retreat. I watched for a moment the net swirling in the waters and wrapping itself round the jagged points of the rocks like a black serpent. This was good-bye to our fish. No chance would arise now to carry the net like a wounded animal to Newlyn. The sea had exacted its revenge.

10

One summer the violets were in the meadow below the cottage which had been a bog when we first arrived, and where Tommy and I had sunk yards of earthenware drainpipes. I was weeding the plants one afternoon when Jeannie, who had gone for a walk over the cliffs, returned highly excited. The delight of her character was the way in which her zest relished our adventure in a manner so natural, so persuasive in its truth, that never at any time did she fail to enthuse even when I, crowding my mind with materialistic fears, blocked her enthusiasm with doubts.

I doubted, for instance, on this occasion when she bubbled the news that the farmer whose land bordered John's to the west, five minutes' walk from Minack, was prepared to rent us two acres. These particular acres together with a cascade of small meadows which fell to the sea below them and which the farmer was to retain for himself, had a reputation in the district of being a potato gold mine. It was a reputation which stemmed from the war when new potatoes fetched ten shillings a pound and daffodils of the most common variety five shillings a bunch. It was early land facing south with the Wolf Rock a finger in the distance, so early that the farmer concerned had never failed to keep his record of sending the first mainland potatoes to market. Thus Pentewan, as the land was called, seemed to provide the chance we were seeking. We were cramped at Minack, but now we could launch out as big growers.

'I wonder why he's giving it up?' I said to Jeannie. My hesitancy was a poor reward for her enthusiasm and she told me so bluntly, nor was my caution to be relied upon. It was a mood which might well be concerned with my dissatisfaction over the growth of the plants I was hoeing, a trivial moment of gloom unfitted to greet a challenge. It certainly was unfair to Jeannie.

'He says there'll be room for four tons of potatoes,' she went on as if she were trying to put a match to my woodiness, 'so that with four tons over here we'll have eight tons of seed next year and at three and a half to one that means twenty-eight tons of potatoes. We could take at least a thousand pounds, and with luck much more!'

If her reasoning sounded optimistic, it also made sense. We had cropped eleven tons of potatoes from three tons of seed during the past season and had averaged £45 a ton; thus Pentewan together with the land we were continuing to reclaim at Minack would put us firmly in sight of establishing ourselves. We would have elbow room, space for more bulbs, be able to grow a greater variety of crops and each on a substantial scale if we so wished. It would counter the disadvantage of Minack where, in view of the endless reclaiming that had to be done, we resembled two people living in a house that was in the process of being built. At Pentewan the meadows awaited us, old hands which knew what was expected of them, a century of sun-drenched labour within their boundaries. I had become as excited as Jeannie.

Meanwhile Jeannie's *Meet Me At The Savoy* for which Danny Kaye had written the foreword had sold as a serial to *John Bull*, and we had invested the proceeds in making the cottage our own particular palace. We installed a petrol-driven pump at the top of the well and became reacquainted with the comfort of a bath and indoor lavatory, having added a wood-built annexe at the far end of the one-time chicken house. This development - hot water came from a Calor gas heater - gave us as much pleasure as that of a millionaire sailing a maiden voyage in his yacht. We revelled in our independence of the weather, and the gush of a tap gave us the same sharp wonderment as that of natives being introduced to the plumbing civilisation for the first time. We still could not afford a sink with running water from a day and night burning stove, nor a hole through the end wall of the cottage with a connecting lobby to the spare room and bathroom; and it was two years before we could do so. Thus, in order to reach the bathroom, we had to go through the front door, a task which was inconvenient but not disastrous; and as far as the washing up was concerned we had to continue to use a basin, then empty the contents over a neighbouring hedge.

I sometimes wonder whether the ghosts of the cottage cast a spell over us, enabling us to accept this abuse of twentieth-century comfort in the way we did. Inconvenience had pervaded the cottage for over five hundred years, so was it inevitable that we should act as if it were natural? The twentieth century decorates life like a Christmas cake, but it still cannot do anything about the basic ingredients; and there seemed to be a starkness in our companionship which enabled us to find a fulfilment without the aid of man-made devices; as if the canvas of each day was so vast that mirror-smooth techniques of living, coma entertainment like television, would only make it unmanageable. We are still without electricity and we remain thankful we have no telephone; yet it would be a pose to pretend that self denial did not seek its compensations.

We have revelled in occasional brisk returns to the life we used to know, being flattered because we were new faces in an old circle or rejoicing in the stimulation of reunions. It was fun being at the first night of A.P. Herbert's musical play 'The Water Gypsies' which he wrote at Minack, to stay at the Dorchester because Richard Aldrich wanted us to be present when his book *Gertrude Lawrence as Mrs A* was launched. All this was the sugar that titivates a day but does not provide its bread; and the basic fact remained that we could not build Minack by playing as if it were an accessory to our life instead of its foundation.

These sorties to an existence which used to be our daily round confirmed the wisdom of our escape, but, at the time we were doped by the paraphernalia of sophistication. We delighted in the silliness, the laughter in cocktail bars, relaxing late in the afternoon over lunch, parties at night. No one could have called us peasants. But when we returned to Minack we looked back on those gilded shadows and were thankful they had passed over us so briefly. We felt pity instead of envy for our contemporaries whose company had regained for us so much pleasure. Success in this age breeds only a rackety happiness, providing little time for its own enjoyment. The bite of competition is too sharp for leisure, so success is either pimped by others to further their own ends or creates its own demoralisation and betrays the truth from which it sprang. There is no freedom in twentieth century achievement for the individual is controlled not by his own deep thinking processes but by the plankton of shibboleths which are currently in fleeting fashion; and by his own desperate need to maintain financial survival in the glittering world he has found himself. Jeannie and I have also to fight for survival, but it is an easy battle compared to that in a city. At least the countryman still possesses the luxury of being able to live at the same leisurely pace of another age.

❄ ❄ ❄

We took over Pentewan meadows and briskly decided to cultivate them by modern methods. They were, for the most part, large sloping meadows which from time immemorial had been shovel-turned in the autumn, shovel-planted with potatoes in early spring, shovel-cropped in the summer. They had never seen a machine, and even the laborious task of hacking the ground into suitable condition before planting had always been done by hand. Obviously my new landlord had found an extra man would be needed on the farm if the meadows were to be worked and unless the wage was that of a coolie profits would be small; and in any case he could not be bothered with the trouble that labour in such circumstances often involves.

I, on the other hand, untrammelled by tradition, was convinced that the answer to the problem was mechanisation; and that once I had gathered around me the correct assortment of machines I would forge ahead with the same relentless success as a gang on a motorway. I was not thinking in terms of the normal sized tractors but of the hand-controlled variety, one of which I had already tried out at Minack; and I thought that if I had a motor-hoe and a motor-driven hedge cutter, tedious time absorbing tasks would be cut to the minimum.

I bought the Minack tractor second-hand, a monstrous looking thing with a plough, and an engine that kicked like a mule every time I started it. Tommy, who could handle any horse, had nothing in common with this example of progress, and he behaved to it always as if he were a fox sniffing danger; and when one day I suddenly saw Tommy careering down the big field towards the cliff, hanging on to the handlebars with the tractor quite out of his control, I decided it was time to get rid of it.

It was exchanged for a second-hand rotovator and this was the machine with which we first went into the attack on the Pentewan meadows. It was a dual purpose machine for if I exchanged the normal small wheels for large ones, removed the rotovator from the engine and substituted a specially designed shaft I could use it with a plough; and a plough can sometimes do work for which a rotovator is useless. For instance some experts will say that a rotovator used often on the same ground will pommel it into uselessness; and that ground should be spared the rotovator and ploughed instead at least once every two years. This probably applies where blades are used but in this instance I had claw-like tines fitted to the machine which churned the soil as if they were forks being used at maniacal speed. The theory was right but the execution wrong, because every time a tine hit a rock hidden beneath the soil it would snap; and as there were many such rocks this method became ridiculously expensive.

I soon found, too, that the machine did not like me; for time and time again when I set out to rotovate, the engine obstinately refused to start. Usually, of course, on such occasions the fault can be quickly corrected by a mechanic, and the mechanic if you possess the most elementary knowledge should be yourself. Check plug, clean carburettor, make sure the ignition is all right. I used to perform these tasks, secure no result, then storm back to Jeannie. 'The bloody thing won't work,' I would shout, 'and I'll have to get them to come and see it.'

'Them' were the Helston people from whom I had bought it, and in due course a kindly mechanic would arrive, tinker an hour or two with the engine, gain no response, then remark; 'I've never known an engine like this before.' My years at Pentewan - and other rotovators behaved in the same way as this first one - are filled with memories of mechanics in various meadows where the rotovator of the moment had broken down, unscrewing things, screwing things up, with me beside them hopefully staring, waiting for them to arrive, or thanking them for coming. 'I can't help thinking,' said one, grimly trying to be cheerful, 'if the firm wouldn't be wise to pitch a tent here.'

Yet this first rotovator had the advantage of being the spearhead of our hopes; and the tantrums were forgiven because we were, in our own minds, revolutionising the cultivation of cliff meadows. Others might think their commercial value was dying out but we were proving that a new outlook, a dashing grasp of experts' advice, would lead them to prosperity. Our landlord had a man called Joe who looked after the cascade of meadows below our own, vineyards of meadows where no machine of any kind could reach, falling to the sea amid hedges of escallonia, apple trees, and banks thick in winter with the fragrance of wild violets; and Joe would leave a meadow which he had been laboriously turning with a shovel, and come to watch me at work; to stare at my method of rotovating or perhaps just to help me with advice on how to get the engine started.

Joe belonged to the cliffs in the same way that a cliff fox or a cliff badger belongs; and he disapproved of change in the same way that anyone disapproves of action that changes something directly concerning his own heart. He distrusted the rotovator. He would stand at the bottom of the meadow where I was working, an old felt hat on his head, a pipe in his mouth, eyes that were set wide apart, young middle age, looking at me bringing the rotovator down the hill then reversing upwards, my foot on the metal cover to keep it from lurching the handlebars high from my grasp. He would watch and say nothing, chewing the stem of his pipe; and then weeks later I would be in some pub, and I would be told: 'I hear that that there rotovator brings all the soil down bottom of meadow.' I do not agree that this view was right; but it made me aware that Joe as he meandered from his own particular world so near the sea, was watching and judging me as I bent the ways of the clinical present to better the integrity of the past; and so I, too, watched and listened.

Joe used to bicycle to the cliffs from his home with Bish his bull terrier trotting at the wheel; and when Bish grew old Joe carried him on the handlebars. Like all his breed Bish was a fierce protector of his owner and of his owner's belongings and as we shared the same hut there were often occasions when Bish would not allow us to enter. The hut was known as the Pink Hut because it was built of corrugated-iron once painted a red which had faded to pink over the years; and as its main function was for the 'shooting' of potatoes it was so designed inside that layer upon layer of boards could be fixed, each layer rising above another which had receive its quota of potato seed. Joe had one half of the hut with its boards, we had the other; and there were times when we wanted to use our half when only Bish was resident in the other. Then Bish, so friendly when nothing of his owner's was threatened, would bare his teeth, snarl, bellow, and frighten us into cupping hands to mouth and shouting downwards towards the seat: 'Joe! Joe! Come up will you? Bish won't let us in!' There would be an answering cry like the hoot of an owl, and in a few minutes Joe would slowly arrive, and Bish would wag his tail and grin at us and apologise.

Joe accepted wild life, not as some countrymen do with the object to kill, but as a means of sharing enjoyment. He hated trapping and when on one occasion he was instructed to do so, he found the next morning in one of the traps a badger. A badger is notoriously, and for obvious reasons, a deadly dangerous animal to release from a trap; and a trapper, if for no other reason except his personal safety, will make certain he has killed it before there is any question of touching it. Not so Joe. He was grievously upset when he found the badger struggling to escape as he walked along the field towards it; and he decided the only thing he could do was momentarily to stun it, then quickly release the foot from the trap. He picked up a stick and hit it, and the badger lay still. Ten minutes later it was still lying there, breathing but without any other signs of life; and so Joe picked it up in his arms, a heavy full grown badger, and carried gently to the Pink Hut.

I came to the hut later in the morning when Joe was having his tea break, and found the badger lying on a bed of sacks, with another sack so folded that it acted as a pillow. Bish was quiet in another corner, Joe puffing his pipe. 'I hit it too hard,' he said to me sadly after he had told me what had happened, 'that's what I did. I hit it too hard.'

Jeannie and I were, at the time, 'shooting' potatoes and this tedious task kept us for hour upon hour in the hut. This gave us the advantage of keeping an eye on the patient as it lay there. It was early in the afternoon over twenty-four hours later that it stirred, an eye opened, and it whimpered. A badger is beautiful to look at in its true setting, a wild path of its own treading, the moon lighting the white streaks of its head, dark shadows its armour; but lying there in the hut, impotent without our help, a heavy immovable body, its appeal was not in its mobility but the common denominator of suffering. I went outside and down the mountain-like track to where Joe was digging. 'It's coming round,' I said. The smile was one of relief rather than pleasure. 'It is?' and he jabbed his shovel into the ground and came back with me to the hut.

The badger was a patient for six weeks, and every day Joe fed him with bread and milk, then when he got stronger shared his sandwiches. Bish was quite unconcerned and showed no jealousy, and the badger in his turn seemed to accept Bish; and then came the time when the badger, gaining confidence, remembering freedom, began to show restlessness. 'To my way of thinking,' said Joe, 'it won't be long before he's ready to go.' In this he was correct but he did not foresee the manner of his going.

At week-ends while Joe remained at home, Jeannie and I used to take over as nurses, and one Sunday evening we fed him as usual, saw that he was comfortable, and shut up the hut. I was first back there in the morning and when I had opened the door, a glance was enough to show the badger had gone. The floorboards had been ripped from the centre of the hut as if a man had been at work with a pickaxe, and as there was only soil underneath, it was then easy for the badger to rejoin the wild where he belonged.

❊ ❊ ❊

Joe used to refer to each meadow as a garden. 'That garden by the quarry is frosty,' he would say. Or: 'I've dug three hundredweight from this garden before May month . . . handsome samples.'

I was in this particular garden one November afternoon during this first year we rented Pentewan, grimly pursuing my task of rotovating the ground. Machines, when seen in a catalogue, appear to perform their duties magically on their own; and if there is a picture of the operator, a broad grin on his face suggests his presence is only a formality. Perhaps it is when the ground is level, but at both Minack and Pentewan the meadows are steep and contracted; and an hour with the rotovator leaves the body pommelled and aching as if it had been stretched on the rack.

The rotovator works the ground downhill and in order to keep the tines deep in the soil, it is necessary to weight the body on the handlebars, at the same time being prepared to lift it if you get warning of an under-the-soil rock. When you return to the top of the meadow you disengage the rotovator, then put the engine in reverse; but in order to control the machine, to prevent the handlebars shooting skywards, you have to do this job by pressing one foot on the cover of the rotovator while hopping backwards on the other; and at all times your arms are also having to force the handlebars downwards. The job is a punishment, a self-inflicted torture which awaits its compensation only when all the land is rotovated, and you rustle the sweet knowledge in your mind that you have achieved in a week what a labourer with a shovel would have done in eight. The pain was repeated twice a year, first in the autumn and then when the potatoes were being planted, the second occasion of course, enabling the shoveller to dig through the soil at great speed; but it is a November afternoon that I am remembering in a garden that Joe once prized as one of his best. As I performed my routine, the engine roaring, my limbs craving for rest, I saw John in the distance with a pair of horses ploughing the field that edged Pentewan and his own.

At the time, he and I were not on speaking terms, and although he had to come Minack way almost every day to collect his horses or pass on down to his cliffs, he never spoke; and when sometimes in a flush of trying to be friends again I wished him good day, my wish was left to hang alone in the air. On this occasion I observed that when he and his horses reached the end of the field and were ready to turn, he would wait a moment or two, and stare across in my direction. His action irritated me, little realising how fortunate, in a few minutes, it would prove to be.

But I was irritated because I had an uncomfortable feeling that he was not wishing me well; he resented our presence at Minack because he did not consider that we belonged there, and he smouldered with vexation that the roughness of the life had not driven us away. Now we had the Pentewan meadows we had become entrenched. He himself would like to have had them. What right had we to move in and collect such a prize?

Physical effort that demands great strain, I have found, creates a pattern of twisted thoughts, the mind is a daytime nightmare, and while the body is being pounded with exhaustion the brain races with a kaleidoscopic jungle of ideas. Such was the course of my thinking as I grimly continued my labour and when, suddenly, while I was reversing , a wheel hit a rock and the machine lurched sideways.

At the same time the catch which disengaged the rotovator slipped out of position and the tines began circulating with great speed. The handlebars shot up skywards and in this instant of my loss of control, my left foot which had been weighting the rotovator cover was twisted under the cover and met the full force of the tines. The next thing I knew was that the machine had turned on its side, the engine had spluttered to a stop, and the tines ceased circulating because my foot and part of my leg was wrapped round the shaft under the cover.

Tommy, I knew, was in a meadow within shouting distance alongside the Pink Hut. I yelled and there was no answer. 'Tommy!' I shouted again. 'Tommy! Tommy! Tommy!' Heavens knows what he was doing, perhaps drowning my cries with some of his own. I lay there immovable, the weight of the tractor on my leg while my foot, I began to realise, was oozing wet in my rubber Wellington boot.

The shock of the accident was now replaced by panic. There was every reason to suppose that no one would hear me; Joe, I knew was in one of his gardens close to the sea while Tommy, if in one of his moods, might well have his mind and ears in another world. I was beginning to have pain. 'Tommy! Tommy! *Tommy!*' I was reaching that hazy, never-never land which heralds a faint when suddenly I heard the beat of running footsteps to the left of me. I twisted my head around and through the grass which brushed my face I saw John.

'All right, mate . . . lie still, I'll get the tractor off you.' He had the strength of a bull and he heaved up the tractor as if it had the weight of a wooden chair . . . but, as the tractor became upright, so it became clear that my foot was hooked on a tine like a joint on a butcher's hook; the point had gone through one side of my foot and out of the other.

'If you could find Tommy,' I said, 'he could go over and fetch Mrs Tangye and get bandages.' John gave me a cigarette, then disappeared; and a few minutes later returned with a scared Tommy who went off across the fields to Minack. I soon found that I could not begin to free my foot until he boot was cut away, and this John proceeded to do, sawing away with a blunt pen-knife at the rubber. It was several minutes before he was successful and by that time my principal anxiety was that Jeannie might arrive while I was still trapped. Unfortunately when the machine turned over and the engine stopped, the rotovator was stalled in gear; and because of the position of the tine that held my foot, my foot could not possibly be freed until he rotovator shaft had been turned several inches. It would not budge.

'You'll have to rock the machine, John,' I said, 'there's nothing else for it.'

At any moment Jeannie would be appearing over the hedge, and I could not bear the thought of her seeing me.

'Rock it to and fro,' I said, 'I often do it when it stalls after getting a stone jammed in the tines.'

He rocked it gently, my leg moving in rhythm, and suddenly the shaft was free. John's cap was pushed on the back of his head, his face was red, the Woodbine dangled out of the corner of his mouth.

'Now be careful, mate,' he said, 'take yer time with the foot.'

It was an occasion when you do not pause to think, for thinking would bring inaction. I noted the shape of the hook, the way it was pointing, the direction I would have to thrust my leg. It was easy. My foot freed itself at the very instant that a startled Jeannie arrived with water, basin, bandages and iodine.

'John here,' I said looking at Jeannie and aware that he would not want me to show gratitude, 'John got me out of this mess.'

11

I was in bed for a fortnight and on crutches or hobbling with a stick for a further six weeks.

Perhaps I should have taken the accident as an omen. What does a shipowner say to himself if a mishap occurs to a new vessel at the moment of launching? I was brought up on the comforting philosophy that single mindedness, a dogged determination to succeed at some specific task inevitably led to conquest; and hence, I remember, I spent hour after hour, week after week, bowling by myself at the nets when I was at Harrow under the misapprehension that it was the road to the Eleven.

That I was laughed at was part of the test, and that I ignored this was part of the philosophy. It is a useful philosphy in the armoury of schoolmasters because boys without talent believe they can gain the same rewards as those who have, and those who have talent are lured to make the most use of it. As far as I am concerned the philosophy has lingered in its influence; and the result has been that, although I have often failed to gain the objectives which from the beginning I had no chance of gaining, my efforts have often brought unexpected but pleasurable rewards. Thus, although I am superstitious enough to be wary of Friday the thirteenth and of walking under ladders, and always feel happier if a black cat crosses my path, I consider omens as incidents to forget however moodily I may greet them. Had I shied from Pentewan as a consequence of my accident Jeannie and I would have been spared countless laborious hours and, for that matter, considerable expense; but we would never have tasted the subtleties of the reward for staying.

Obstinacy is, of course, both a virtue and a fault, and the art lies in identifying the dividing line; and in this tussle of identification you can be called courageous one moment, a fool the next, and brilliant the one after that

– if your objective has been achieved.

One particular obstinacy at Pentewan was to heave our energy and enthusiasm against the weather, and every time it knocked us out, to bob up again, roll up our shirt-sleeves and defy it once more. You cannot treat the weather that way. It always wins. It obliterates a thousand hours of effort in a night, with the same abandoned power of a finger smudging a mosquito on a window-pane.

Should we have packed up after the first wail of defeat? We met a little barrel of a man in a pub shortly after we had taken over the meadows who for many years had worked the selfsame meadows himself. 'Expect,' he said, in a piping voice, 'a bumper harvest once in every four years.' He did not intend to be gloomy. He was giving the glad news that we would make so much money in one year that it would not matter what happened in the other three. Old men of the countryside appear to novices as oracles; as if the lines on their faces, the horizon look in their eyes, the slow motion of their movements harken a confidence within you that echoes your belief in the Prophets. Thus each time the weather struck we revived ourselves with the words of high promise: 'Expect a bumper harvest in every four years . . .'

We needed, however, that good harvest the first year; and our optimism excited us to expect it. It was indeed vital that it should be a good one. The hazy honeymoon with escapism was being replaced by the conventional necessities of day to day existence, our commitments were increasing, our reserves dwindling. We took on Pentewan knowing it would vastly increase our expenses, but saying to ourselves that if we planned with vision, courage and care, all we would then require would be to have luck on our side; for endeavour, however painstakingly pursued, can rarely receive its accolade unless a magic bestows it.

Yet we were aware that there was something else at stake besides material victory; there was the continuing challenge to prove that we were not flirting with the tedium of manual labour, that our enthusiasm had not been checked by reverses or by the roughness of the life, that we possessed staying power which could earn respect. It was a simple ambition and some would call it a valueless one, but within it there was the prospect of peace of mind born of permanence. There is no permanence in the conventional ambitions that hasten you up the pyramid of power, each step killing one ambition and creating another, leading you by a noose to a pinnacle where, too late, you look back on the trampled path and find the yearning within you is the same as when you were young.

We knew, therefore, that we could not impose ourselves on the countryside but had to be absorbed by it, creating by our efforts an intangible strength that became an element of the beauty, of the wildness, and of the peace around us; and we would then begin to feel and to see the gossamer secrets that are for ever hidden from the casual passer-by. I was about twelve when my father took me to see an old man who lived in a cottage in the woods near Bodmin; why we went or who he was I do not remember; but I remember the untamed setting and how, when we went inside, what seemed to be a cluster of birds flew out of the window. I was disappointed because I had never known birds in a house before, and I wanted to see them flying around.

'Will they come back?' I asked? 'Not till you have gone, I'm afraid,' said the old man, 'you see I've been here a long time and I am accepted like that old fir tree out there.' The incident has always been to me a lesson in living.

My foot had recovered when the time came for planting the potatoes . . . eight tons of them. It had been a mammoth task in the first place, when they arrived at the end of October, to put them away ends up; partly in the Pink Hut and partly at Minack, and as I for most of the time was out of action, the tedious job was shared between Jeannie and Tommy. They were an incongruous couple to be together and I awaited expectantly at home her report on their latest conversation.

'Tommy is in one of his silent moods,' she would say, 'hasn't said a word all morning' Or: 'Tommy's bought a camera and he's spent the afternoon telling me how he's going to take pictures through his telescope.' Or: 'Tommy's in a terrible state. The police called on him yesterday evening. The camera he bought was a stolen one!' Or: 'Tommy wants us to get a portable tent which he can take along with him as he goes on working in the rain!'

Tommy was undismayed by the quantity of potatoes we were planting, and on one occasion as he was silently putting them away he suddenly roared with laughter.

'What's funny?' asked Jeannie. 'Just you think,' he answered, 'what they are going to say when they see all these going off to the station!' He was foreseeing the harvest, and 'they' were John and any of his previous bosses. 'They won't like it,' he added, 'won't like it at all.'

Tommy was sensitive to the cost of the venture as I had warned him that we would have to take at least £500 before we showed any profit, and that the profit would have to be large enough to pay for our keep and his, for another six months in any case. As a result he became very concerned with the rats which penetrated through the floorboards of the Pink Hut and of the mice which entered the Minack potato hut. 'Every potato they damage,' he said earnestly, 'means a half-crown thrown away next summer . . . we must have poison down all the time.'

Sometimes, mild as the climate may generally be, we have bitter cold snaps which catch us unawares and the frost bites inside the potato huts; as a result some of the potatoes are either squashed into uselessness or are 'chilled', which means they will never grow a full crop. One night Jeannie and I had gone to bed when we heard a knock at the door, followed by Tommy's stentorian voice. 'I've come to tell you it's freezing!' He had walked a mile from his caravan to warn us, and to help us carry the paraffin heaters to the potato huts.

It was, however, a comparatively mild winter and we were able to start planting early in January and carry on, except when it was wet, for day after day until all eight tons were in the ground by the first week in March. We had prepared the soil according to advice from experts; heavily liming the Pentewan soil in the autumn because the analysis showed it had not been given any lime in years; and dressing each meadow as we came to plant it with a compound chemical fertiliser. Our allotted tasks were for Jeannie to cut the potatoes and fill the baskets, Tommy to shovel them in, while I rotovated a piece of ground ahead of Tommy, carried the baskets from the hut to the meadow concerned, and dropped the potatoes in the drill Tommy had opened up.

These tasks may seem straightforward, but they caused arguments. We were so anxious now that we had suddenly become big potato growers to perform the planting according to the best advice available that we confused ourselves with a plethora of advisers. We were soon told, for instance, that we should be using fish manure and not the compound fertiliser of which we had bought two tons.

'You want body in this ground, not chemicals,' said one esteemed farmer of the neighbourhood. This worry, however, had come too late to concern us; and we consoled ourselves with remembering the opposite view of the agricultural adviser who told us that chemicals were the only fertiliser for the early crop as they acted so much more quickly. Next came the pros and cons about cutting the potatoes. Then the question of space intervals in planting, and how much soil should cover the potatoes. As in other more important matters, the experts contradicted each other. Cut each potato in as many pieces as there are shoots, was the advice of one old farmer who had grown potatoes in the district for thirty years. His neighbour, on the other hand, asserted with equal confidence that potatoes should not on any account be cut, unless planting was in March. Plant them seven inches apart and fifteen inches between the rows said one; plant them twelve inches apart and eighteen inches between the rows said another. Cover them with plenty of soil, cover them so there is only a shallow layer above the shoots. The opposites briskly met each other and left us bewildered referees.

It is easy to understand that the more you cut the potatoes, the more plants you will have as a result; and thus greed encouraged us to cut them. But the anti-cutters maintained that a cut potato produced a vulnerable plant, a plant that had no reserve to fall back on if it were pulverised by frost or lambasted by a gale . . . and Pentewan, its meadows lying facing the threatening sweep of the sea, suffered constantly the prospect of obliteration.

'Ah,' said an old pro-cutter appearing to be wise, 'it all depends on weather.'

This wisdom also applied to the advantages and disadvantages of shallow planting. A potato likes to be near the surface of the ground to bask in the warmth of an early spring sun and, in times of dry weather to drink the benefits of dews and light showers.

'But,' said a saturnine farmer, 'I've known all shallow planted potatoes be rotted because of a freeze-up.'

Thus, it seemed, the gods had to be on your side if you engaged in cutting or shallow planting, and Jeannie and I were not prepared to trust them. We would play for safety. We would cut only the biggest of potatoes, and we would cover them liberally with soil; but there was still the question of space intervals in planting.

We were, in any case, concerned as to whether we had enough cultivated land for our eight tons; and so the variation between the theories of space intervals in planting were important to us. The difference, for instance, between a seven inch space interval and a twelve inch, would mean that the latter would require nearly twice as much land; and then there was still the difference of fifteen or eighteen inches between rows to worry about. Such closeness of planting is a joke to the normal potato grower who expects to have two feet between the rows and perhaps eighteen inches between each potato; but on the cliff it is different. The pundits declare that the more closely the potatoes are planted, the more likely they are to protect each other because the green tops sway in a solid phalanx in a gale, instead of each green top being whipped on its own; and that in a period of drought, the shadow of the leaves hides the sun from the moisture which is in the soil.

Jeannie and I listened to the profusion of advice like foreign students at an English lecture; we made notes, held discussions, but in the end felt lost because experience could be the only interpreter. Nobody seemed to know what were the best methods. There was no standard law. Each season had different growing conditions. Every section of the cliff had a special character of its own; and even the meadows had individual personalities.

'It takes a bit of time to get to know them,' said Joe glumly to me one day, 'and half a meadow is sometimes different to the other half.'

Thus, it appeared, old meadows were as temperamental as human beings; and ours at Pentewan, time seemed to prove, were like overworked clerks in need of a holiday. They were exhausted. After a hundred years of hard labour in producing potatoes, they chose to rebel when Jeannie and I arrived as their masters. The soil was sick of potatoes and wanted a rest; but we in our innocence believed they were the mirror of our future prosperity, and when I dropped the last potato of the eight tons behind Tommy's shovel I celebrated. I was now a big grower, probably the largest grower of cliff potatoes west of Penzance, and I mused happily over my succulent objective – the Cornish new potatoes which would surprise the townsmen like the advent of fresh garden peas, bringing us the cash which would ensure security.

Jeannie holds the view that the pleasantest part of the growing season is when the land has just been ploughed, or a crop just planted. Then there is nothing to worry about, the soil looks clean and rich and the mind is full of comfortable calculations of the prosperity to come. It was in this mood that we surveyed our handywork of the past two months and each day, wresting time from daffodil bunching, we toured the meadows with Monty trotting along with us. Gradually we began to notice the green buttons bursting out of the soil, and we started to use the language of potato growers: 'The meadow below the gate is in rows' or 'The meadow above the Pink Hut looks backward.'

The Minack meadows had been the first to be planted and thus the first to be peppered with green but the Pentewan meadows, aided by the extra hour of the sun they received as they stared south towards the Wolf Rock, were quick to catch up. Soon, in the ideal mild weather, the plants were growing so fast that the pundits were talking of the earliest potato season on record; and Jeannie and I rejoiced that it seemed we were scheduled for beginner's luck. John was happy enough to smile and volunteer good mornings, and Joe's boss – the farmer who rented us Pentewan – forgot his quiet self and made jokes. There was a pleasant camaraderie on the cliffs, and confidence that all would share unenviously in the prosperity ahead.

One afternoon, it was Thursday March 27th, we heard a chiff-chaff making its monotonous call, the first of the year, the wonder of its African journey transferred to Minack woods; and it gave us the cool pleasure of confidence in ourselves and our surroundings. The cry followed us: 'Chiff Chaff! Chiff Chaff!' – and the sound of its limited note amid trees pinking with buds, moss brightening with growth on old rocks, primroses a secret ecstasy unless unexpectedly discovered, pools of ragged robin and bluebells . . . the sound of its limited note derided the tyranny of the automaton age and the warped values that advance the putrid aims of the dodgers of truth, the cynical commentators of the passing scene, the purveyors of mass inertia. The dull two notes of the tiny bird trumpeted defiance of the fake and the slick, bringing to the shadows in the woods the expanse of its own achievement; until the sound gently entered the evening, and as night fell, hid among the trees.

It was suddenly cold, and as I came back from shutting up the chickens a sudden breeze hit the branches above my head, a sharp thrust from the east. Indoors Jeannie was stirring soup on the stove while Monty was behaving as if scissors were after his tail and dinosaurs awaiting his pounce.

'What on earth's wrong with Monty tonight?' And I bent down and tried to pick him up. He darted to the door and when I moved to open it, rushed to the sofa, forking his claws in the side raking the material, and earning a 'Shut up, Monty!' from Jeannie. There was a sound outside as if a car was driving up to the cottage. 'Listen,' I said, and we paused, tense. 'It's a plane,' said Jeannie, relieved. There it was again, a rushing, moaning sound. 'It isn't,' I answered knowledgeably, 'it's the wind.'

It was the sound of the scouts, the fingers of the wind, stretching ahead probing the hills and woods, the rocks and hedges, the old cottages, the lonely trees acting as sentinels of the land. They probe and jab, searching for flying leaves, decaying branches ready to fall, for flowers youthfully in bloom, for the green swath of the potato tops; and finding, they rush on searching for more, magnificently confident that the majesty of the gale which follows will crush and pound and obliterate. And when they have gone there is an instant of stillness to remind you of a quiet evening, the passing assurance of a safe world, and you wait; you wait and wonder if you were wrong and the wind is innocent; you listen, your mind peeling across the green meadows whose defences are impotent; then suddenly the slap of the face and the braying hounds of hell and the heaving mountain of maniacal power.

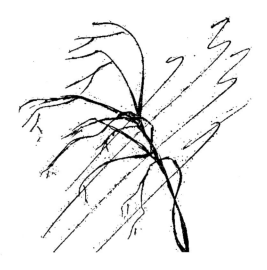

12

The gale roared without pause till the afternoon of March 29th, vicious, friendless and with frost in its scream; here was man as helpless as the foam on the rocks, centuries of rising conceit contemptuously humbled, the joke of the tempest. Action was masochistic. We struggled heads down as if fighting a way through invisible jungle grass, buffeted, pushed back soundless in our shouting, kneeling to the ground to gape at a meadow in its progress towards obliteration, then hustled home as if our coats were kites, running without effort, feathers in air.

We sat and waited. The vapid wait, droning the hours away with our fears, calculating losses, listening to the ships' waveband as vessels neared Land's End ('I don't fancy going round the corner'), unknown voices sharing our company, leaping to the window when the noise for a second abated, hearing the sea hissing like a coastline of cobras, sleeping with demons in our dreams. Waiting, waiting, waiting. And when it was over, when our ears were still humming with the beating drums of fury and the sea still heaved in mud-grey valleys, we went out into an afternoon that had suddenly become as caressing as a summer's day; as if a lost temper had been replaced by shame and the cost of havoc was being guiltily assessed.

The Minack meadows were a pattern of black stumps; in pocket-size havens the wind had entered like a tornado, and there were gaps where not even stumps were to be seen. At Pentewan the army of green, the plants the size of cabbages had become a foot-high petrified forest drooping in the sunshine like melting black candles. Black also was the grass on the banks, filmed as if with tar, and the stinging nettles which once taunted us to scythe them down; and here and there wild daffodils stared forlornly with petals shredded into tea-stained strips; or with necks broken, their heads drooped against the stems like victims of the gallows. The desolation looked up at the blue sky and the fleck of a lark singing. A magpie flew by coarsely chattering, and for a second I saw a fox silhouetted on a rock above the quarry. A boat chugged by outward bound to the fishing grounds beyond the Isles of Scilly, and we looked down at the men on deck as if we were on a hill and they in a valley. Normality was returning even if the thrash of the whip was still in our ears; ideas began to form, the warm challenge born of disaster quickened our minds, the sense of comradeship which frays in tedious defeat but sharpens in sudden defeat, became exhilarated, and I greeted Joe as if victory was our companion.

He was standing gloomily by the Pink Hut at the head of the path that corkscrewed steeply downwards to the sea, wearing his mildewed green trilby, an unlit pipe in his mouth and incongruously an old telescope slung from his shoulder. Bish was at his feet and she wagged white body and tail as I approached, whimpering a greeting.

'Does a gale like this often happen?' I asked with mock humour. Joe, after all, had been part of this cliff for seventeen years and he would have the answer to the permutation of emergencies.

'I've known nothing like it,' he said glumly, then grinned as if this might be a shield against the consequences, and went on: 'Coming so late with taties up like that they'll never recover … I don't think so, not in time at any rate.'

The tone in which he spoke sent a chill through me. Up to then my instincts had been charging me to get to grips with retrieving the disaster by discovering what wise old farmers would do and by energetically putting their proposals into effect. As simple as that. It was a setback not a finality, and means were available, if I could learn about them, which would put things right. But Joe had talked about time, and time had not entered into my calculations.

Now I suddenly saw that time was the vital factor in my recovery. The cliff no longer held the advantage over the inland potato growers stretching up the country to the great potato areas of Lincolnshire. The cliff potatoes would have to pause, summon strength to send out new shoots, push out into a second cluster of leaves . . . and all this before there could be any question of making actual potatoes. Instead of being ahead they would be behind in the race. The inland potatoes would be still underground or just breaking through, and thus they would continue to grow with the speed which comes of normality; and the avalanche of their harvest would crush the markets while the cliff was still being jabbed with shovels. The prospect scared me.

During the following days inland farmers roamed the cliff in the same way some people like to visit and stare at the scene of an accident. They were solicitous, but one suspected their sudden appearance was connected with assessing how our misfortune might result in their good fortune. They got on Tommy's nerves. 'Serve 'em, right,' he snorted, 'if they have hard frost after Buryan feast.'

Feast Day was the second Sunday in May and it was traditional that frost could be expected up to that date but not afterwards; and so Tommy was wishing them ill at a time when their potatoes would be at the same advanced stage as ours had been. But Tommy's personal chip of revenge was no reply to the predicament with which we were faced. We had gambled so heavily on the prospect of a harvest with handsome returns that failure inevitably would drain the last of our capital reserves. We would either have to return to London or Tommy would have to go, and leave us to carry on with the work on our own. It was the kind of situation which lies naggingly at the back of your mind but which you refuse to accept seriously while an element of hope still exists; and both Jeannie and I could not believe that such total defeat was possible. Our armour was our enthusiasm and, just as useful, our ignorance. We were, therefore, both determined to attack the next few weeks as if energy provided the certainty of victory.

But there was little we could do. Convalescence cannot be successful over-night, nor can plants grow with the speed of those in a nature film; and the only action we could take was to dose the meadows with nitro-chalk. Among potato growers nitro-chalk is considered a menace by some and a blessing by others. Its purpose is that of a pep pill and given convenient conditions such as warm and damp weather, the effect begins to show within a fortnight by veining the leaves with dark green; thus strength enters the leaves which, on reaching maturity, return it to the developing potatoes. This description sounds like the alluring advertisement of a quack medicine, and it possesses in degree the same deception; for the success of nitro-chalk depends on conditions over which you have little control at the time of sowing. Moreover, and this is the chief objection against it, nitro-chalk though increasing the size of the crop does so at the expense of making it later. Thus if a spell of dry weather follows the time of sowing before rain comes to wash it in, the crop will be later than ever.

'I wouldn't use it if I were you,' said one. 'I'd certainly sow nitre,' said another. My final decision was based on the fact the plants looked so battered and terrible that I felt compelled to take some kind of action to help them; and, as it happened, that was the only satisfaction I had. The nitro-chalk on this occasion provided no sudden elixir of potato life; and to prove it there were two meadows side by side one of which had received its quota of nitro-chalk, while the other had been spared it. Six weeks later the tops of both were still the size of mushrooms, and by this time the grim fact had emerged that the harvest would resemble that of peas rather than potatoes. The plants had been unable to recover, not even our caution in leaving the seed uncut had been able to save them.

We had, however, an ace up our sleeves. It is an obvious calculation that the sum total of man hours required to dig potatoes is the same if there is one man at work or four. Thus one man would take four hours to perform a task which would take four men an hour; and so the pursuit of this idea inevitably led us to the tempting prospect that if we were able to engage two men to help us, the harvest would be cleared in half the time it would take Tommy and myself; and that more extra men would further reduce the time in proportion. Thus, according to this theory, we still had a chance to save the situation by disposing of our miserable harvest when the price was still high; and it could mean, we argued cheerfully to ourselves, that we could take just as much money as with a crop twice the size but half the price.

Our neighbours, however did not agree with these views. They never had spent any money on extra labour and they were not going to do so now. It was an attitude that pleased us. It gave us an understandable source of contentment that we had a chance to show our teachers that we had the intelligence to cope with a crisis. The problem was, however, where to find the men to help us.

It was now that we had a stroke of luck. We remembered the miners from St Just, Jack and Maurice, who had dug us the well, and off we went to see them.

St Just is a solid town which revolves around the Geevor tin mines and spreads a spider's web of grey cottages with the square as its centre, the sea on one side, and the wild hilly moorland on the others. It is unique for a town of its size in that it is five miles from the nearest railway station, Penzance, and this fact, along with the Atlantic fogs which sweep through the streets in winter, seems to exude a sturdy self-sufficiency among its inhabitants. They are tough, reliable, kind, and aim to see a good day's work performed before they add up the money which rewards it.

Jack and Maurice promptly agreed to help but they would only be able to do so between shifts at Geevor. They therefore proposed they should organise a succession of miners, and that by running a shuttle service in the Land Rover we would collect and return them at times to dovetail with each shift. Thus we could if we so wished collect one group at eight in the morning after the night shift, another at three in the afternoon after the early morning shift, and another at six in the evening after the day shift, the latter working on till dusk. We were also able to engage a retired miner called Willie and a postman, Eddie, both of whom were ready to come full time - the latter taking his annual holiday specially to do so. This galaxy of manpower so excited Jeannie and myself that we marvelled with gratitude that the fates should so generously come to our rescue.

Within a week we had cleared the Minack cliff, sent away five tons and had grossed £250. We were up to schedule both on time and price. But the tight little meadows restricted the use of our full labour force, and only Willie, Eddie, Jack and Maurice provided the extra help. It was a scouting force compared to the army to come, and which proceeded to descend on the larger sloping meadows of Pentewan.

I now had what I thought was an excellent idea. The method of gathering potatoes in a field is for a tractor to drive its length while the pickers-up are each given a station of perhaps twenty yards for which they are responsible. I decided to adjust this method to the meadow. I fixed the plough and the large wheels on my hand-controlled tractor, gave each miner a station, then grimly drove the machine in such a way that the plough tipped each row to one side where hands seized the tops, shook them, and picked up the potatoes.

It was a method suitable for a flat field, but I had chosen meadows that were square, oblong, round, steep in one direction then in another, with rocks as obstacles, requiring strength and ingenuity even to get the tractor with its large wheels to enter them. Obstinately I stuck to my task, stripped to the waist, my hands ripped with blisters, my body aching with fatigue, dazedly going on and on in the belief that I was the instrument of speed.

It was a delusion. The tractor broke down and when, in its place, shovels were used, the primitive once again proved its superiority over the modern.

Two shovellers each took a row, and racing each other up the meadow, they tossed the plants to one side, leaving the rest of us to scramble our hands through the soil bruising our fingers against the stones, chaffing each other with mock accusations.

'Hey, Eddie, have you gone home?' meaning that he had been slower to pick up than the rest of us. Or if a shoveller had sliced a few potatoes as he thrust up the meadow, 'We've got the chips, Willie, so now you'd better catch the fish.' The forced jokes which come with monotonous tasks, remarks which are contrived to bolster minds and bodies which are tiring. 'Dick's in love . . . that's why he's leaving them all behind.' 'Them' being potatoes and Dick being a hunk of a miner who had just got engaged. Long silences, then inconsequent comments on sport. 'Good boy Peter May . . . he's a good boy Peter.'

Periodically Jeannie would appear with tea, cakes and sandwiches, heavy loads which she carried over from Minack, balancing them as if they were jewels while she clambered over the hedges; then a break for everyone, and afterwards Jeannie would join the pickers-up, in shorts, with delicate hands and quicker than any of them. A group had to go back to Geevor and another collected. 'Don't you ever need sleep?' I'd say, 'Well we can last till Saturday.' Tough, cheerful, unsparing in their willingness to help, I felt a tiring sadness that the rarity of their unstinting capacity of giving was tainted by the inevitability of failure.

The price had begun to drop. 'What is it today?' one of them would ask. 'Gone down to thirty-five,' I would answer, and there would be silence; and although they would be getting their pay at the end of the day, such was their rugged, honest independence that they did not feel at peace that they should gain and we should lose.

Jeannie and I became unaware of days and nights, we blazed with the fanatic's zeal to remove every potato from Pentewan in time . . . we were up at dawn to weigh and address the bags, then one of us would collect the first group from St Just, then load up the Land Rover two or three times until yesterday's digging had been driven to the place where Carbis, the St Buryan carrier, would load them on his lorry and take them to the station. Waiting for the post and prices, tea and sandwiches, drive a group back to St Just and collect another, more tea and sandwiches, another drive to St Just, then in the evening rough cider with the sandwiches and jokes afterwards: 'Maurice is seeing so many double taties that he can't pick up one.' Then back to St Just with the last group, and because we were both very tired we would go together.

We were aware soon after beginning Pentewan that we were doomed. Minack meadows had survived in some degree because they were new, the soil was fresh to production and had reserves to face the wound from the slash of a knife, but those at Pentewan were like tired old men who saw no virtue in fighting nor possessed the capacity for doing so. The crop almost uniformly was the size of marbles; and when the shovellers had disposed of a meadow and I looked up in my record book to compare the seed potatoes we had planted and the harvest we had gathered, I found it more comforting to keep the information to myself.

Yet speed might still save us. Jeannie and I clung to the belief that time was our ally, that our town-inspired briskly intelligent ideas would outweigh the true facts. We maintained the illusion until one night, after returning the last of our friends to St Just, we called in on the way home at a pub whose outward fame is its name, the First and Last (pub in Britain), but whose inward fame was provided by the Lancashire brothers who had kept it for twenty-five years. 'You've heard the news?' said Jesse Fox, one of the brothers, as I raised my glass, 'taties have hit the floor. They're £6 a ton at Bristol.'

Next morning I looked at Tommy when he arrived, the old shabby clothes, the faded Panama hat, and I said to myself: 'Why does he look so distinguished? It would be so much easier if he looked sour and bad tempered.' He performed the motions of his job seemingly unaware that his time with us was at an end. I delayed. When it was all over and Eddie and Willie, Maurice, Jack and our passing friends like Tommy May, nightwatchman at Geevor and collector of sea debris by day, and Dick and all the others . . . when I had said good-bye to all these, I was faced with the vacuum of telling Tommy Williams that his time with us was over.

I had braved myself to do so when, as I was leaving the cottage, a man arrived whom I had casually met a few days before. He was a brisk, efficient young man possessed with the certainty that his current opinions would secure his advancement. He was like hail on a summer's day, and as I watched him, uninvited, undo his knapsack, then heard him say: 'It's quite all right, don't worry about me, I've got my own sandwiches . . . I felt only too ready to brain him.

But, and this was the irritation of the occasion, there was a security about his behaviour which mocked the unreasonableness of our own. He represented sense and an arid existence, while Jeannie and I had nothing to show him or anyone else except an intangible happiness. Thus, unknowingly, he provided me with an angry brashness, a reaction to his own normality, when at last I saw Tommy and said I could not pay him any more. 'I knew that was coming,' he said, and his eyes were looking far out over Mount's Bay; 'I'll go back to Birmingham where I was for a time during the war. I'll get a good job there in Birmingham Parks.'

He was down the bottom of the cliff when I told him, and I had a long way up to walk with the knowledge that an unpleasant task had been achieved. I did not feel despair but anger, as if the zest which had led us to the kind of life we had chosen had been stung into fury by conformism pirouetting in self-justification. Ah, you fool, I heard voices mocking, you should have stayed with the herd, the herd breathes safely in the expanse of the plains, its thoughts locked in convention, moving through time sheltered in the security of dullness. The herd does not look for trouble as you have done. The herd is content, it is not greedy like you.

I climbed slowly up the cliff path and found Jeannie waiting for me at the top. 'He took it very well,' I said, 'he's going to sell his caravan and go north. He says he's certain to get a job with what he calls Birmingham Parks.' I spoke with assurance as if I were certain that Tommy was thankful his mind had been made up for him. 'It's funny,' I added, 'but I've always had an idea he hankered after Birmingham Parks and he's only stayed with us because of a queer notion it meant scoring a revenge over the farmers he detested.'

Jeannie did not reply and we began to walk arm in arm up the field towards the cottage. The silence hurt both of us. We had been consumed by the mission I had just fulfilled, and now we were left with thoughts that frightened us. We had not only lost our gamble, but were faced with retrieving its cost without anyone to help us. We had not bargained for failure when we left London, and its arrival, the sudden barefacedness of its arrival, brought unbearable depression.

And then, just as we gloomily reached the old stone stable and the slope which led up to the cottage, Jeannie suddenly said in a voice that sounded as if our problems had been solved: 'Look! There's a gull on the roof!'

13

The gull on the roof is called Hubert. He joined Monty as a witness of our endeavour and the pleasure that has come with it. He watched us fight back at Minack working for a year on our own. He saw us beginning to succeed then rushed by the elements into retreat, then forward again. He is old now, his feathers have lost their sheen, and when he gathers himself to fly away he is like a rheumaticky old man shuffling to rise from an armchair.

He was old when he arrived, or so we thought. 'They come to man when they're ailing,' Joe had told us, 'you won't see him for long.' But the years have passed and he is still with us, and it is only on days when a gale is raging that he fails to spread his wings over the cottage and alight on the roof. Then when I see him again I will say, 'The gale is over. Hubert's back.'

A. P. Herbert came to stay a few days after his first appearance, and A.P.H. was the instrument which gave him his name. We were in the main street of Penzance one morning when first one person then another asked A.P.H. for his autograph. A little crowd gathered among whom was a young girl who, we noticed, was pushed forward by a friend. 'Can I have your autograph?' she asked, holding out notebook and pencil. A.P.H. bowed ceremoniously, then asked kindly, 'And whose autograph are you expecting?' The girl looked at him doubtfully, 'Sir Hubert . . . or something.' And for that slight reason Hubert became Hubert.

A.P.H. has always remained Hubert's admirer and on this occasion he bought a gaily painted toy bucket with the idea of filling it with limpets for Hubert's benefit. He would clamber down the cliffs to the rocks, spend an hour or two unclamping the limpets, then return to the cottage where he would spend another hour cleaning them from the shells . . . so that Hubert could gobble them in a few seconds.

One evening we were listening to a broadcast performance of Cesar Franck's Symphony in D Minor conducted by Sir Malcolm Sargent when Hubert began to cry like a baby screaming for attention. A.P.H. went to the door and looked up to the roof. 'Shush, Hubert,' he said, 'or I'll tell Sir Malcolm.' Hubert miraculously remained silent for the remainder of the performance, and the following morning A.P.H. wrote to Malcolm Sargent to inform him of the incident. A few days later there came a solemn reply. 'I'm delighted to hear of my new and unusual fan. Tell him I hope he enjoys Tchaikovsky's Fifth next Monday.'

Hubert provided us not only with the jest of his companionship but also, in this period of defeat, he showed us the prize of our way of life. This attention from the untamed was an antidote to loss of confidence. It revealed that eyes in the sky watched our comings and goings and now accepted our presence as shadows on the landscape. We were no longer strangers. We had nudged our way into a kingdom that had the passage of time as its passport; no easy short cuts, no synthetic substitutes, no man-made device can breed the trust of the wild. You have to wait.

Others followed Hubert. He remained king of the roof and would savagely attack any usurper, but during the hours he was absent strangers began to call until they too became friends. They came singly, wary of rivals, plummeting down on the ridge of the roof, then peering into the garden to see if we had noticed their approach. They flew out of the anonymity of the sky, from the vast gatherings on the rocks along the coast, and became in their own way rebels against conformism. We know them now as one knows animals on a farm; and if we are a field or two away and a gull is winging towards the cottage we can often name it by the manner of its flight; or if we are on the other side of the valley and we see a silhouette below the chimney the size of a fist we are quite likely to be right when one of us says; 'Knocker's waiting for us.'

Knocker, Peter, Philip, Squeaker, Gregory, these join Hubert as our regular visitors and, although sometimes they are away for a month or two, they return and are easily recognised. Knocker announces his arrival by rapping on the roof with his beak, so loudly and briskly that time and again we are deceived into thinking someone is at the door. He has an uncanny sense of knowing when we are in, or perhaps it is that after alighting on the roof he waits to hear our voices before he begins to knock; for we have watched him arrive from afar off and he perches, head erect, waiting; but when we return and go indoors, a minute later the knocking begins.

Peter is shy, he stretches his neck this way and that eyeing us nervously, as if he felt guilty of trespassing. Philip has a confident, lazy, 'no harm can come to me' kind of attitude, and when he is in the mood he will follow us on our walks. Squeaker is a silly bird who has never grown up. He still makes the same piping, wheedling noise that he made when he first began visiting us as a first year bird in mottled grey plumage. He sits on the roof endlessly squeaking, bending his head up and down in the same manner as a nestling demands food from its parents. We throw up a piece of bread, hope for silence, then when the whine continues I am driven to shout: 'Shut up! Shut up!' And afterwards, when he has flown away, I am sorry I have been so abrupt.

Gregory has one leg, the other presumably lost long ago in a trap; and because the source of his strength is unbalanced he has become barrel chested like a plump duck. He is the easiest to recognise when in flight because his chest seems to protrude like the front cone of an aircraft. He is a lonely gull. I have often seen him attacked by others and driven twisting and turning across the moorland to the sea; and there was one occasion when he was caught unawares on the roof and bullied screaming off it so that he fell in the garden. Hubert was the villain and I rushed out and stood by, until Gregory had recovered sufficiently to hop away to the path and take flight. Usually he calls about an hour before dusk but if someone else is still on the roof I see him waiting and watching in a field across the valley, a white speck against the soil. Then, when the roof is bare, he is with us.

I am wondering now whether I should not have written about Gregory in the past tense. We have not seen him for months. He has been absent before now for several weeks on end, usually in the summer, and we have mocked him on his return. 'You've been cadging from the visitors,' we have accused him, 'you've been hopping on the beach luring them to say "we must feed that poor bird with one leg." ' But he has never been away for so long and we are worried. Has a fox caught him as he hopped in a field? Or has his own kind swooped and battered him into the sea?

I wonder, too, whether Hubert is nearing the end of his reign as king of the roof; age becomes driftwood wherever it may be. Once he had only to bellow a screeching warning for any gull on the roof to flee at his approach. But the other day I watched him being himself attacked, pounced on by a newcomer as he was warming himself on the chimney; and the newcomer, a brash, bossy gull who, without being friendly, greedily demands his food, unbalanced poor Hubert in such a manner that he fell like an untidy parachute to the grass below.

Hubert is fussy. He dislikes shop bread, tosses it in disgust in the air if he is given it, and insists instead on Jeannie's home-made variety. He loves cheese, but his favourite dish is bacon rinds. 'Let me know when Hubert arrives,' Jeannie will say, 'I've got bacon rinds for him today.' In wintry weather his visits are brief, long enough to have a meal, then he flies majestically away towards the sea, sloping his flight down the valley to the rocks below the cliffs which are his home. In normal weather he may stay with us for most of the day announcing his arrival with a squeak; then he will squat on the wide rugged stones of the chimney as if on a nest, or he will stand looking bored and disconsolate on the ridge of the roof, or walk to and fro along it like a sentry on a parapet. He observes us. We are always aware of his scrutiny.

In the beginning Monty was irritated rather than jealous of him. Monty would doze in the garden, look up when Hubert started to cry, then curl his upper lip in a soundless snarl. Or if we were having breakfast on the white seat below the cottage and Hubert was strutting within throwing distance of a piece of toast, Monty would lie and stare; then as if he thought some gesture of defiance was required on his part, he would gently growl like a dog. In time they became friendly enough to ignore each other.

Monty was indifferent to birds and we were never made anxious by the sight of him stalking. He once caught a wren but it was hardly his fault. He was lying somnolent on the grass by the apple tree while a covey of baby wrens flew around him, teasing him as if they were flies and he a tired old horse. I saw him flick his tail in impatience, then pounce, and a wren was in his mouth; but his actions were so gentle that when I rushed to the rescue, shouting at him, he let it go and it flew away unharmed.

He had other temptations but there was a placid quality in his nature that helped him to ignore them. We had, for instance, the usual company of tom-tits, blue-tits, dunnocks, buntings and sparrows flitting about the garden in expectation of crumbs, and he took no notice of any of them; but in particular we had Charlie the chaffinch and Tim the robin.

Charlie attached himself to us soon after the arrival of Hubert, and like

134

Tim he is still with us. He is a bird with a dual character; that of the spring and summer when he is resplendent in plumage of slate-blue, pink, chestnut, black and white wings and tail, is boastful and demanding; that of the winter when his feathers have the drabness of faded curtains, is apologetic, as if surprised he was worthy of any attention. In spring and summer his call is as loud as a trumpet, in winter it is that of a squeak. He has an endearing personality. We may be anywhere in the environment of Minack and suddenly find him hopping about beside us or flitting in the trees as we walk through the wood. We seldom see him any distance from the cottage though once I found him on the edge of the Pentewan meadows. I said: 'Hello Charlie, what are you doing here?' in the tone of voice that might have greeted a friend I thought was in London. Then, when I started back to the cottage, he came with me.

There was one winter, however, when he disappeared for four or five months and we sadly concluded he was dead. But one March morning when Jeannie was in the chicken run which we had moved to a clearing in the wood, she suddenly heard 'cheep, cheep' from a branch above her head. It was Charlie; and she rushed back to the cottage to tell me. 'Charlie's back!' she said excitedly, 'I must get him a biscuit!' And by that time Charlie had followed her and was sitting on the bird-table cheeping away like a dog barking a welcome. Where had he been? In the autumn hordes of migrating chaffinches sweep along the coast past Minack on the way to Southern Ireland, so perhaps Charlie went along with the group. It does not seem the trip was a success. He has never gone away for the winter again.

Charlie is a diffident character compared with Tim. Charlie never comes inside the cottage whereas Tim will perch on the back of a chair and sing us a song. Charlie, when we are bunching flowers, will cheep on the doorstep of the flower house while Tim is inside hopping about on the shelves. Charlie shies away if you put out a hand, Tim will stand on my outstretched palm until my arm aches.

One November, Tim, like Charlie, disappeared. Tim's territory consisted of the cottage, about forty yards of the lane beyond Monty's Leap, and a field bordering it. One morning a few days after we had noticed Tim's disappearance we observed another robin, a nervous robin, flying about the same territory. Robins, of course, compete with each other for desirable territories, so we looked at this robin and wondered whether he had driven Tim away or moved into the territory because Tim was dead. We did not look with favour, for whatever happened was distressing.

It was a fortnight later that we saw Tim again. We were strolling along a cliff path a half mile from the cottage when suddenly, perched on a twig of quickthorn, I saw Tim. There was no mistaking him. He was perched with his feathers fluffed out, motionless, watching us. 'Tim!' Jeannie said with delight, 'what are you doing here?' I had a few crumbs in my pocket which I held out on the palm of my hand. A second later I felt the touch of his legs, as if two matchsticks were standing upright.

The following day we returned to the same place. There was no Tim. We pushed our way through the brush calling his name, walking in ever widening circles. At Minack he always used to answer to his name. We would stroll a few steps down the lane calling, 'Tim!' – and a few moments later he would be with us. But this time there was no sign of him, nor the next day, nor the day after. 'Well,' I said to Jeannie. 'I hope that hawk which has been around hasn't had him.' Jeannie did not like the casual way I spoke. Tim was as much a friend as any human could be.

You can, of course, always win the attention of birds by throwing them crumbs, and you reap the pleasant reward of watching them; but it is when an individual bird enters the realm of companionship that the soul is surprised by a gossamer emotion of affection. Tim was not greedy. He did not call on us just because he was hungry. I have seen him time and time again flutter at the window of the flower house, then, when we have let him in, mooch around for a couple of hours among the jars full of flowers, warble a little, perch on a bloom with feathers fluffed out watching us at work.

'Where's Tim?' I would ask Jeannie.

'He was up on the top shelf among the King Alfreds a moment ago.'

We missed him when February came and daffodils began filling the flower house again. We would be silently bunching when one of us would break the silence; 'I wonder what *did* happen to Tim?' We knew we would never see him again.

But we were wrong. One afternoon in the last week of February we had gone into the cottage for tea and left the door of the flower house open. Twenty minutes later we returned and quietly continued to bunch. You get in a daze doing the job, picking the daffodils out of the jars, building them three at a time into a bunch, stacking the bunches into galvanised pails where they will stay overnight before they are packed. Your hands move automatically. You only pause to count the number you have done. I had turned to pick out three blooms for the first layer of a bunch when I happened to look up at the beam which crossed the house.

'Jeannie!' I said, 'look on the beam!'

Gazing down at us serenely confident, head on one side and in best spring plumage, was Tim.

14

Hubert up there on the roof looks down on greenhouses now at Minack. First a small one thirty feet long and twelve feet wide; then another, one hundred feet long and twenty-two feet wide; then two mobiles, dutch light type glasshouses which are pushed on rails covering two sites and two separate crops in a year, each seventy feet long and eighteen feet wide; and two more the same length but twenty feet wide.

We now work some of the land which John used to have, for John has left the district to go to a farm of his own. Walter and Jack have taken his place; and these two, and Bill who has the other farm which pivots from the collection of buildings, are neighbours who are always ready to help.

We have changed our pattern of growing. Our hands no longer grovel after potatoes in the soil, and we have returned Pentewan to its owner. We have learnt to hate potatoes. Once they promised to be the crop of our prosperity, and instead they have absorbed money, patience and countless aching hours of our labour. 'Once in four years you can expect a bumper harvest,' said the old man with the piping voice when we took over Pentewan. We waited and it never came.

The weather was too dry or too cold or too windy. The weather was always exceptional. 'Never known an April so dry' – and the potatoes instead of swelling would remain the size of golf balls. 'Never known such bad weather in February' - and instead of getting on with our planting we had to wait, knowing the farmers in their fields would catch us up. 'Never known a spring so cold' . . . Every year the old men in the pubs would drag out from their memories their gloomy comparisons. At first it was comforting to know the season was exceptional, then irritating, then a threat to enthusiasm.

As the cost of production has risen so have the prices fallen. Foreign potatoes flood the markets during the period when those of the Cornish cliff used to reign by themselves. Palates are jaded, and size rather than flavour is the arbiter of purchase. The Cornish cliff new potato is no longer a desirable delicacy; the shovels in the tiny meadows beside the sea, the tedious walks up the cliffs with a chip in each hand, the neatly packed chips being loaded at Penzance station . . . these are the actions of another age. Thus along with the remarks about exceptional weather, there are those about exceptional prices. 'Down to £30 already? I've never known anything like it.'

We were the first to break with tradition. Others have followed us, and Joe no longer haunts the cliffs that have known him for seventeen years. It is sad when hopes are slowly battered, and events burrow reality into your mind. It is sad, even when the cause is the humble potato.

Flowers, tomatoes and lettuces are the crops we grow at Minack. We plant every year an acre of winter flowering wallflowers, one hundred thousand anemone corms, a half acre of calendulas and four thousand violet plants. We have fifteen tons of daffodil bulbs. The greenhouses have forget-me-nots, freesias, iris, polyanthus and stocks during the winter; and three thousand tomato plants during the summer. We aim to sell forty thousand lettuces between April and October.

Such is the blueprint of our annual output. Unfortunately, a market garden for the most part is like a factory with workshops open to the sky. The sky is the ceiling. There are production problems as in a factory, selling problems as in any business; but however clever you may be in overcoming these, it is always the weather which dictates your prosperity. Thus I may pay staff for several months of preparatory labour - preparing land, planting, weeding - but lose everything in a hard frost, a few gales, or as in the case of some crops, a period of wet muggy weather.

Or it may be a hot spell at the wrong time which has hit us. An excessively warm March defeated our Wedgewood iris gamble. The thirty-six thousand which we had planted in one of the greenhouses were scheduled to be marketed before the outside Wedgewood in the Channel Islands came into bloom. But a March resembling mid-summer brought both indoor and outdoor iris into the markets together, deluging the salesmen and bringing despair to the growers. 'Well,' I said to Jeannie, 'we'll never grow iris again.' But we did. The best course a grower can take is to follow one year's bad market with the same crop the next.

Frost, gales, muggy weather, unseasonable heat-waves . . . sometimes Jeannie and I wonder whether we should ever expect normality. Of these frost is the least of our worries, for it is very seldom indeed that there is a persistent hard frost in West Cornwall. Gales, however, will chase us to the end of our days though sometimes they seem to take a rest and leave us in comparative peace. They blow but lack viciousness, or they launch an attack at a time when there are no crops to harm. Such a period lulls us into forgetfulness, and we deceive ourselves into thinking that optimism is a substitute for realism; and so we plant a crop in a meadow which is doomed as soon as a frenzied gale blows again.

The first time we grew anemones in any great number was following a winter that was as gentle as a continuous spring, when our flowers had bloomed in steady profusion and we were happy in the confidence born of success. So confident indeed that we proceeded to act as if gales were no longer an enemy.

We decided that the Dairyman's Meadow at Pentewan would be ideal for the anemone crop, and that another meadow over there would be suitable for the cloches we had recently bought. The Dairyman's meadow, so called because the use of it was once the perk of the man who looked after the cows on the farm, sloped south, dipping downwards from a high bank to the crest of the cliff. The other meadow, known as the thirty lace meadow because of its size, was more exposed but being flat it was exactly what we required for the cloches, We were going to use them as a cover for winter-growing lettuces.

By October the anemones were in full bloom, long stems and brilliant colours; and we congratulated ourselves on our good fortune. 'There you are,' I said to Jeannie, 'it just proves we *do* sometimes know more than the old hands.' For the old hands, in the person of Joe, had warned us that nobody had ever succeeded in growing anemones on the cliff.

That year we had advertised a private box service, sending flowers direct to the home; and the anemones proved such a success that time and again they were specially asked for in repeat orders. We were particularly delighted when one lady ordered twenty dozen . . . to decorate a house for a wedding reception; and she carefully instructed us to be certain they arrived the day before, December the first.

We never sent them, nor did we send any more anemones away that season. The gales had returned, blasting away the illusions that we could grow anemones on the cliff. A monster had roared in from the sea during the night of November the twenty-ninth, and when we reached the meadow in the morning it was as if a khaki coloured carpet had been spread across it. Not an anemone, not a green leaf was to be seen. The meadow was a desert.

It was another monster, three months later, that sent the cloches skidding across the thirty lace meadow. Never before or since have I known a gale which blew so hard as on that March morning, so hard that I had to crawl on my hands and knees in order to make any progress against it. Glass seemed to be flying like swallows skimming the cliff, and there was nothing for me to do except watch and curse and wait.

And as I waited, sheltered a little by a hedge, I suddenly saw Jeannie fighting her way towards me. It was her birthday and I was miserable that it should have begun so disastrously. There was no reason why she should have joined me. I had not asked her nor expected her. She was joining me because it was in her nature that trouble should be shared.

'Here,' she said as she reached me, 'I've brought you a flask of tea . . . I thought you might need it.' I most certainly did. 'And I've put Glucose in it to help you keep warm.' I poured out a cup, spilling some of it in the wind, then took a gulp. It was awful. It tasted like quince. 'You've poisoned me, Jeannie!' I shouted jokingly into the gale, 'what on earth did you put in it?'

When we returned to the cottage we found the lid was firmly pressed down on the Glucose tin; that of the Epsom salts lay loose on the table.

Gales, then, will always be our enemy but they are an enemy which attacks without guile; and it is easier to deal with a man who boasts his hate rather than with one who hides it. Muggy weather, warm wet sticky sea fog which covers the fields like a dirty stream achieves its destruction by stealth.

It creeps into the greenhouses sponging the tomato plants with botrytis and mildew, or blearing the freesias with tiny brown smudges making them useless for sale. Outside, it browns the tips of the anemone blooms, and sometimes does this so slyly that the damage is revealed only after the flowers have been picked and have remained in their jars overnight.

But it is at daffodil time that muggy weather can gain its great victories. A gale can beat at a wall but on the other side you can rest in its shelter. Muggy weather gives no chance of such rest. It envelops the daffodils in a damp cocoon and brushes the petals, either in bud or in bloom with the smear of its evil. There is no defence. You have to put up your hands in surrender.

There was one year when we lost eighty per cent of our daffodils in this way, and the compost heaps were piled high with their stems. The previous year had been a bumper one. We had bought ten tons of bulbs and in two months had earned their capital outlay. Thus our expectations were high when the new season began; but instead, basket after basket brought in from the meadow had blooms which were unworthy of being despatched to market.

This dismal experience had a curious feature, a feature which only affected those daffodils within a half mile or so of the sea. First there was a brown mark on the petal, the next day it had turned green, and the third day there was a tiny hole in the same place as if it had been burnt by a red hot pin. The experts were evasive. They could give us no exact explanation. 'Looks like daffodil flu,' was all they murmured.

Nor could they explain the unhappy events that followed. For two years the affected bulbs were sterile, scarcely a bloom was to be found among them; and those of us who lived on the coast, as well as the Scilly Islanders, disconsolately stared at our meadows of green foliage while growers inland were rushing their blooms to market.

Jeannie had her own interpretation of what happened. Shortly before the daffodils were attacked, canisters of atomic waste were dumped off Land's End; and one of the canisters, it was reported, burst during the dumping. Jeannie blames our misfortunes on its contents being blown back on to the coast mingled in spray. It is as good an explanation as any provided by the experts.

Few people pass Minack at any time of the year, and even at the height of the summer when conventional places are awash with humanity, a figure on the landscape cries out for our comment. 'Somebody's on the Carn!' I'll call to Jeannie . . . Or we will shout the absurd alarm of Alan Herbert: 'White men! White men!'

The occasional hikers plod by, some delighting in the untamed nature of their walk, some indignant that a highway through the undergworth along the coast is not maintained for their benefit; some stimulated by the need for initiative, some at a loss. 'I've never had my legs so scratched in all my years of walking,' said one furious lady . . . then, as if it were my fault, flinging the threat at me, 'I'm going to write to *The Times!*'

Sometimes we have seen strangers who have had a menacing air about them, as if belonging to the mechanism of progress from which we sought to remain free. Men who have come to survey the district, men walking by who were too well dressed to be hikers, two or three who have spent their days hammering holes in the rocks; and there was one threatening week when an aeroplane flew up and down each section of the coast towing a box-like contraption behind it. On such occasions we bristled with suspicion. Others in beautiful, lonely places have watched such activities, waited and wondered, then found themselves faced with the roar of a motorway, or on the site of some other monument to progress.

One day a man called at the cottage and said he was studying rock conditions in our area on behalf of a certain Ministry. He asked for permission to study those on our land.

'Of course you can, I said, then added suspiciously, remembering the other activities, 'if you are looking for uranium I hope you won't find it'

The man stared at me. 'But my dear sir,' he said loftily, 'if I found uranium just think how rich you would be!'

Jeannie was with me at the time and it was she who answered him. 'Had we the choice,' she said, 'between a uranium mine and Minack, I can assure you we would choose Minack.' The man retreated to his duties and Jeannie and I set off to weed the anemones.

We know now there is no possibility of any part of this area being exploited. Buildings and caravans are forbidden, there is no place for a motorway to go, it is too inaccessible even to fear the prospect of an atomic power station; and the scientists have announced the region is bare of uranium. Perhaps I am being over-confident. Such remoteness will always tempt someone to plot its destruction.

But today we can go out of the cottage and shout to the heavens and no one will hear; or lie on the rocks with only cormorants, oyster catchers and gulls as companions; or stroll in the wood with Charlie hopping from branch to branch above our heads, or pause to talk to Tim, or say to each other: 'the gannets are passing along the coast early this year' . . . 'I saw the first whitethroat this morning' . . . 'If you look to the left of those quickthorns you will see a fox sunning itself in the bracken' . . . 'The Seven Stone lightship was towed past this morning' . . . 'We'll have lunch on the rocks and watch the seal in the bay' . . .

These belong to the pleasures which have pleased since the beginning of time. They await in remoteness, hiding their secret in solitude, unhurt by man-made glitter and away from his intrigue, seemingly insignificant moments which enrich the soul. They live with us at Minack so that whatever material disappointments we may have, however hard may be the consequences of a failed harvest, they take us forward again. It is a way of life which belongs to the ages instead of ourselves.

Monty was fifteen years old when he began to ail. There was nothing sudden about his illness, and as the weeks went by there were times when we made ourselves believe that we were worrying unnecessarily. Sometimes he was his old jaunty self, following us in our walks round Minack, then sitting purring on my knees in the evening. We made the customary remarks that are made by those who watch the sick. 'I think the medicine has done him a lot of good' . . . 'He really enjoyed his walk this morning.' And then quite suddenly the sickness within him began to hurry.

He died on a May morning, a morning that was soft and warm and full of sweet scents, the sort of morning Jeannie would have said to me: 'Let's take Monty a walk before breakfast.' As I was dressing he had begun to cry, and I knew instinctively there was nothing more that we could do. I went away to telephone the vet and when I returned I found Jeannie had carried him out into the sun. He was lying, breathing gently, stretched out on the grass; and, strangely, Charlie was on the ground within a yard of him, Tim was perched on a rosebush two feet from his head, and Hubert was up there on the roof. All were silent.

Monty was the only cat I had ever known and my loyalty was to him and not to his breed. One day during his illness I was telling him that I would never have another to replace him. I was in fact thinking of those sympathetic meaning people who hasten to replace an old friend with a substitute. 'The only exception,' I said, and this I wrote down in my diary, 'is if a black cat whose home could never be traced cried outside the door in a storm.'

At the beginning of March the following year, Jeannie and I became aware of a black cat running wild on our land. We scarcely took notice of it except to observe, after a time, that it was always on our land and never on that of our neighbours. But it was so wild that it was only a black dash in the distance.

One evening, at the beginning of April, Jeannie was sitting after dinner talking of Monty. A gale was blowing and rain lashed the cottage. Suddenly I said: 'Did you hear a cry?' And without waiting for Jeannie to answer I went and opened the door.

In came the black cat. She is beside me now as I end this story.

THROUGHOUT their many years at Dorminack Derek and Jeannie only held the property - the cottage and its meadows - via a lease. In fact originally they didn't even have that - they had no more security than a verbal agreement with the farmer that owned the lease. By a combination of chance and good fortune though, they eventually came to own the freehold of some adjacent land. This came about when they found out that their peace and tranquillity, so jealously guarded, was at dire risk. They already called the land that adjoined Minack's cultivated meadows *'Oliver Land'*, because it was where they'd first seen a wild black cat that they'd then adopted and given the name of Oliver. This land constituted their view across to Carn Barges in the east; 20 acres of wild scrub that they walked across and came to regard almost as their own. Then one day they heard from Margaret Smith that it had been put up for sale and permission was being sought for a caravan and a cess pit. This could be the thin edge of a wedge of development that would have been a disaster for them. They made an immediate offer to buy it for themselves, and to their great relief, courtesy of funds raised with the help of a friendly bank manager, were successful. As Derek later wrote *"Oliver Land was OUR land, 20 acres of it and we decided that any money we had when we died should be devoted to its preservation..."* And Jeannie added:*"It must be preserved for the natural inhabitants, the multitude of wild creatures, insects, butterflies, foxes, badgers, nesting birds. It mustn't be preserved for human beings, except those who seek solitude."*

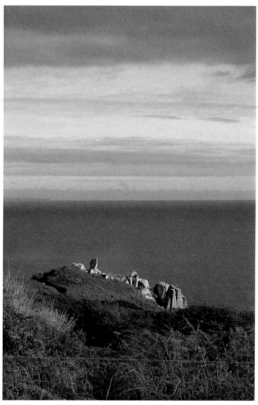

Oliver Land looking out to Carn Barges.

It's clear that they were both already very conscious of their own mortality and realised that Oliver Land could eventually be left as their gift to a world that would increasingly need places like this. Although their time at Minack was transitory and would eventually fade into the past, Oliver Land, as a place where human beings could share in and respect the natural world, represented the future.

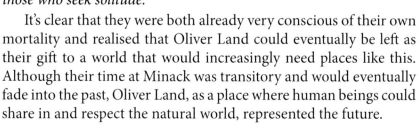

Jeannie died first, in 1986, at just 66 years of age, her life at Minack tragically cut short by cancer. Derek had found it very difficult to openly acknowledge how ill she was, and consequently her death came as a shock to many of their friends. Just before she died, at St Michael's Hospital in Hayle, Derek had shown her a sign he'd had made to be placed at the entrance to Oliver Land. The dark green wooden sign was inscribed in yellow lettering with the following words:

THE DEREK AND JEANNIE TANGYE
MINACK CHRONICLES
NATURE RESERVE
A Place for Solitude

He knew that this final gift would fulfill her dearest wish, that these precious acres would remain unchanged forever and provide a haven, not only for wildlife, but for those individuals that wanted to experience for themselves the spiritual healing that solitude in a wild and beautiful place can bring. Derek had also promised her that he would never leave Minack, a promise he kept, staying there until his own death at the cottage on 26th October, 1996.

On Friday 4th April 1997, the auction rooms of David Lay in Penzance were packed for a very special sale. People had come from all over the country in the hope of buying a special memento from amongst the items of Derek's estate that were going under the hammer that day. Derek and Jeannie had no children, so once the bequests in Derek's will had been settled and his trustee, Anne Sutton, had dealt with the vast archive of sensitive or personal material that he had kept in what he aptly called the 'Confusion Room', the residue of Derek's belongings were put up for auction. There was a huge number of lots, varying from furniture and paintings to scrapbooks, tobacco tins and photographs. Derek's friends and readers were vying for the lots with professional dealers and the auction went on all day. A large number of documents were purchased by the Trust themselves as a permanent archive and these are now kept at the Morrab Library in Penzance. It's a home that they would have approved of - as a private subscription library the Morrab is

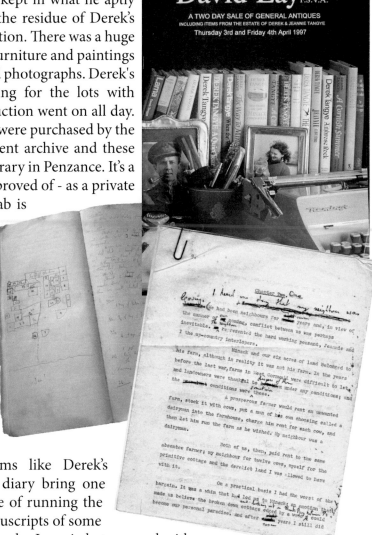

an increasingly rare species - there are only nineteen now left in the entire United Kingdom. Set in the sub-tropical Morrab Gardens, it houses a marvellous series of collections which have gradually been acquired since it was founded in 1818. Its small band of friendly volunteers take good care of the Tangye archive and ensure it is permanently available to the public. Items like Derek's carefully recorded gardening diary bring one close to the everyday minutiae of running the flower farm, and the draft manuscripts of some of the books, carefully typed up by Jeannie but covered with scores of hand written and barely decipherable revisions by Derek, give one a unique insight into the sheer physical labour involved in the production of a book before the age of the computer or word processor.

Some fourteen years have now passed since Derek left Minack for the last time. As we have seen, before he died Derek took the necessary steps to safeguard Oliver Land and his literary work by means of a Trust and asking a small group of his most valued and trusted friends to act as his Trustees. Registered as a charity, its primary aims are *"to advance the education of the public about the Minack Chronicles......and in particular by preserving Oliver Land as a place of solitude to which the public may have access..."*. The creation of this Trust put a legal seal on his pledge to Jeannie to protect Oliver Land permanently from the encroachments of the modern world. The Trust also supports various other charities, in particular making donations to smaller local animal charities to help with veterinary expenses, and providing an annual bursary for those, who having been inspired by the Minack Chronicles, are seeking a literary or artistic career. The Trust continues to perform those duties, but within a few years of Derek's death it became clear that the administrative responsibilities of dealing with requests from hundreds of readers was a heavy burden on the individual trustees. When the independent *'Friends of Minack Society'* was formed, it began to supplement the role of the Trust in maintaining contact with Derek's readers and keeping interest in the books alive. FOMS has since grown to an organisation with members and supporters all over the world, and although there is no formal connection between the two organisations, a few years ago the Trust, reluctantly having to reduce its public information role, recommended that those who wished to maintain contact with other Minack Chronicles readers should get in touch with the Friends of Minack Society.

During the final years of his life Derek had not been able to work the land and by 1998, when the owners, the Tregothnan Estate, appointed Jane Bird and her partner Peter Clough as the new tenants, the cottage itself had also been empty for some time. Consequently there was much work to be done - Jane can be heard on John Coles' DVD talking at this time of her plans to restore Minack's land back to life and of

Jane and Peter tackling the gorse on Oliver Land

just how much she'd wanted this opportunity to return there. Since Peter's premature death, Jane undertakes all this work alone, so is unable to attend to visitors, although the cottage can still be seen from the adjacent Oliver Land. *"When Derek invited me to be a Trustee,"* she told me, *"it was with a special remit to protect the Oliver Land from becoming a 'zoo' or a park, and to ensure it remained protected by 'nature's barbed wire' - the brambles and gorse."* Consequently, under her supervision, the Trust now manages Oliver Land with a light touch, partly by using ponies to keep down some of the vegetation, and then trimming the hedges and pathways only at times when it doesn't affect nesting birds. In line with other local conservation societies it has recently initiated a programme of maintenance that should encourage parts of Oliver Land to revert to heathland, and small patches of heather have already reappeared. Bracken is being discouraged in places in favour of grasses, which the ponies will help to keep close cropped. This work,

Dorminack ponies

undertaken in conjunction with the *Royal Society for the Protection of Birds* and *Natural England* as part of the *Chough Project*, could open up the exciting prospect that the chough, Cornwall's iconic national bird, may once again be seen here. Up to the end of the last century the chough had been extinct for decades in Cornwall, the last birds being seen at around the time the Tangyes first came to Minack in the early 1950s. These are wonderful, acrobatic birds of the cliffs which, according to legend, bear the spirit of King Arthur - once the bird comes back, so the legend goes, the ancient king will also return to lead Cornwall to nationhood.

Attempts in the latter part of the last century at reintroduction by breeding and releasing captive birds failed, but in 2001 the first wild birds returned and nested on the very southern tip of the Lizard. It is likely that it was the reintroduction of grazing on the cliffs that produced the environment and the food supply that they liked, and they have returned to this site each year since. More recently they have also nested at a site at Botallack, near Cape Cornwall on our most westerly coast - the chicks being the first recorded in west Penwith for many decades. At the end of 2009 there were 21 Cornish birds, and individual birds had been seen within a few miles to the west of Minack, at Gwennap Head. This small population is genetically very fragile though, and more wild birds are needed to join them and expand their gene pool. If they can be encouraged to nest on the south western coast around Minack it could link the Lizard and Botallack nesting sites and perhaps lead to choughs returning to west Cornwall in large numbers. Derek had a great interest in the bird life at Minack, often making notes about the arrival and departure of summer visitors or the sighting of different species on the cliffs or out at sea. How wonderful it would be to see choughs nesting along this part of the coast - a privilege that even Derek and Jeannie wouldn't have had, but which their legacy may help to realize.

Cornish Choughs

Whilst the Trust has continued its vital conservation role at Oliver Land, the Friends of Minack Society has worked alongside them in maintaining public interest in Derek and Jeannie's work. In doing that we've been acutely aware that there is always a conundrum to be faced when publicising wild and little known places. On the one hand, public understanding and knowledge is encouraged and consequently with it their support for the survival of such places. Ignorance often breeds indifference, and many valuable things have been lost by the indifference of previous generations. On the other hand a delicate balance has to be maintained to ensure that public access doesn't then destroy the very thing we are trying to preserve. Derek himself faced this dilemma every time he published one of the books and even more so when he was twice offered contracts by television companies to make a series based on the Chronicles. He kept publishing the books, but he knew that the TV offers would potentially take Minack's public profile to a different level. One of the offers fell through anyway when the ITV company concerned lost its franchise. The other offer was from the BBC, but despite the potential financial benefits, he turned it down when it became apparent from the screenplay that they intended to trivialize their story to widen its audience appeal. He still rather liked the idea that it required more than a little effort to find the way to Minack, for then he could be assured that those who did so were more likely to be on what he called their 'wavelength'.

The Minack Chronicles Revisited has been sponsored by FOMS in that same spirit. The cost of bringing it to publication was met by personal donations from a great many members and from the hard work of fundraising over a period of three years by a great many more. It was clearly Derek's wish that the Chronicles should remain in print and available to as wide a readership as possible. Likewise, it was clearly Derek and Jeannie's wish that Oliver Land should be open to the public. But it was most emphatically not their intention that it should be seen as some sort of 'visitor attraction' - the idea that large groups of tourists might turn up, 'doing' Oliver Land and Minack as part of a whistle stop tour of West Penwith, would have horrified them both. Those words of Jeannie's that I quoted earlier - *"It mustn't be preserved for human beings, except those who seek solitude"* - are an important reason in support of access now being limited to an entrance on the coastal path. By this route it can be visited any day of the year, by walking from Lamorna or St Loy and locating the gateway between Carn Barges and Tater Du, but it doesn't link Oliver Land to the 'winding lane', which in any event

belongs to the tenancy of Dorminack rather than to the Trust. Although this restricted access is disliked by some, it ensures that Oliver Land is protected and, by not being linked to any other right of way, it cannot become simply a conduit for hikers passing through.

People do indeed still visit Oliver Land throughout the year, often regardless of the weather, which in winter can be as wild as the setting. In spring though, which comes early here, dog violets, celandine and pink campion line the pathways and the pocket meadows still come alive with Tangye daffodils. Summer brings buttercups, sea thrift, the tall purple stems of foxgloves and the sweet scent of honeysuckle. In places the gorse may sometimes form an inpenetrable barrier to people, but not to the badgers whose ancient pathways become tunnels through the dense undergrowth. Gorse, the 'furze' that would have provided fuel to the earliest inhabitants of Minack, flowers in patches throughout the year, but in summer its yellow blossom is in abundance and its balmy scent, smelling strangely of coconut, fills the air as you brush against it. Visitors will then quite frequently be seen, often alone, wandering

Wild flowers on Oliver Land ~ Above: gorse Left: honeysuckle Below: sea thrift.

around the meadows or sitting, quietly reflecting, on the huge granite stone that Jeannie had given one of her special names. Derek had uncovered this rock when, having just secured ownership of the land, he had been clearing the dense undergrowth so that they could have a *"celebration path"* to stroll along. Their resident cat at the time, Ambrose, had decided to follow them all the way, and as they sat on the rock, Ambrose jumped up with them as if to join the celebration of their good fortune. Jeannie had just christened the land itself as 'Oliver Land' after one of their cats, and defended herself against Derek's comment that *"some people might call it sentimental"*. She couldn't have cared less what they thought and now, as they sat dangling their feet on this natural granite bench, revelling in the knowledge that Oliver Land was safe, she turned to Derek and told him she'd never forget this moment. *"Do you know what I'm going to call this rock?"* she said - *"the Ambrose Rock."*

"The agelessness of the grey granite rocks lying half hidden by the greening undergrowth."
The Ambrose Rock

If you enjoyed reading *A Gull on the Roof*, I hope you will feel moved to read more of the books that make up The Minack Chronicles. It makes more sense to read them in sequence, but it really isn't essential, as each one stands alone and Derek would often achieve this by repeating parts of the earlier story to put things into context. He has often been criticised for this, perhaps with some justification, but he knew his readers and, if sales are anything to go by, they didn't mind at all.

Mim and I never did visit Minack whilst either Jeannie or Derek was still alive. Although we knew where it was and over the years were often nearby, we invariably had our children in tow and had a natural reticence about turning up, unknown, uninvited and unannounced at someone's home. Now that we live so close and have spoken to those that did visit, we both regret not doing so, as many people have told us of the welcome they received there.

As well as being a vehicle for telling a host of small stories, Derek constantly used his books to express his thoughts and philosophy on life. As he filled the pages of the Chronicles with the narrative of Minack's passing seasons and their daily lives, using words to draw vignettes of the simplest of life's pleasures, he returned again and again to his theme of shedding the trappings of materialism.

"Simplicity," he wrote *"is what one should seek. Bury the myriad theoretical dogmas which have brought such distress in the past, and strive to achieve simplicity in behaviour towards others, in one's thoughts, in one's daily life. The final test of religion is not religiousness, but Love."* In his later, less mobile years he would sit quietly in his porch at Minack enjoying the company of visitors, many of whom came seeking advice or solace for some personal misfortune. David Cornwell had often personally witnessed this and commented that *"to the converted, his personal power of empathy verged on the hypnotic".*

———⟊———

How, or for that matter, whether, in this increasingly transient world, the work of Derek and Jeannie Tangye will be remembered only time will tell. Although the Minack Chronicles are still widely read, they have been out of print now for several years. The Friends of Minack Society provides a service for sourcing second hand copies, from cheap paperback versions to signed hard back copies, which are in such demand that they now fetch quite high prices. At the time of writing, FOMS has plans for a number of events to celebrate, in March 2011, the 50th anniversary of the publication of *A Gull on the Roof*. Amongst these, apart from the launch of this book and an accompanying DVD, is the unveiling of two new daffodil varieties, named after Derek and Jeannie, at the Penzance Flower Show. It's difficult to think of a more fitting, or lasting, tribute and FOMS is grateful to Ron Scamp, of specialist growers *R.A. Scamp Quality Daffodils* for creating them.

The new Tangye Daffodils

If you do decide to visit west Penwith and come to Lamorna, please take a little time out for refreshments in the tea rooms of the Lamorna Pottery, whose treacle tart must float down from heaven each morning on a sunbeam, and where you can view the books, DVDs and other items for sale at *'Tangye Corner'*. Better still, whilst there, buy another copy of this book for a friend and help FOMS in its efforts to get more of the Chronicles back into print.

The South West Coastal Path is one of the gems of Cornwall, and our section can be joined at either Lamorna Cove, or from a permissive path via the private lane that starts opposite the Lamorna Wink and climbs up the side of the valley, past the Cove Hotel and eventually leads down to join the coastal path at Carn Barges. From there, you will get exactly the same view that Derek and Jeannie had when they first set eyes on Minack and Jeannie exclaimed *"Look, there it is...!"*

The entrance to the Minack Chronicles Trust Nature Reserve at Oliver Land is between Carn Barges and the Tater Du lighthouse, but please do respect the privacy of Dorminack itself by keeping within the bounds of the Reserve, and above all remember Derek and Jeannie's wishes - that Oliver Land is intended to be *A Place for Solitude* and a haven for the wild creatures. Please, take nothing away but memories and leave nothing behind but your footprints.

The spirits of Minack
Welcome you
To their world of Forever
Where life continues
And death is never

Jeannie Tangye

ACKNOWLEDGEMENTS

THE **Minack Chronicles Revisited** is the result of the time and efforts of more people than I can accurately acknowledge here. I'll give it my best shot though, and apologise in advance to anyone I've missed out.

The project couldn't have been attempted at all without the sponsorship of *The Friends of Minack Society*, of which I am privileged to be Chairman. Funds were raised largely through book sales at 'Tangye Corner' and online book sales via the FOMS website. Additional finance was raised by an appeal to FOMS members for sponsorship, and all those individuals that responded so generously are listed at the front of this book. The nitty gritty of production - all the scanning, retouching, typesetting, artwork and endless revisions when I couldn't make my mind up, were handled with infinite patience by my wife Mim, who thought she was coming to Cornwall to get away from scanning, retouching, typesetting, artwork and endless revisions. Mim was assisted in the re-keying of *A Gull on the Roof* by FOMS' secretary Gloria Townsin, who also did sterling work keeping the rest of the FOMS show on the road whilst I was faffing about being creative. I was ably assisted in proofreading by Patricia Wilnecker - any errors are probably on the pages I checked. The line drawings throughout *A Gull on the Roof* are the original ones by Jeannie Tangye herself. I'm grateful to the executors of Derek Tangye's estate for permission to use these drawings, to scan and photograph some of the archive material, and to reproduce the text of *A Gull on the Roof*. Jenny Murrish played a major role, via Tangye Corner, in raising the funds for this book, as did Linda and Jeff Hartley, in raising sponsorship via the FOMS website. Our Membership Secretary, Mary Ackroyd, and our Treasurer, Yasmin Donlon, also each played a vital part in raising and looking after funds.

Last, but not least, I'm grateful to Jane Bird and Moira Tangye, Trustees of The Minack Chronicles Trust, and especially to Anne & Malcolm Sutton, former Trustees, for their support and encouragement.

PHOTOGRAPHY

Amongst the contemporary shots a few are mine, but the best ones are by the two professional photographers that worked with me, John Coles and Sue Searle, who each contributed their work without charge. *(See also separate list below for full photography credits.)*

JOHN COLES John has long been an admirer of The Minack Chronicles and contributed a number of shots and some invaluable advice. Along with his wife Anna, he is releasing a separate DVD to go with the book. Also entitled *'The Monack Chronicles Revisited'*, it includes a fascinating compilation of pictures, interviews and music about Minack. John and Anna have previously released audio recordings under the title of '*The Sounds of Minack*'.

John owns and works from **Dazzle Studios** at 31 St Thomas Road, Launceston, Cornwall PL15 8DA Tel: 01566 773535 website: www.dazzlestudios.co.uk

SUE SEARLE I see Sue quite regularly, as we're both members of the *Lamorna Valley Group* of artists and craftspeople. Her photographs show her enduring love for the landscape of west Penwith in all its varied forms and colours. She is especially familiar with Lamorna as she was brought up at Borah Farm, close to Minack. Rather disconcertingly, she told me that her dad would not have been at all impressed with her contribution - he'd often complained to Derek about the large number of visitors that kept turning up at Borah, having lost their bearings trying to find Minack! Sue now lives and works in the heart of the Lamorna valley at Lamorna Vean, Lamorna, Penzance TR19 6NY email: sue.lamornavean@btinternet.com

THE FRIENDS OF MINACK SOCIETY (FOMS)

The Society was founded in 1999 by Pauline Ruffles and Tony Finn. It now has members all over Britain as well as in Europe, Canada, USA, South Africa and Australia. Derek had asked people to remember Minack on Jeannie's birthday, March 23rd, so large numbers of members gather each year on the nearest weekend to this for the Society's AGM. Held at the Queen's Hotel in Penzance, it includes a programme of events covering four days. The FOMS magazine, '*Wavelength*' is published three times a year - full of news, views,

pictures and letters, and is free to all members, including overseas. Members keep in touch constantly throughout the year via the Society's website, online forum and Facebook page. Non members can take part in the very active Forum and Facebook page, or find out anything about the Society by going to the website:

www.friendsofminack.org.uk

You can join FOMS directly from here, or by writing to our Membership Secretary: Mrs Kath Mulligan, 33, Eaves Knoll Road, New Mills, High Peak, Derbyshire, SK22 3DN

Email address – kathmulligan@yahoo.co.uk   Tel: 01663 741989

THE DEREK AND JEANNIE TANGYE MINACK CHRONICLES NATURE TRUST

Management of Oliver Land is now in the hands of Cornwall Wildlife Trust.

'TANGYE CORNER' at the LAMORNA POTTERY

This is FOMS' permanent display in the tea rooms of the Lamorna Pottery, where you can buy further copies of this book and John Coles' DVD; second hand copies of The Minack Chronicles; DVDs, and a number of other related items. FOMS membership forms are also available here. For many years it has been run for us by Jenny Murrish, but more lately by Patricia Wilnecker. The space is provided with the kind permission of Pottery owner Andrea Bennetts.

Lamorna Pottery, Lamorna, Penzance, Cornwall TR19 6NY

Tel: 01736 810330   website: www.lamornapottery.co.uk

THE MORRAB LIBRARY

A private subscription library that looks after the Tangye Archive. Access for library members is free, but non-members can use the library for a daily rate of £3, or view the archive by appointment and payment of a fee of £5. Housed in a fine early 19th century building and set in the sub-tropical Morrab Gardens, it's well worth a visit for the ambience alone.

Open Tuesday to Friday 10am to 4pm, Saturday 10am to 1pm

Morrab Library, Morrab Gardens, Penzance, Cornwall TR18 4DA

Tel: 01736 364474   website: www.morrablibrary.org.uk

THE TANGYE DAFFODILS

These two special varieties are named after Derek and Jeannie and were specially developed for FOMS by daffodil and bulb specialist, Ron Scamp. Ron has had 37 years experience in the selective breeding of daffodils and has won awards at exhibitions all over the country. The Tangye Daffodils are available from him at R.A.Scamp Quality Daffodils, 14, Roscarrack Close, Falmouth, Cornwall. TR11 4PJ. Tel: 01326 317959 Email: info@qualitydaffodils.com http://www.qualitydaffodils.com

FURTHER READING

Apart from the rest of the Minack Chronicles, for further reading there is also **'TANGYE'** by David Power. It's a powerful and sometimes critical biography of Derek that one reviewer called *"compassionate and honest"* and an *"emotional recounting of the love story that he and his wife Jeannie shared"*. Essential reading for anyone that wants a unique personal viewpoint, by one of their friends, into what made Derek and Jeannie's relationship tick. I'm very grateful to David for allowing me to take advantage of his meticulous research.
Publisher: Book Guild Ltd; ISBN-10: 1857766865.

PHOTOGRAPHS & ILLUSTRATIONS

Line drawings, B/W archive photos, scans and shots of documents are by kind permission of the Derek Tangye Estate. Photos of individuals are reproduced by their permission.

Colour photographs:

John Coles: p17 Carn Barges; p20 Dorminack Cottage; p 47 Oliver Land looking out to Carn Barges; p48 Solitude Gate; p50 Jane and Peter; p51 Dorminack ponies; p53 Honeysuckle; Thrift; p54 The Ambrose Rock; p56 Dorminack from Oliver Land.

Sue Searle: p26 Merry Maidens; p28 The Mill, Daffodils at cottage door; p29 Lamorna Stream; p30 Lamorna Quay, Sunrise over Carn Dhu.

John Nash: Front cover photo; p18 Look there it is! p25 St Michael's Mount; p26 Pensans sign; p27 St Helen's Chapel; p28 Lamorna Wink; p53 Gorse flowers

Woman's Weekly Magazine: p46 Derek, Jeannie and donkeys at Minack reproduced by their permission.

Kath Mulligan: p8 'Time was Mine' cover.

Jeff & Linda Hartley: pp21-23 Minack Chronicles and 'Meet Me At The Savoy' book covers

Robert and Carol Moule: p29 View of Carn Dhu from Chygurno Gardens

Gloria Townsin: p55 Tangye Daffodils; xi FOMS website header photo

David Cornwell: p33 photograph reproduced by his permission

The Friends of Minack Society